C000193955

Бжⷭ҇твенная литꙋргі́а и҆́же во ст҃ы́хъ ѻ҆тца̀ на́шегѡ васі́лїа вели́кагѡ

The Divine Liturgy
of Our Father among the Saints
Basil the Great

Изда́тельство
Свѧто-Тро́ицкагѡ Монасты́рѧ.
тѷпогра́фїѧ преп. І҆́ѡва Поча́евскагѡ.
Джорданви́лль, Н.І̇.

Printed with the blessing of His Eminence,
Metropolitan Hilarion, First Hierarch of the
Russian Orthodox Church Outside of Russia

The Divine Liturgy of Our Father Among the Saints
Basil the Great: Slavonic-English Parallel Text
© 2020 Holy Trinity Monastery,

PRINTSHOP OF
SAINT JOB OF POCHAEV

An imprint of

HOLY TRINITY PUBLICATIONS
Holy Trinity Monastery
Jordanville, New York 13361-0036
www.holytrinitypublications.com

ISBN: 978-0-88465-434-6

Library of Congress Control Number 2019952925

Table of Contents

Чи́нъ

бж҃е́ственныѧ лїтꙋргі́и

и҆́же во ст҃ы́хъ

ѻ҆тца̀ на́шегw

васі́лїа вели́кагw.

The Order
of
The Divine Liturgy
of
Our Father Among the Saints
Basil the Great

Бжⷭ҇твенндѧ літꙋргі́а
и҆́же во ст҃ы́хъ ѻ҆тцⷶ на́шегѡ
васі́лїа вели́кагѡ

Проскомі́дїа

Хотѧ́й сщ҃е́нникъ бжⷭ҇твенное соверша́ти
тайнодѣ́йствїе, до́лженъ є҆́сть перва́е
оꙋ҆́бѡ примире́нъ бы́ти со всѣ́ми, и҆
не и҆мѣ́ти что̀ на кого̀, и҆ се́рдце
же, є҆ли́ка си́ла, ѿ лꙋка́выхъ блюстѝ
по́мыслѡвъ, воздержа́тисѧ же съ
ве́чера, и҆ трезви́тисѧ да́же до вре́мене
сщ҃еннодѣ́йствїѧ. Вре́мени же наста́вшꙋ,
вхо́дитъ въ хра́мъ и҆ соедини́всѧ со
дїа́кономъ, творѧ́тъ вкꙋ́пѣ къ восто́кꙋ
предъ ст҃ы́ми две́рьми поклонє́нїѧ трѝ.

The Divine Liturgy
of Our Father among the Saints
Basil the Great

The Proskomedia

The priest that desires to celebrate the
Divine Mysteries must first be at peace
with all, having nothing against anyone,
and insofar as is within his power, keep his
heart from evil thoughts, be continent from
the evening before, and be vigilant until the
time of the divine service. When the time
is come, he goes into the church, together
with the deacon, and together they make
three bows to the waist towards the east
before the holy doors.

Та́же глаго́летъ дїа́конъ: Бл҃гословѝ, влады́ко.

Сщ҃е́нникъ: Бл҃гослове́нъ бг҃ъ на́шъ всегда̀, ны́нѣ и҆ при́снѡ, и҆ во вѣ́ки вѣкѡ́въ. А҆ми́нь.

Начина́етъ глаго́лати дїа́конъ: Цр҃ю̀ нб҃е́сный: Трис҃то́е: по О҆́ч҃е на́шъ:

Сщ҃е́нникъ: Я҆́кѡ твоѐ є҆́сть цр҃тво:

Та́же глаго́лютъ: Поми́лꙋй на́съ, гд҃и, поми́лꙋй на́съ: всѧ́кагѡ бо ѿвѣ́та недоꙋмѣ́юще, сїю̀ тѝ мл҃твꙋ ꙗ҆́кѡ вл҃цѣ грѣ́шнїи прино́симъ: поми́лꙋй на́съ.

Сла́ва: Гд҃и поми́лꙋй на́съ, на тѧ́ бо оу҆пова́хомъ, не прогнѣ́вайсѧ на ны̀ ѕѣлѡ̀, нижѐ помѧнѝ беззако́нїй на́шихъ: но при́зри и҆ ны́нѣ ꙗ҆́кѡ бл҃гоꙋ́тробенъ, и҆ и҆зба́ви ны̀ ѿ вра́гъ на́шихъ: ты́ бо є҆сѝ бг҃ъ на́шъ, и҆ мы̀ лю́дїе твоѝ, всѝ дѣла̀ рꙋкꙋ̀ твое́ю, и҆ и҆́мѧ твоѐ призыва́емъ.

И҆ ны́нѣ: Милосе́рдїѧ две́ри ѿве́рзи на́мъ, бл҃гослове́ннаѧ бг҃оро́дице, надѣ́ющїисѧ на тѧ̀ да не поги́бнемъ, но да и҆зба́вимсѧ

Deacon: Bless, master.
Priest: Blessed is our God, always, now and ever, and unto the ages of ages. Amen.

The deacon begins: O Heavenly King...,
Trisagion to Our Father...

Priest: For Thine is the kingdom...
Then they say: Have mercy on us, O Lord, have mercy on us, for at a loss for any defence, this prayer do we sinners offer unto Thee as Master: have mercy on us.

Glory... Lord, have mercy on us, for we have hoped in Thee. Be not angry with us greatly, neither remember our iniquities; but look upon us now as Thou art compassionate, and deliver us from our enemies; for Thou art our God, and we, Thy people; all are the works of Thy hands, and we call upon thy name.

Both now... Open unto us the doors of compassion, O blessed Theotokos, for, hoping in thee, may we not perish, through thee

тобою ѿ бѣ́дъ, ты̀ бо є҆сѝ спасе́нїе ро́да хрⷭ҇тїа́нскагѡ.

Та́же ѿхо́дать ко і҆кѡ́нѣ хрⷭ҇то́вѣ и҆ цѣлꙋ́ютъ ю҆̀, глаго́люще:

Пречⷭ҇то́мꙋ твоемꙋ̀ ѻ҆́бразꙋ покланѧ́емсѧ бл҃гі́й, просѧ́ще проще́нїѧ прегрѣше́нїй на́шихъ, хрⷭ҇тѐ бж҃е: во́лею бо бл҃говоли́лъ є҆сѝ пло́тїю взы́ти на крⷭ҇тъ, да и҆зба́виши, ꙗ҆̀же созда́лъ є҆сѝ, ѿ рабо́ты вра́жїѧ, тѣ́мъ бл҃года́рственнѡ вопїе́мъ тѝ: ра́дости и҆спо́лнилъ є҆сѝ всѧ̑ сп҃се на́шъ, прише́дый сп҃стѝ мі́ръ.

Та́же цѣлꙋ́ютъ и҆ і҆кѡ́нꙋ бц҃ы глаго́люще тропа́рь:

Милосе́рдїѧ сꙋ́щи и҆сто́чникъ, ми́лости спо-до́би на́съ, бц҃е, при́зри на лю́ди согрѣши́в-шыѧ, ꙗ҆вѝ ꙗ҆́кѡ при́снѡ си́лꙋ твою̀, на тѧ̀

may we be delivered from adversities, for thou art the salvation of the Christian race.

Then they approach the icon of Christ and kiss it, saying:

We worship Thine immaculate Icon, O Good One, asking the forgiveness of our failings, O Christ God; for of Thine own will Thou wast well-pleased to ascend the Cross in the flesh, that Thou mightest deliver from slavery to the enemy those whom Thou hadst fashioned. Wherefore, we cry to Thee thankfully: Thou didst fill all things with joy, O our Saviour, when Thou camest to save the world.

Then they kiss the icon of the Theotokos, saying the troparion:

As thou art a well-spring of compassion, vouchsafe mercy unto us, O Theotokos. Look upon a sinful people; show forth, as always, thy power. For, hoping in thee, we cry 'Rejoice!' to thee, as once did Gabriel,

бо ѹпова́юще, ра́дꙋйсѧ вопїе́мъ ти̏, ꙗ́коже и҆ногда̀ гаврїи́лъ, безпло́тныхъ а҆рхїстрати́гъ.

Та́же приклонѣ̀ главꙋ̀, і҆ере́й глаго́летъ:

Гдⷭ҇и, низпослѝ рꙋ́кꙋ твою̀ съ высоты̀ ст҃а́гѡ жили́ща твоегѡ̀, и҆ ѹ҆крѣпѝ мѧ въ предлежа́щꙋю слꙋ́жбꙋ твою̀: да неѡсꙋжде́ннѡ предста́нꙋ стра́шномꙋ прⷭ҇то́лꙋ твоемꙋ̀, и҆ безкро́вное сщ҃еннодѣ́йствїе совершꙋ̀. Ꙗ́кѡ твоѧ̀ є҆́сть си́ла и҆ сла́ва во вѣ́ки вѣкѡ́въ. А҆ми́нь.

Та́же творѧ́тъ и҆ къ ликѡ́мъ покло́ны по є҆ди́номꙋ: и҆ та́кѡ ѿхо́дѧтъ въ же́ртвенникъ, глаго́люще:

Вни́дꙋ въ до́мъ тво́й, поклоню́сѧ ко хра́мꙋ ст҃о́мꙋ твоемꙋ̀ въ стра́сѣ твое́мъ. Гдⷭ҇и, наста́ви мѧ пра́вдою твое́ю, вра̑гъ мои́хъ ра́ди и҆спра́ви пред̾ тобо́ю пꙋ́ть мо́й. Ꙗ́кѡ нѣ́сть во ѹ҆стѣ́хъ и҆́хъ и҆́стины, се́рдце и҆́хъ сꙋ́етно, гро́бъ ѿве́рстъ горта́нь и҆́хъ, а҆зы̑ки свои́ми льща́хꙋ. Сꙋдѝ и҆̀мъ, бж҃е, да ѿпадꙋ́тъ

the supreme commander of the bodiless hosts.

Then, with bowed head, the priest says:

O Lord, stretch forth Thy hand from Thy holy place on high, and strengthen me for this, Thine appointed service; that, standing uncondemned before Thy dread altar, I may celebrate the bloodless ministry. For Thine is the power and the glory unto the ages of ages. Amen.

Then they make a bow to each choir, and go into the altar, saying:

I will come into Thy house, in Thy fear will I worship toward Thy holy temple. Lead me, O Lord, in Thy righteousness; because of mine enemies, make my way plain before Thee. For there is no truth in their mouth; their heart is vain; their throat is an open sepulcher; they flatter with their tongue. Judge them, O God; let them fall through their own

ѿ мы́слей свои́хъ: по мно́жествꙋ нече́стїѧ и҆́хъ и҆зри́ни ѧ̀, ꙗ҆́кѡ преѡгорчи́ша тѧ̀, гдⷭ҇и. И҆ да возвеселѧ́тсѧ вси ᲂу҆пова́ющїи на тѧ̀, во вѣ́къ возра́дꙋютсѧ, и҆ всели́шисѧ въ ни́хъ: и҆ похва́лѧтсѧ ѡ҆ тебѣ̀ лю́бѧщїи и҆́мѧ твоѐ. Ꙗ҆́кѡ ты̀ блгⷭ҇ослови́ши пра́ведника, гдⷭ҇и, ꙗ҆́кѡ ѻ҆рꙋ́жїемъ блговоле́нїѧ вѣнча́лъ є҆сѝ на́съ.

Вше́дше же во ст҃и́лище, творѧ́тъ покло́ны трѝ пред ст҃о́ю трапе́зою и҆ цѣлꙋ́ютъ ст҃о́е є҆ѵⷢ҇лїе и҆ ст҃ꙋ́ю трапе́зꙋ. Та́же прїе́млютъ въ рꙋ́ки своѧ̀ кі́йждо стїха́рь сво́й, и҆ творѧ́тъ покло́ны трѝ къ восто́кꙋ, глаго́люще въ себѣ̀ кі́йждо:

Бж҃е, ѡ҆чи́сти мѧ̀ грѣ́шнаго и҆ помилꙋ́й мѧ̀.

Та́же прихо́дитъ ко сщ҃е́нникꙋ дїа́конъ, держа̀ въ деснѣ́й рꙋцѣ̀

imaginations; cast them out according to the multitude of their ungodliness; for they have embittered Thee, O Lord. And let all them that put their trust in Thee be glad; they shall ever rejoice; and Thou shalt dwell in them and they that love Thy name shall be joyful in Thee. For Thou wilt bless the righteous, O Lord, for with the shield of Thy favorable kindness hast Thou crowned us.

Having entered into the sanctuary, they make three prostrations before the Holy Table and kiss the Holy Gospel and the Holy Table. Then each one takes his sticharion in his hands, and they make three bows to the waist toward the east, while saying to themselves with each bow:

O God, cleanse me a sinner and have mercy on me.

Then the deacon comes to the priest, holding in his right hand the sticharion

стїхáрь со ѡрарémъ, и поклони́въ є҆мꙋ̀
главꙋ̀, глагóлетъ:

Блгослови́, влады́ко, стїхáрь со ѡрарémъ.

Сщéнникъ глагóлетъ:

Блгословéнъ бгъ нáшъ всегда̀, ны́нѣ и҆
при́снѡ и҆ во вѣ́ки вѣкѡ́въ.

Тáже ѿхóдитъ дїáконъ во є҆ди́нꙋ странꙋ̀
ст҃и́лища, и҆ ѡблачи́тсѧ въ стїхáрь,
молѧ́сѧ си́це:

Возрáдꙋетсѧ дꙋша̀ моѧ̀ ѡ гдѣ̀, ѡблечé бо
мѧ̀ въ ри́зꙋ спсéнїѧ, и҆ ѡдéждею весéлїѧ ѡдѣ́ѧ
мѧ̀, ꙗ҆́кѡ женихꙋ̀ возложи́ ми вѣнéцъ, и҆
ꙗ҆́кѡ невѣ́стꙋ оу҆краси́ мѧ красотóю.

И҆ ѡрáрь оу҆́бѡ цѣловáвъ, налагáетъ на
лѣ́вое рáмо. Нарꙋкáвницы же налагáѧ на
рꙋ́ки, на деснꙋ́ю оу҆́бѡ, глагóлетъ:

with the orarion, and bowing his head
before the priest, says:

Bless, master, the sticharion with the orarion.

The priest says:

Blessed is our God, always, now and ever,
and unto the ages of ages.

Then the deacon goes to one side of the
sanctuary, puts on the sticharion, praying
in these words:

My soul shall rejoice in the Lord, for He hath
clothed me in the garment of salvation, and
with the vesture of gladness hath He covered me; He hath placed a crown upon me
as on a bridegroom, and He hath adorned
me as a bride with comeliness.

And then kissing the orarion, he places it
on the left shoulder. Then putting the cuffs
on the hands, starting with the right cuff he
says:

Десни́ца твоа̀, гд҃и, просла́вися въ крѣ́пости: десна́а твоа̀ рꙋка̀, гд҃и, сокрꙋши́ врагѝ, и̇ мно́жествомъ сла́вы твоеѧ̀ сте́рлъ є̇сѝ сꙋпоста́ты.

На лѣ́вꙋю же, глаго́летъ:

Рꙋцѣ̀ твоѝ сотвори́стѣ мѧ̀ и̇ созда́стѣ мѧ̀: вразꙋми́ мѧ, и̇ наꙋ́чꙋсѧ за́повѣдемъ твои́мъ.

Та́же ѿше́дъ въ предложе́нїе, ѹ̇готовлѧ́етъ сщ҃е́ннаѧ. Ст҃ый ѹ̇́бѡ дїскосъ поставлѧ́етъ ѿ шꙋ́юю странꙋ̀, потꙋ́ръ же, є̇́же є̇́сть ст҃ꙋ́ю ча́шꙋ, ѿ деснꙋ́ю, и̇ про́чаѧ съ ни́ми.

Сщ҃е́нникъ же си́це ѡ̇блача́итсѧ: прїе́мль стїха́рь въ лѣ́вꙋю рꙋ́кꙋ, и̇ поклони́всѧ три́жды къ восто́кꙋ, ꙗ̇́коже рече́сѧ, назна́менꙋетъ, глаго́ла:

Thy right hand, O Lord, is become glorious in power; Thy right hand, O Lord, hath dashed in pieces the enemy, and in the abundance of Thy glory Thou hast wiped out Thine adversaries.

And continuing with the left, he says:

Thy hands have made me and fashioned me; O give me understanding, and I shall learn Thy commandments.

Then, going to the Table of Oblation, he prepares the holy vessels. He places the holy diskos on the left side; the chalice, that is, the holy cup, on the right; and the rest (the spoon, spear, etc.) with them.

And the priest vests himself thus: taking the sticharion in his left hand, and bowing three times toward the east, as mentioned before, he signs it with the sign of the Cross, saying:

Бл҃гослове́нъ бг҃ъ на́шъ всегда̀, ны́нѣ и҆
при́снѡ, и҆ во вѣ́ки вѣкѡ́въ. А҆ми́нь.

Та́же ѡ҆блачи́тсѧ, глаго́лѧ:

Возра́дꙋетсѧ дꙋша̀ моѧ̀ ѡ҆ гд҃ѣ, ѡ҆блече́ бо
мѧ̀ въ ри́зꙋ спcе́нїѧ, и҆ ѻ҆де́ждею весе́лїѧ ѡ҆дѣ́а
мѧ̀, ꙗ҆́кѡ жениⷯꙋ̀ возложѝ мѝ вѣне́цъ, и҆
ꙗ҆́кѡ невѣ́стꙋ ᲂу҆краси́ мѧ красото́ю.

Та́же прїе́мь є҆пїтрахи́ль и҆ назна́менавъ,
ѡ҆блага́етсѧ є҆́ю, глаго́ла:

Бл҃гослове́нъ бг҃ъ и҆злива́ай бл҃года́ть свою̀
на сщ҃е́нники своѧ̀ ꙗ҆́кѡ мѵ́ро на главѣ̀,
сходѧ́щее на брадꙋ̀, брадꙋ̀ а҆арѡ́ню, сходѧ́щее
на ѡ҆ме́ты ѡ҆де́жди є҆гѡ̀.

Та́же прїе́мъ по́ѧс и҆ ѡ҆поѧ́сꙋѧсѧ,
глаго́летъ:

Blessed is our God, always, now and ever, and unto the ages of ages. Amen.

Then he vests himself, saying:

My soul shall rejoice in the Lord, for He hath clothed me in the garment of salvation, and with the vesture of gladness hath He covered me; He hath placed a crown upon me as on a bridegroom and He hath adorned me as a bride with comeliness.

Then taking the epitrachelion and signing it, he puts it on, saying:

Blessed is God Who poureth out His grace upon His priests, it is like the myrrh upon the head, that runneth down upon the beard, even Aaron's beard, and goeth down to the fringes of his clothing.

Then taking the belt and girding himself, he says:

Блгословéнъ бг҃ъ препоясуàй мà си́лою, и҆ положѝ непорóченъ пу́ть мóй, совершàай нóзѣ моѝ ꙗ҆́кѡ є҆лéни, и҆ на высóкихъ поставлàай мà.

Нарꙋка́вницы же, ꙗ҆́кѡ вы́ше речéса. Та́же прїéмь набéдренникъ, а҆́ще и҆́мать, и҆ блгослови́въ и҆̀, и҆ цѣловáвъ, глагóлетъ:

Препоѧ́ши мéчь твóй по бедрѣ̀ твоéй, си́льне, красотóю твоéю и҆ добрóтою твоéю, и҆ налѧцы̀, и҆ ꙋ҆спѣвáй, и҆ цр҃твꙋ́й, и҆́стины рáди и҆ крóтости и҆ прáвды, и҆ настáвитъ тà ди́внѡ десни́ца твоѧ̀, всегдà, ны́нѣ и҆ при́снѡ и҆ во вѣ́ки вѣкѡ́въ. А҆ми́нь.

Та́же прїéмь фелóнь и҆ блгослови́въ, цѣлꙋ́етъ, глагóлѧ си́це:

Сщ҃éнницы твоѝ, гд҃и, ѡ҆блекꙋ́тсѧ въ прáвдꙋ, и҆ преподóбнїи твоѝ рáдостїю возрáдꙋютсѧ всегдà, ны́нѣ и҆ при́снѡ и҆ во вѣ́ки вѣкѡ́въ. А҆ми́нь.

Blessed is God that hath girded me with strength, and made my way perfect, that maketh my feet like harts' feet, and setteth me up on high.

Then the cuffs, in the manner described. Then taking the epigonation, if he has it, and having blessed and kissed it, he says:

Gird Thy sword upon Thy thigh, O Thou Most Mighty, according to Thy splendor and Thy beauty, and bend Thy bow, and prosper, and reign, for the sake of truth, and meekness, and righteousness; and Thy right hand shall guide Thee wonderfully, always, now and ever, and unto the ages of ages. Amen.

Then taking the phelonion, and having blessed and kissed it, he says:

Thy priests, O Lord, shall be clothed with righteousness, and Thy saints shall rejoice, always, now and ever, and unto the ages of ages. Amen.

Та́же ѿше́дше въ предложе́нїе, оу҆мыва́ютъ
ру́ки, глаго́лz:

Оу҆мы́ю въ непови́нныхъ ру́цѣ мои̑, и҆ ѡ҆бы́дꙋ
же́ртвенникъ тво́й, гд҃и, є҆́же оу҆слы́шати
ми гла́съ хвалы̀ твоеѧ̀, и҆ повѣ́дати всѧ̑
чꙋдеса̀ твоѧ̑. гд҃и, возлюби́хъ бл҃голѣ́пїе до́мꙋ
твоегѡ̀, и҆ мѣ́сто селе́нїz сла́вы твоеѧ̀. да
не погꙋби́ши съ нечести́выми дꙋ́шꙋ мою̀, и҆
съ мꙋ́жи крове́й живота̀ моегѡ̀: и҆́хже въ
рꙋка́хъ беззакѡ́нїz, десни́ца и҆́хъ и҆спо́лнисz
мзды̀. а҆́зъ же неѕло́бїемъ мои́мъ ходи́хъ,
и҆зба́ви мѧ, гд҃и, и҆ поми́лꙋй мѧ. нога̀ моѧ̀
ста̀ на правотѣ̀, въ цр҃квахъ бл҃гословлю̀
тѧ̀, гд҃и.

Та́же поклоне́нїz три̑ пред предложе́нїемъ
сотво́рше, глаго́лютъ кі́йждо:

Бж҃е, ѡ҆чи́сти мѧ грѣ́шнаго и҆ поми́лꙋй
мѧ. и҆: и҆скꙋпи́лъ ны̀ є҆сѝ ѿ клѧ́твы
зако́нныz честно́ю твое́ю кро́вїю: на
крⷭ҇тѣ̀ пригвозди́всz и҆ копїе́мъ прободе́z,

Then, having gone to the sacristy, they
wash their hands, saying:

I will wash my hands in innocency, O Lord,
and so will I go round about Thine altar; That
I may hear the voice of Thy praise, and tell of
all Thy wondrous works. Lord, I have loved
the beauty of Thy house, and the dwelling-
place of Thy glory. O destroy not my soul
with the ungodly, nor my life with the blood-
thirsty; in whose hand is wickedness, and
their right hand is full of bribes. But as for
me, I have walked innocently; deliver me, O
Lord, and have mercy upon me. My foot hath
stood on the right; in the churches I will bless
Thee, O Lord.

Then making three bows to the waist
before the Table of Oblation, each says:

O God, cleanse me a sinner and have mercy
on me. And: Thou hast redeemed us from
the curse of the law by Thy precious Blood:
nailed to the Cross and pierced with a spear,

безсме́ртїе источи́лъ є҆сѝ человѣ́кѡмъ: сп҃се на́шъ, сла́ва тебѣ̀.

Та́же глаго́летъ дїа́конъ:

Бл҃гословѝ, влады́ко.

И҆ начина́етъ сщ҃е́нникъ:

Бл҃гослове́нъ бг҃ъ на́шъ всегда̀, ны́нѣ и҆ при́снѡ и҆ во вѣ́ки вѣкѡ́въ.
Дїа́конъ: А҆ми́нь.

Та́же прїе́млетъ сщ҃е́нникъ лѣ́вою оу҆́бѡ руко́ю просфору̀, десно́ю же ст҃о́е копїѐ, и҆ зна́менуꙋ и҆́мъ три́жды верху̀ печа́ти просфоры̀, глаго́летъ:

Въ воспомина́нїе гд҃а и҆ бг҃а и҆ сп҃са на́шегѡ і҆и҃са хрⷭ҇та̀. [Три́жды.]

И҆ а҆́бїе водружа́етъ копїѐ въ десну́ю страну̀ печа́ти, и҆ глаго́летъ рѣ́жꙋ:

Thou hast poured forth immortality upon mankind, O our Saviour, glory to Thee.

Then the deacon says:

Bless, master.

And the priest begins:

Blessed is our God, always, now and ever, and unto the ages of ages.
Deacon: Amen.

Then the priest takes a prosphora in his left hand, and in his right hand the holy spear, and making with it the sign of the cross thrice over the seal of the prosphora, he says:

In remembrance of our Lord and God and Saviour, Jesus Christ. Thrice.

And immediately he thrusts the spear into the right side of the seal, and cutting it, he says:

Ꙗ́кѡ ѻ҆вча̀ на заколе́нїе веде́сѧ.

Въ лѣ́вꙋю же:

И҆ ꙗ́кѡ а҆́гнецъ непоро́ченъ, пра́мѡ стригꙋ́щагѡ є҆го̀ безгла́сенъ, та́кѡ не ѿверза́етъ ᲂу҆́стъ свои́хъ.

Въ го́рнюю же странꙋ̀ печа́ти:

Во смире́нїи є҆гѡ̀ сꙋ́дъ є҆гѡ̀ взѧ́тсѧ.

Въ до́льнюю же странꙋ̀:

Ро́дъ же є҆гѡ̀ кто̀ и҆сповѣ́сть;

Дїа́конъ же взира́ѧ бл҃гоговѣ́йнѡ на сицево́е та́инство, глаго́летъ на є҆ди́нѣмъ ко́емждо рѣ́занїи:

Гдꙋ̀ помо́лимсѧ:

держа̀ и҆ ѻ҆ра́рь въ рꙋцѣ̀. По си́хъ глаго́летъ:

Возмѝ, влады́ко.

Сщ҃е́нникъ же, вложи́въ ст҃о́е копїѐ ѿ ко́свенныѧ десны́ѧ страны̀

He was led as a sheep to the slaughter.

And into the left side:

And as a blameless lamb before his shearer is dumb, so He openeth not his mouth.

And into the upper side of the seal:

In His humiliation His judgment was taken away.

And into the lower side:

And who shall declare his generation?

And the deacon, gazing reverently at this Mystery, says at each of these incisions:

Let us pray to the Lord;

holding also his orarion in his hand. After this he says:

Take away, master.

And the priest, having thrust the holy spear obliquely into the right side of the

просфоры̀, взима́етъ ст҃ы́й хлѣ́бъ,
глаго́ля си́це:

Ꙗ҆́кѡ взе́млется ѿ землѝ живо́тъ є҆гѡ̀.

И҆ положи́въ и҆̀ взна́къ на ст҃ѣ́мъ ді́скосѣ,
ре́кшꙋ дїа́конꙋ:

Пожрѝ, влады́ко.

Жре́тъ є҆гѡ̀ крестови́днѡ,
си́це глаго́ля:

Жре́тся а҆́гнецъ бж҃їй, взе́мляй грѣ́хъ мі́ра,
за мїрскі́й живо́тъ и҆ сп҃се́нїе.

И҆ ѡ҆браща́етъ горѣ̀ дрꙋгꙋ́ю странꙋ̀,
и҆мꙋ́щꙋю кр҃тъ.

Дїа́конъ глаго́летъ:

Прободѝ, влады́ко.

Сщ҃е́нникъ же, прободая и҆̀ въ деснꙋ́ю странꙋ̀
копїе́мъ, глаго́летъ:

prosphora, takes away the holy bread,
saying thus:

For His life is taken away from the earth.

And the priest having laid it inverted on
the holy diskos, the deacon says:

Sacrifice, master.

And he cuts it in the form of the Cross,
while saying:

**Sacrificed is the Lamb of God that taketh
away the sin of the world, for the life and
salvation of the world.**

And he turns upward the other side, which
has the sign of the Cross.

The deacon says:

Pierce, master.

And the priest, piercing also in the right
side with the spear, says:

Е҆ди́нъ ѿ во́инъ копїе́мъ ре́бра є҆гѡ̀ прободѐ, и҆ а҆́бїе и҆зы́де кро́вь и҆ вода̀: и҆ ви́дѣвый свидѣ́тельствова, и҆ и҆́стинно є҆́сть свидѣ́тельство є҆гѡ̀.

Дїа́конъ же, прїе́мь вїно̀ и҆ во́дꙋ, глаго́летъ ко сщ҃е́нникꙋ:

Блгⷭ҇овѝ, влады́ко, ст҃о́е соедине́нїе.

One of the soldiers with a spear pierced His side, and forthwith came there out blood and water. And he that saw it bare witness, and his witness is true.

The deacon, taking wine and water, says to the priest:

Bless, master, the holy union.

Й взе́мъ на́дъ ни́ми блгослове́нїе, вливае́тъ во ст҃ы́й поти́ръ ѿ вїна̀ вкꙋ́пѣ и воды̀.

[Е҆гда̀ же и҆ въ проскомі́дїи і҆ере́й, глаго́ля словеса̀ сїѧ̑: а҆бі́е и҆зы́де кро́вь и҆ вода̀, воды̀ ма́лѡ не влїе́тъ, є҆ще́ же по ѡ҆сщ҃е́нїи ст҃ы́хъ та́йнъ во своѐ вре́мѧ, є҆гда̀ влага́етъ во ст҃ы́й поти́ръ ча́сть ст҃а́гѡ а҆́гнца, не влїе́тъ ма́лѡ те́плыѧ воды̀, и҆ли вмѣ́стѡ те́плыѧ хла́днꙋю влїе́тъ во́дꙋ, сме́ртнѡ, ꙗ҆́кѡ престꙋ́пникъ цр҃ко́внагѡ преда́нїѧ, согрѣши́тъ.

Вливати же во́дꙋ въ проскомі́дїи, и҆ли по соверше́нїи во поти́ръ, до́лжно съ ве́лїимъ тща́нїемъ смотрѣ́ти, є҆́же бы вїнꙋ̀ сво́йственнагѡ вкꙋ́са не и҆змѣни́ти въ во́дный: и҆́бо та́йна въ сицево́мъ вїнѣ̀, є҆́же во вкꙋ́съ во́дный и҆змѣни́тсѧ, не соверши́тсѧ, и҆ слꙋжа́й та́кжѡ сме́ртнѡ согрѣши́тъ.]

And receiving the blessing upon them,
he pours wine together with water
into the holy chalice.

[If the priest, having said the following
words: "**and forthwith came there out blood
and water**", does not pour in a little water,
and also if, after the consecration of the
Holy Mysteries in its proper time, when he
puts into the holy chalice a piece of the Holy
Lamb, he does not pour in a little warm
water, or instead of warm water pours cold
water, he is committing a mortal sin as one
who breaks a tradition of the Church.

When the priest pours the water into the
chalice during the Proskomedia, or after
the consecration, he must with great care
be sure that the wine does not lose its
natural taste and begin tasting like water:
for in such wine, when its taste changes
to that of water, the Mystery shall not be
celebrated, and the celebrant shall commit
a mortal sin.]

Сще́нникъ, прїе́мь въ ру́цѣ вторꙊ́ю
просфорꙊ́, глаго́летъ:

Въ че́сть и па́мать пребл҃гослове́нным
вл҃чцы на́шем бц҃ы и приснодѣ́вы марі́н,
є҆а́же моли́твами прїнмѝ, гд҃н, же́ртꙊ сїю̀
въ пренбⷭ҇ный тво́й же́ртвеннкъ.

И҆ взе́мъ части́цꙊ, полага́етъ ю̀
ѡ҆деснꙊ́ю ст҃а́гѡ хлѣ́ба, бли́зъ среды̀
є҆гѡ̀, глаго́ла:

Предста̀ цр҃и́ца ѡ҆деснꙊ́ю тебѐ, въ ри́зы
позлаще́нны ѡ҆дѣ́анна, преꙋкраше́нна.

Та́же прїе́мь тре́тїю просфорꙊ́, глаго́летъ:

Честна́гѡ сла́внагѡ пррⷪ҇ка, предте́чн н
крⷭ҇ти́тела і҆ѡа́нна.

И҆ взе́мъ пе́рвꙊ́ю части́цꙊ, полага́етъ ю̀ ѡ
шꙋ́юю странꙊ́ ст҃а́гѡ хлѣ́ба, творѧ̀ нача́ло
пе́рвагѡ чи́на.

The priest, taking in his hand the second prosphora, says:

In honor and remembrance of our most blessed Lady, the Theotokos and Ever-Virgin Mary, through whose intercessions do Thou, O Lord, receive this sacrifice upon Thy most heavenly altar.

And taking out a particle, he places it on the right side of the holy bread, near its middle, saying:

Upon Thy right hand did stand the Queen; in garments of gold is she vested, wrought about with divers colors.

Then taking the third prosphora, he says:

Of the honorable glorious Prophet, Forerunner, and Baptist John.

And taking out the first particle, he places it on the left side of the holy bread, making the beginning of the first row.

Та́же глаго́летъ:

Ст҃ы́хъ сла́вныхъ про҇ро́кѡвъ: моѷсе́а и҆ а҆арѡ́на, и҆лїи́, и҆ є҆лїссе́а, дави́да и҆ і҆ессе́а: ст҃ы́хъ трїе́хъ ѻ҆трокѡ́въ, и҆ данїи́ла про҇ро́ка, и҆ всѣ́хъ ст҃ы́хъ про҇ро́кѡвъ.

И҆ взе́мъ ча́стицꙋ, полага́етъ ю҆ до́лѣ пе́рвыѧ бл҃гочи́ннѡ.

Та́же па́ки глаго́летъ:

Ст҃ы́хъ сла́вныхъ и҆ всехва́льныхъ а҆п҇лъ петра̀ и҆ па́ѵла, и҆ про́чихъ всѣ́хъ ст҃ы́хъ а҆п҇лѡвъ.

И҆ та́кѡ полага́етъ тре́тїю ча́стицꙋ до́лѣ вторы́ѧ, сконча́ва́ѧ пе́рвый чи́нъ.

Та́же глаго́летъ:

И҆́же во ст҃ы́хъ ѻ҆те́цъ на́шихъ, ст҃и́телей: васі́лїа вели́кагѡ, григо́рїа бг҃осло́ва и҆ і҆ѡа́нна златоꙋ́стагѡ: а҆ѳана́сїа и҆ кѷри́лла а҆леѯандрі́нскихъ, нїкола́а мѷрлѷкі́йскагѡ, мі҆ха́ила кі́евскагѡ, петра̀, а҆леѯі́а, і҆ѡ́ны,

Then he says:

Of the holy glorious prophets: Moses and Aaron, Elias and Elisseus, David and Jesse; of the Three holy Youths, of Daniel the Prophet, and of all the holy prophets.

And taking out a particle, he places it below the first, in the proper order.

Then he says again:

Of the holy glorious and all-praised Apostles Peter and Paul, and of all the other holy apostles.

And thus he places the third particle below the second, completing the first row.

Then he says:

Of our fathers among the saints, the holy hierarchs: Basil the Great, Gregory the Theologian, and John Chrysostom; Athanasius and Cyril of Alexandria; Nicholas of Myra in Lycia; Michael of Kiev; Peter, Alexis, Jonah,

фiлiппа, е҆рмоге́на, и҆ тv́хѡна моско́вскихъ, нiкíты новгоро́дскагѡ, леѡ́нтïа росто́в_ скагѡ, и҆ всѣ́хъ ст҃ы́хъ ст҃и́телей.

И҆ взе́мъ четве́ртꙋю ча́стицꙋ, полага́етъ ю҆ бли́зъ пе́рвыꙗ ча́стицы, творѧ̀ второ́е нача́ло.

Та́же па́ки глаго́летъ:

Ст҃а́гѡ а҆п҃ла, первомч҃нка и҆ а҆рхïдïа́кона стефа́на, ст҃ы́хъ вели́кихъ мч҃нкѡвъ дими́трïа, геѡ́ргïа, ѳеѡ́дѡра тv́рѡна, ѳеѡ́дѡра стратила́та, и҆ всѣ́хъ ст҃ы́хъ мч҃нкъ, и҆ мч҃нцъ: ѳе́клы, варва́ры, кv́рïакíн, е҆v҆фи́мïн и҆ параске́vы, е҆катери́ны, и҆ всѣ́хъ ст҃ы́хъ мч҃нцъ.

И҆ взе́мъ пѧ́тꙋю ча́стицꙋ, полага́етъ ю҆ до́лѣ пе́рвыꙗ, сꙋ́щïѧ нача́ломъ втора́гѡ чи́на.

Та́же глаго́летъ:

Philip, Hermogenes, and Tikhon of Moscow; Nicetas of Novgorod; Leontius of Rostov; and of all the holy hierarchs.

And taking a fourth particle, he places it near the first particle, making the beginning of the second row.

Then again he says:

Of the holy Apostle, Protomartyr, and Arch-deacon Stephen; the holy Great martyrs Demetrius, George, Theodore Tyro, Theodore Stratelates, and of all holy martyrs; and of the women martyrs: Thecla, Barbara, Kyriake, Euphemia, and Paraskeve, Catherine, and of all the holy women martyrs.

And taking a fifth particle, he places it below the first which is at the beginning of the second row.

Then he says:

Прпⷣбныхъ и҆ бг҃оно́сныхъ ѻ҆ц҃ъ на́шихъ: а҆нтѡ́нїа, є҆ѵѳѵ́мїа, са́ввы, ѻ҆нꙋ́фрїа, а҆ѳана́сїа а҆ѳѡ́нскагѡ, а҆нтѡ́нїа и҆ ѳеодо́сїа пече́рскихъ, се́ргїа ра́донежскагѡ, варлаа́ма хꙋ́тынскагѡ, серафі́ма саро́вскагѡ, и҆ всѣ́хъ прпⷣбныхъ ѻ҆ц҃ъ, и҆ прпⷣбныхъ ма́терей: пелагі́н, ѳеодо́сїн, а҆наста́сїн, є҆ѵпраѯі́н, февро́нїн, ѳеодꙋ́лїн, є҆ѵфроси́нїн, марі́н є҆гѵ́птаныни, и҆ всѣ́хъ ст҃ыхъ прпⷣбныхъ ма́терей.

И҆ та́кѡ взе́мъ шестꙋ́ю ча́стицꙋ, полага́етъ ю҆ до́лѣ вторы́а ча́стицы, во и҆сполне́нїе втора́гѡ чи́на.

По си́хъ же глаго́летъ:

Ст҃ыхъ и҆ чꙋдотво́рцевъ, безсре́бренꙋкъ космы̀ и҆ дамїа́на, кѵ́ра и҆ і҆ѡа́нна, пантелеи́мѡна и҆ є҆рмола́а, и҆ всѣ́хъ ст҃ыхъ безсре́бренꙋкѡвъ.

И҆ взе́мъ седмꙋ́ю ча́стицꙋ, полага́етъ ю҆ верхꙋ̀, творѧ̀ тре́тїе нача́ло, по чи́нꙋ.

Of our venerable and God-bearing fathers: Anthony, Euthymius, Sabbas, Onuphrius, Athanasius of Athos, Anthony and Theodosius of the Caves, Sergius of Radonezh, Barlaam of Khutyn, Seraphim of Sarov, and of all the venerable fathers; and of the venerable mothers: Pelagia, Theodosia, Anastasia, Eupraxia, Febronia, Theodulia, Euphrosyne, Mary of Egypt, and of all the venerable mothers.

And taking out a sixth particle, he places it below the second particle, in completion of the second row.

Then he says:

Of the saints and wonderworkers, the Unmercenaries: Cosmas and Damian, Cyrus and John, Panteleimon and Hermolaus, and of all the holy unmercenaries.

And taking out a seventh particle he places it at the top, making the beginning of the third row.

Та́же па́ки глаго́летъ:

Ст҃ы́хъ и пра́ведныхъ бг҃оотє́цъ їwакі́ма и а́нны: и ст҃а́гw и҆́мк҃ [є҆гẃже є҆́сть хра́мъ и҆ є҆гẃже є҆́сть де́нь] ст҃ы́хъ равноап҃льныхъ меѳо́дїа и кѷрі́лла, оу҆чи́телей славе́нскихъ: ст҃ы́хъ равноап҃льныхъ вели́кагw кн҃а́за влади́мїра, и҆ всѣ́хъ ст҃ы́хъ, и҆́хже моли́твами посѣти́ ны̀, бж҃е.

И҆ полага́етъ о҆́смꙋю части́цꙋ до́лѣ пе́рвыа бл҃гочи́ннw.

Є҆щѐ же къ си́мъ глаго́летъ:

И҆́же во ст҃ы́хъ о҆тца̀ на́шегw васі́лїа вели́кагw, а҆рхїепⷭ҇кпа кесарі́н каппадокі́нскїа.

И҆ та́кw взе́мъ девѧ́тꙋю части́цꙋ, полага́етъ ю҆̀ въ коне́цъ тре́тїагw чи́на, во и҆сполне́ніе.

Та́же прїе́мъ четве́ртꙋю просфорꙋ̀, глаго́летъ:

Помѧнѝ, влⷣко чл҃вѣколю́бче, вели́кагw господи́на и҆ о҆тца̀ на́шего ст҃ѣ́йшаго

Then again he says:

Of the holy and Righteous Ancestors of God, Joachim and Anna; and of Saint(s) N. (whose temple it is and whose day it is); of the holy Equals to the Apostles Methodius and Cyril, teachers of the Slavs; of the holy Equals to the Apostles Great Prince Vladimir, and of all the saints, through whose intercessions do Thou visit us, O God.

And he places the eighth particle below the first, in the proper order.

After this he says:

Of our father among the saints, Basil the Great, Archbishop of Caesarea in Cappadocia.

And then taking out a ninth particle, he places it at the end of the third row, completing it.

Then taking a fourth prosphora, he says:

Remember, O Master, Lover of Mankind, our great lord and father, the Most Holy

патріа́рха и҆м҃къ, и҆ господи́на на́шего высоко-
преѡсще́нн҃ѣйшаго митрополі́та и҆м҃къ,
первоїера́рха р꙾сскіѧ зар꙾бе́жныѧ цр҃кве, и҆
господи́на на́шего высокопреѡсще́нн҃ѣйшаго
а҆рхїепи́скопа [и҆лѝ преѡсще́нн҃ѣйшаго е҆пи́скопа]
и҆м҃къ [е҆гѡ́же е҆па́рхїа], честно́е пресвv́терство,
во хр҃тѣ̀ дїа́конство и҆ ве́сь сще́нническїй
чи́нъ, [а҆́ще во ѻ҆би́тели: а҆рхїмандрі́та и҆лѝ
и҆г꙾мена и҆м҃къ:], и҆ всю̀ бра́тїю на́ш꙾, ꙗ҆́же
призва́лъ е҆сѝ во твоѐ ѻ҆бще́нїе, твои́мъ
бл҃гоу҆тро́бїемъ, всебл҃гі́й вл҃ко.

И҆ взе́мъ ча́стиц꙾, полага́етъ ю҆̀ до́лѣ ст҃а́гѡ
хлѣ́ба.

Та́же помина́етъ и҆̀же во вла́сти с꙾́ть,
глаго́лѧ си́це:

Помѧнѝ гд҃и бг҃охрани́м꙾ю стран꙾̀ рѡссі́йск꙾ю
и҆ правосла́вныѧ лю́ди е҆ѧ̀ во ѻ҆те́чествїи и҆
въ разсѣ́ѧнїи с꙾́щіѧ, стран꙾̀ сїю̀, вла́сти и҆
во́инство е҆ѧ̀ и҆ всѣ́хъ вѣ́рою и҆ бл҃гоче́стїемъ
жив꙾́щихъ въ не́й.

Patriarch N.; and our lord, the Very Most Reverend Metropolitan N., First Hierarch of the Russian Church Abroad; and our lord, the Most Reverend Archbishop (or Bishop) N. (whose diocese it is); the honorable priesthood, the diaconate in Christ and all the priestly order, (if in a monastery: Archimandrite or Abbot N.), and all our brethren whom, in Thy compassion, Thou hast called into Thy communion, O All-good Master.

And taking out a particle, he places it below the holy bread.

Then he commemorates those who are in authority, saying thus:

Remember, O Lord, the God-preserved Russian land, and its Orthodox people in the homeland and in the diaspora, this land, its authorities and armed forces, and all who in faith and piety dwell therein.

Та́же помина́етъ, и҆́хже и҆́мать живы́хъ,
по и҆́мени и҆ на ко́еждо и҆́мѧ взе́млетъ
ча́стицꙋ, глаго́лѧ:

Помѧнѝ, гдⷭ҇и, и҆́мⷬ҇къ:

И҆ та́кѡ взе́мъ ча́стицы, полага́етъ а҆̀ до́лѣ
стⷢ҇а́гѡ хлѣ́ба.

Та́же взе́мъ пѧ́тꙋю просфорꙋ̀, глаго́летъ:

Ѽ па́мѧти и҆ ѡ҆ставле́нїи грѣхѡ́въ
стⷯ҇ѣ́йшихъ патрїа́рхѡвъ правосла́вныхъ
и҆ блгⷪ҇чести́выхъ црⷬ҇е́й и҆ блгⷪ҇чести́выхъ
црⷬ҇и́цъ, бл҃же́нныхъ созда́телей стⷢ҇а́гѡ хра́ма
сегѡ̀ [а҆́ще во ѡ҆би́тели: стⷯ҇ы́ѧ ѡ҆би́тели сеѧ̀].

Та́же помина́етъ рꙋкоположи́вшаго
є҆го̀ а҆рхїере́а и҆ дрꙋги́хъ, и҆́хже хо́щетъ,
оу҆со́пшихъ по и҆́мени. На ко́еждо
и҆́мѧ взима́етъ ча́стицꙋ,
приглаго́лѧ:

Помѧнѝ, гдⷭ҇и: и҆́мⷬ҇къ.

И҆ коне́чнѣ глаго́летъ си́це:

Then he commemorates those that are living, by name, and at each name he takes out a particle, saying:

Remember, O Lord, N.

And having taken out a particle, he places it below the holy bread.

Then taking a fifth prosphora, he says:

In commemoration and for the remission of sins of the most holy Orthodox patriarchs, of pious kings and pious queens; and of the blessed founders of this holy church (if it be a monastery: **of this holy monastery**).

Then he commemorates the departed, by name: the bishop that ordained him (if he is among the departed), and others, whomsoever he wills. At each name he takes out a particle, saying:

Remember, O Lord, N.

And finally he says thus:

Й всѣхъ въ надѣжди воскрⷭ҇нїѧ, жизни вѣ́чныѧ й твоегѡ̀ Ѻ҆бщѣ́нїѧ ѹ҆со́пшихъ правосла́вныхъ ѻ҆тє́цъ й бра́тїй на́шихъ, чл҃вѣколю́бче гдⷭ҇и.

Й взима́етъ ча́стицꙋ.

По се́мъ глаго́летъ:

Помѧни̑, гдⷭ҇и, й моѐ недосто́инство, й прости̑ ми всѧ́кое согрѣшѣ́нїе, во́льное же й нево́льное.

Й взима́етъ ча́стицꙋ.

Й прїе́мъ гꙋбꙋ̀, собира́етъ на дї́скосъ ча́стицы до́лѣ ст҃а́гѡ хлѣ́ба, ꙗ҆́коже бы́ти во ѹ҆тверже́нїи, и не испа́днꙋти чесомꙋ̀.

Та́же дїа́конъ, прїе́мь кади́льницꙋ й ѳѷмїа́мъ вложи́въ въ ню̀, глаго́летъ ко сщ҃е́нникꙋ:

Бл҃гословѝ, влады́ко, кади́ло.

Й а҆́бїе са́мъ глаго́летъ:

And of all our Orthodox fathers and brethren who have departed in the hope of resurrection, life eternal, and communion with Thee, O Lord, Lover of mankind.

And he takes out a particle.

Then he says:

Remember, O Lord, also mine unworthiness, and pardon me every transgression, both voluntary and involuntary.

And he takes out a particle.

And taking the sponge, he gathers the particles together on the diskos below the holy bread, so that they are secure, and none of them fall off.

Then the deacon, taking the censer and having placed incense in it, says to the priest:

Bless the incense, master.

And immediately the deacon himself says:

Гдꙋ помо́лимсѧ.

И сщё́нникъ
моли́твꙋ кади́ла:

Кади́ло тебѣ̀ принóсимъ хрⷭ҇тѐ бж҃е на́шъ, въ воню̀ бл҃гоꙋха́нїѧ дꙋхóвнагѡ, є҆́же прїе́мь въ пренбⷭ҇ный твóй же́ртвенникъ, возниспослѝ на́мъ бл҃года́ть прест҃а́гѡ твоегѡ̀ дх҃а.

Дїа́конъ: Гдꙋ помо́лимсѧ.

Сщё́нникъ, покади́въ ѕвѣздицꙋ, полага́етъ верхꙋ̀ ст҃а́гѡ хлѣ́ба, глагóлѧ:

И пришéдши ѕвѣзда̀, ста̀ верхꙋ̀, и҆дѣ́же бѣ̀ Ѻ҆троча̀.
Дїа́конъ: Гдꙋ помо́лимсѧ.

Іере́й покади́въ пéрвый покрóвецъ, покрыва́етъ ст҃ый хлѣ́бъ съ дíскосомъ, глагóлѧ:

Гдⷭ҇ь воцри́сѧ, въ лѣ́потꙋ ѡ҆блече́сѧ: ѡ҆блече́сѧ гдⷭ҇ь въ си́лꙋ, и҆ препоѧ́сасѧ. И҆́бо оꙋтвердѝ вселéннꙋю, ꙗ҆́же не подви́житсѧ.

Let us pray to the Lord.

And the priest says the
Prayer of the Incense:

Incense do we offer unto Thee, O Christ
our God, as an odour of spiritual fragrance;
accepting it upon Thy most heavenly altar, do
Thou send down upon us the grace of Thy
Most Holy Spirit.

Deacon: Let us pray to the Lord.

The priest, having censed the asterisk,
places it over the holy bread, saying:

And the star came and stood over where the
young Child was.

Deacon: Let us pray to the Lord.

The priest, having censed the first veil,
covers the holy bread and the diskos,
saying:

The Lord is King, He is clothed with majesty;
the Lord is clothed in strength, and hath girt
Himself, for He hath made the whole world

Готовъ прⷭ҇то́лъ тво́й ѿто́лѣ, ѿ вѣ́ка ты̀ є҆сѝ. Воздвиго́ша рѣ́ки, гдⷭ҇и, воздвиго́ша рѣ́ки гла́сы своѧ̀: во́змꙋтъ рѣ́ки сотре́нïѧ своѧ̀, ѿ гласѡ́въ во́дъ мно́гихъ. Ди́вны высѡ́ты морскі́ѧ, ди́венъ въ высо́кихъ гдⷭ҇ь, свидѣ́нïѧ твоѧ̀ ѹ҆вѣ́ришасѧ ѕѣлѡ̀: до́мꙋ твоемꙋ̀ подоба́етъ ст҃ы́нѧ гдⷭ҇и въ долготꙋ̀ дні́й.

Дïа́конъ: Гдꙋ̀ помо́лимсѧ. Покры́й влады́ко.

Îере́й же, покади́въ вторы́й покро́вецъ, покрыва́етъ ст҃ы́й поти́ръ, глаго́лѧ:

Покры̀ нб҃са̀ добродѣ́тель твоѧ̀ хрⷭ҇тѐ, и҆ хвалы̀ твоеѧ̀ и҆спо́лнь землѧ̀.

Дïа́конъ: Гдꙋ̀ помо́лимсѧ. Покры́й влады́ко.

Îере́й же, покади́въ покро́въ, си́рѣчь возд꙳ꙋхъ, и҆ покрыва́ѧ ѻ҆бо́ѧ, глаго́летъ:

so sure, that it shall not be moved. From the beginning is Thy throne prepared; Thou art from everlasting. The rivers are risen, O Lord, the rivers have lift up their voices. The rivers shall stir up their havoc; from the voices of many waters, Wonderful are the heights of the sea; wonderful is the Lord on high. Thy testimonies are very sure; holiness becometh Thine house, O Lord, unto length of days.

Deacon: Let us pray to the Lord. Cover, master.

And the priest, having censed the second veil, covereth the holy chalice, saying:

Thy virtue covered the heavens, O Christ, and the earth is full of Thy praise.

Deacon: Let us pray to the Lord. Cover, master.

Then the priest, having censed the veil, i.e. the aer, covers both the holy diskos and the holy chalice, saying:

Покры́й на́съ кро́вомъ крилꙋ̀ твое́ю, и̑ ѿженѝ ѿ на́съ всѧ́кагѡ врага̀ и̑ сꙋпоста́та: ѹ̑мирѝ живо́тъ на́шъ, гдⷭ҇и, поми́лꙋй на́съ, и̑ мі́ръ тво́й, и̑ спасѝ дꙋ́шы на́шѧ, ꙗ҆́кѡ бл҃гъ и̑ чл҃вѣколю́бецъ.

Та́же прїе́мь сщ҃е́нникъ кади́льницꙋ, кади́тъ предложе́нїе, глаго́лѧ три́жды:

Бл҃гослове́нъ бг҃ъ на́шъ, си́це бл҃говоли́вый, сла́ва тебѣ̀.

Дїа́конъ же на ко́емждо глаго́летъ:

Всегда̀, ны́нѣ и̑ при́снѡ, и̑ во вѣ́ки вѣкѡ́въ. А҆ми́нь.

И̑ покланѧ́ютсѧ бл҃гоговѣ́йнѡ ѻ�҆́ба, три́жды.

Та́же прїе́мь дїа́конъ кади́льницꙋ, глаго́летъ:

Ѡ̑ предложе́нныхъ честны́хъ дарѣ́хъ, гдꙋ҃ помо́лимсѧ.

Сщ҃е́нникъ же мл҃твꙋ предложе́нїѧ:

Shelter us with the shelter of Thy wings, and drive away from us every enemy and adversary. Make our life peaceful, O Lord, have mercy on us, and on Thy world, and save our souls, for Thou art good and the Lover of mankind.

Then, taking the censer, the priest censes the offering, saying thrice:

Blessed is our God Who is thus well pleased, glory to Thee.

And the deacon says each time:

Always, now and ever, and unto the ages of ages. Amen.

And both bow reverently, thrice.

Then, taking the censer, the deacon says:

For the precious gifts set forth, let us pray to the Lord.

And the priest says the Prayer of Oblation:

Бж҃е, бж҃е на́шъ, нб҃ный хлѣ́бъ, пи́щꙋ всемꙋ̀ мі́рꙋ, гд҃а на́шего и҆ бг҃а і҆и҃са хрⷭ҇та̀ посла́вый сп҃са, и҆ и҆збавителѧ и҆ блг҃одѣ́телѧ, блг҃ословѧ́ща и҆ ѡ҆сщ҃а́юща на́съ, са́мъ блг҃ословѝ предложе́нїе сїѐ, и҆ прїимѝ є҆̀ въ пренбⷭ҇ный тво́й же́ртвенникъ. Помѧнѝ, ꙗ҆́кѡ бл҃гъ и҆ чл҃вѣколю́бецъ, прине́сшихъ, и҆ и҆́хже ра́ди принесо́ша: и҆ на́съ неѡсꙋжде́ны сохранѝ во сщ҃еннодѣ́йствїи бж҃е́ственныхъ твои́хъ та́инъ. Ꙗ҆́кѡ ст҃и́сѧ и҆ просла́висѧ пречⷭ҇тно́е, и҆ великолѣ́пое и҆́мѧ твоѐ, ѻ҆ц҃а̀, и҆ сн҃а, и҆ ст҃а́гѡ дх҃а, нн҃ѣ и҆ при́снѡ, и҆ во вѣ́ки вѣкѡ́въ. А҆ми́нь.

И҆ посе́мъ твори́тъ ѿпꙋ́стъ та́мѡ, глаго́лѧ си́це:

Сла́ва тебѣ̀, хрⷭ҇тѐ бж҃е, оу҆пова́нїе на́ше, сла́ва тебѣ̀.

Дїа́конъ: Сла́ва, и҆ нн҃ѣ: Гдⷭ҇и поми́лꙋй, три́жды. Блг҃ословѝ.

O God, our God, Who didst send forth the Heavenly Bread, the food of the whole world, our Lord and God, Jesus Christ, the Saviour and Redeemer and Benefactor Who blesseth and sanctifieth us: Do Thou Thyself bless this offering, and accept it upon Thine altar above the heavens. As Thou art good and the Lover of mankind, remember those that offer it, and those for whose sake it was offered; and keep us uncondemned in the ministry of Thy Divine Mysteries. For hallowed and glorified is Thy most honorable and majestic name: of the Father, and of the Son, and of the Holy Spirit, now and ever, and unto the ages of ages. Amen.

And after this he pronounces the dismissal there, saying:

Glory to Thee, O Christ God, our hope, glory to Thee.
Deacon: Glory . . . both now . . . Amen. Lord have mercy. Thrice. Bless.

Сщенникъ глаголетъ ѿпꙋстъ:

Аще ᲂу҆бѡ є҆́сть недѣ́ла: Воскрⷭ҇ый и҆з̾ мє́ртвыхъ:

Аще ли же ни: Хрⷭ҇то́съ и҆́стинный бг҃ъ на́шъ, мл҃твами пречⷭ҇тыꙗ своеѧ̀ мт҃ре, и҆́же во ст҃ых̾ ѻ҆ц҃а̀ на́шегѡ васі́лїа вели́кагѡ, а҆рхїепⷭ҇кпа кесарі́и каппадокі́нскіѧ, и҆ всѣ́хъ ст҃ых̾, поми́лꙋетъ и҆ спасе́тъ на́съ, ꙗ҆́кѡ бл҃гъ и҆ чл҃вѣколю́бецъ.

Дїа́конъ: А҆ми́нь.

По ѿпꙋстѣ́ же кади́тъ дїа́конъ ст҃о́е предложе́нїе. Та́же ѿхо́дитъ, и҆ кади́тъ ст҃ꙋ́ю трапе́зꙋ крꙋго́мъ крⷭ҇тови́днѡ, глаго́лѧ въ себѣ̀:

Во гро́бѣ пло́тски, во а҆́дѣ же съ дꙋше́ю ꙗ҆́кѡ бг҃ъ, въ раѝ же съ разбо́йникомъ, и҆ на прⷭ҇то́лѣ бы́лъ є҆сѝ, хрⷭ҇тѐ, со ѻ҆ц҃е́мъ и҆ дх҃омъ, всѧ̑ и҆сполнѧ́ѧй неѡпи́санный.

The priest says the dismissal:

If it be Sunday: May Christ our true God, Who rose from the dead, . . .

If not: May Christ our true God, through the intercessions of His most pure Mother; of our father among the saints Basil the Great, Archbishop of Caesarea in Cappadocia; and of all the saints, have mercy on us and save us, for He is good and the Lover of mankind. Deacon: Amen.

After the dismissal, the deacon censes the holy offering. Then he goes and censes the Holy Table round about in the shape of a cross, saying silently:

In the grave bodily, but in Hades with Thy soul as God; in Paradise with the thief, and on the throne with the Father and the Spirit wast Thou Who fillest all things, O Christ the Inexpressible.

Та́же ѱало́мъ н҃-й, Поми́лꙋй мѧ бж҃е: въ не́мже и покади́въ ст҃и́лище же и хра́мъ ве́сь, вхо́дитъ па́ки во ст҃ы́й Ѻлта́рь, и покади́въ ст҃ꙋ́ю трапе́зꙋ па́ки, и сщ҃е́нника, кади́льницꙋ оу҆́бѡ ѿлага́етъ на мѣ́сто своѐ, са́мъ же прихо́дитъ ко і҆ере́ю. И҆ ста́вше вкꙋ́пѣ пред̾ ст҃о́ю трапе́зою, покланѧ́ютсѧ три́жды, въ себѣ̀ молѧ́щесѧ, и҆ глаго́люще:

Цр҃ю̀ нбⷭ҇ный, оу҆тѣ́шителю, дш҃е и́стины, и́же вездѣ̀ сы́й, и҆ всѧ̑ и҆сполнѧ́ѧй, сокро́вище бл҃ги́хъ и҆ жи́зни пода́телю: прїидѝ и҆ всели́сѧ въ ны̀, и҆ ѡ҆чи́сти ны̀ ѿ всѧ́кїѧ скве́рны, и҆ сп҃сѝ, бл҃же, дꙋ́шы на́шѧ.

Сла́ва въ вы́шнихъ бг҃ꙋ, и҆ на землѝ ми́ръ, въ чл҃вѣ́цѣхъ бл҃говоле́нїе. в҃-жды.

Гдⷭ҇и, оу҆стнѣ̀ моѝ ѿве́рзеши, и҆ оу҆ста̀ моѧ̑ возвѣстѧ́тъ хвалꙋ̀ твою̀.

Та́же цѣлꙋ́ютъ, сщ҃е́нникъ оу҆́бѡ ст҃о́е є҆ѵⷢ҇лїе, дїа́конъ же ст҃ꙋ́ю трапе́зꙋ.

Then the 50th Psalm: **Have mercy on me,
O God** . . . during which, having censed
the sanctuary and the whole temple, he
enters again into the holy altar, and having
again censed the Holy Table, and the priest,
he puts aside the censer into its place,
and approaches the priest. And standing
together before the Holy Table, they bow
down thrice, while praying secretly, saying:

O Heavenly King, Comforter, Spirit of
Truth, Who art everwhere present and fillest
all things, Treasury of good things and Giver
of life: Come and dwell in us, and cleanse us
of all impurity, and save our souls, O Good
One.

Glory to God in the highest, and on earth
peace, good will among men. Twice.

O Lord, open Thou my lips, and my
mouth shall show forth Thy praise.

Then the priest kisses the Holy Gospel,
and the deacon the Holy Table.

Й посе́мъ подклони́въ діа́конъ свою́ главꙋ̀ сщ҃е́нннкꙋ, держа̀ и ѡра́рь треми́ пе́рсты десны́ѧ рꙋкѝ, глаго́летъ:

Вре́мѧ сотвори́ти гд҃ви, влады́ко, бл҃гослови́.

Сщ҃е́нникъ знаменꙋ́ѧ є҆го̀ глаго́летъ:

Бл҃гослове́нъ бг҃ъ на́шъ, всегда̀, ны́нѣ и҆ при́снѡ, и҆ во вѣ́ки вѣкѡ́въ.

Та́же діа́конъ: Помоли́сѧ ѡ҆ мнѣ̀ влады́ко ст҃ы́й.

Сщ҃е́нникъ: Да и҆спра́витъ гд҃ь стѡпы̀ твоѧ̀.

Й па́ки діа́конъ: Помѧни́ мѧ, влады́ко ст҃ы́й.

Сщ҃е́нникъ: Да помѧне́тъ тѧ̀ гд҃ь бг҃ъ во цр҃твїи свое́мъ, всегда̀, ны́нѣ и҆ при́снѡ, и҆ во вѣ́ки вѣкѡ́въ.

Дїа́конъ же: А҆ми́нь.

Й поклони́всѧ, и҆схо́дитъ сѣ́верными две́рьми, поне́же црⷦкїѧ две́ри до вхо́да не ѿверза́ютсѧ. Й ста́въ на ѻ҆бы́чнѣмъ мѣ́стѣ, прѧ́мѡ ст҃ы́хъ двере́й, покланѧ́етсѧ со бл҃гоговѣ́нїемъ, три́жды, глаго́лѧ въ себѣ̀:

After this, the deacon, bowing his head
to the priest, and holding his orarion with
three fingers of his right hand, says:

It is time for the Lord to act. Master, bless.

The priest, signing him with the sign of the
Cross, says:

Blessed is our God, always, now and ever,
and unto the ages of ages.

Then the deacon: Pray for me, holy master.

Priest: May the Lord direct thy steps.

And again the deacon: Remember me, holy
master.

Priest: May the Lord God remember thee
in His kingdom, always, now and ever, and
unto the ages of ages.

Deacon: Amen.

And having bowed, he goes out by the north
door, because the royal doors are not opened
until the entrance. And standing in the usual
place, directly before the holy doors, he bows
reverently thrice, saying secretly:

Гдⷭ҇и, оу҆стнѣ̀ моѝ ѿве́рзеши, и҆ оу҆ста̀ моѧ̀ возвѣстѧ́тъ хвалꙋ̀ твою̀.

И҆ посе́мъ начина́етъ глаго́лати:

Бл҃гословѝ, влады́ко.

И҆ начина́етъ сщ҃е́нникъ:

Бл҃гослове́но црⷭ҇тво:

В҆ѣ́дати подоба́етъ: а҆́ще бе́зъ дїа́кона слꙋ́житъ і҆ере́й, въ проскомі́дїи дїа́конскихъ сло́бъ, и҆ на лїтꙋргі́и пред̾ є҆ѵⷢ҇лїемъ, и҆ на ѿвѣ́тъ є҆гѡ̀: Бл҃гословѝ влады́ко, и҆ Проводѝ влады́ко, и҆ Вре́мѧ сотвори́ти, да не глаго́летъ, то́чїю є҆ктенїѝ и҆ чино́вное предложе́нїе.

А҆́ще же собо́ромъ слꙋ́жатъ сщ҃е́ннїи мно́зи, дѣ́йство проскомі́дїи є҆ди́нъ і҆ере́й то́кмѡ да твори́тъ, и҆ глаго́летъ и҆з̾ѡбраже́ннаѧ. Про́чїи же слꙋжи́тели ничто́же проскомі́дїи ѻ҆со́бнѡ да глаго́лютъ.

O Lord, Thou shalt open Thou my lips, and my mouth shall show forth Thy praise.

And afterwards he begins, saying:

Bless, master.

And the priest begins:

Blessed is the kingdom . . .

It is important to note that if a priest serves without a deacon, the words of the deacon in the Proskomedia, and during the Liturgy before the Gospel, and his response: Bless, master, and Pierce, master, and It is time to act, . . . are not said, but only the litanies and the rite of the Proskomedia.

If many priests concelebrate, the rite of the Proskomedia is celebrated by only one priest who says what is set forth. None of the other celebrants, however, shall say anything of the Proskomedia themselves.

Вѣждь, ꙗкѡ сїа бж҃твенная лїтꙋргїа великагѡ васілїа не всегда поетсѧ, но во времѧ оу҆чинненное, си́рѣчь, въ недѣлахъ великїѧ четыредесѧ́тницы, [кромѣ недѣли ва́їй:] и҆ во ст҃ы́й вели́кїй четверто́къ, въ вели́кꙋю сꙋббѡ́тꙋ, и҆ въ наве́черїи рж҃тва̀ хр҃то́ва, и҆ бг҃оѧвле́нїй, и҆ въ де́нь пра́здника ст҃а́гѡ васі́лїа. Сказа́нїе же и҆ оу҆ста́въ сегѡ̀ сщ҃еннодѣ́йствїа то́жде е҆́сть, е҆́же и҆ ст҃а́гѡ і҆ѡа́нна златоꙋ́стагѡ.

This Divine Liturgy of Basil the Great
is not always celebrated, but on the
appointed days, namely: the Sundays of
Great Lent, not including Palm Sunday;
on Holy and Great Thursday and on Holy
Saturday; on the eves of the Nativity of
Christ and of Theophany; and on the Feast
of St Basil. The order and rule of this
Divine Service are the same as that of St
John Chrysostom.

Бжественнаѧ Літургіа

Дїа́конъ: Бл҃гослови́, влады́ко.

Їере́й:

Бл҃гослове́но ца́рство, Ѻ҆ц҃а̀, и҆ сн҃а, и҆ ст҃а́гѡ дх҃а, ны́нѣ и҆ при́снѡ, и҆ во вѣ́ки вѣкѡ́въ.

Ли́къ: А҆ми́нь.

Дїа́конъ: Ми́ромъ гд҃у помо́лимсѧ.

Ли́къ: Гд҃и поми́луй.

Дїа́конъ: Ѽ свы́шнемъ ми́рѣ, и҆ спасе́нїи ду́шъ на́шихъ, гд҃у помо́лимсѧ.

Ли́къ: Гд҃и поми́луй.

Дїа́конъ: Ѽ ми́рѣ всегѡ̀ ми́ра, бл҃гостоѧ́нїи ст҃ы́хъ бж҃їихъ цр҃кве́й, и҆ соедине́нїи всѣ́хъ, гд҃у помо́лимсѧ.

Ли́къ: Гд҃и поми́луй.

The Divine Liturgy

Deacon: Bless, master.

Priest:

Blessed is the kingdom of the Father, and of the Son, and of the Holy Spirit, now and ever, and unto the ages of ages.

Choir: Amen.

Deacon: In peace let us pray to the Lord.

Choir: Lord, have mercy.

Deacon: For the peace from above, and the salvation of our souls, let us pray to the Lord.

Choir: Lord, have mercy.

Deacon: For the peace of the whole world, the good estate of the holy churches of God, and the union of all, let us pray to the Lord.

Choir: Lord, have mercy.

Дїа́конъ: Ѡ ст҃е́мъ хра́мѣ се́мъ, и҆ съ вѣ́рою, бл҃гогове́нїемъ и҆ стра́хомъ бж҃їимъ входѧ́щихъ во́нь, гд҃у помо́лимсѧ.

Ли́къ: Гд҃и поми́луй.

Дїа́конъ: Ѡ вели́комъ господи́нѣ и҆ ѻ҆тцѣ̀ на́шемъ ст҃е́йшемъ патрїа́рсѣ и҆м҃къ, и҆ ѡ господи́нѣ на́шемъ высокопреѡсщ҃е́н-нѣйшемъ митрополи́тѣ и҆м҃къ, первоїера́рсѣ ру́сскїѧ зарубе́жныѧ цр҃кве, и҆ ѡ господи́нѣ на́шемъ высокопреѡсщ҃е́ннѣйшемъ а҆рхїе-пі́скопѣ [и҆лѝ преѡсщ҃е́ннѣйшемъ є҆пі́скопѣ] и҆м҃къ, честнѣ́мъ пресвv́терствѣ, во хрⷭ҇тѣ̀ дїа́констѣ, ѡ все́мъ при́чтѣ и҆ лю́дехъ, гд҃у помо́лимсѧ.

Ли́къ: Гд҃и поми́луй.

Дїа́конъ: Ѡ странѣ̀ се́й, власте́хъ и҆ во́инствѣ є҆ѧ̀, и҆ всѣ́хъ вѣ́рою и҆ бл҃гоче́стїемъ живу́-щихъ въ не́й, гд҃у помо́лимсѧ.

Ли́къ: Гд҃и поми́луй.

Дїа́конъ: Ѡ бг҃охрани́мѣй странѣ̀ рѡссі́йстѣй и҆ правосла́вныхъ лю́дехъ є҆ѧ̀ во ѻ҆те́чествїи и҆ разсѣ́ѧнїи су́щихъ и҆ ѡ сп҃се́нїи и҆́хъ, гд҃у помо́лимсѧ.

Deacon: For this holy temple, and for them that with faith, reverence, and the fear of God enter herein, let us pray to the Lord.

Choir: Lord, have mercy.

Deacon: For our great lord and father, the Most Holy Patriarch N.; for our lord, the Very Most Reverend Metropolitan N., First Hierarch of the Russian Church Abroad; for our lord the Most [or Right] Reverend Archbishop [or Bishop] N.; for the venerable priesthood, the diaconate in Christ, for all the clergy and people, let us pray to the Lord.

Choir: Lord, have mercy.

Deacon: For this land, its authorities, and armed forces, and all who with faith and piety dwell therein, let us pray to the Lord.

Choir: Lord, have mercy.

Deacon: For the God-preserved Russian land and its Orthodox people both in the homeland and in the diaspora, and for their salvation, let us pray to the Lord.

Ли́къ: Гди помилꙋй.

Дїа́конъ: Ѡ є́же и҆зба́вити лю́ди своѧ̑ ѿ вра̑гъ ви́димыхъ и҆ неви́димыхъ, въ на́съ же ѹ҆тверди́ти є҆диномы́сліе, братолю́біе и҆ бл҃гоче́стїе, гдꙋ помо́лимсѧ.

Ли́къ: Гди помилꙋй.

Дїа́конъ: Ѡ гра́дѣ се́мъ [и҆лѝ ѡ ве́си се́й, и҆лѝ ѡ ст҃ѣй ѻ҆би́тели се́й], всѧ́комъ гра́дѣ, странѣ̀, и҆ вѣ́рою живꙋ́щихъ въ ни́хъ, гдꙋ помо́лимсѧ.

Ли́къ: Гди помилꙋй.

Дїа́конъ: Ѡ бл҃горастворе́нїи воздꙋ́ховъ, ѡ и҆з̑оби́лїи пло́дѡвъ земны́хъ, и҆ време́нѣхъ ми́рныхъ, гдꙋ помо́лимсѧ.

Ли́къ: Гди помилꙋй.

Дїа́конъ: Ѡ пла́вающихъ, пꙋтеше́ствꙋю_щихъ, недꙋ́гꙋющихъ, стра́ждꙋщихъ, плѣне́н_ныхъ, и҆ ѡ спасе́нїи и҆̀хъ, гдꙋ помо́лимсѧ.

Ли́къ: Гди помилꙋй.

Дїа́конъ: Ѡ и҆зба́витисѧ на́мъ ѿ всѧ́кіѧ ско́рби, гнѣ́ва и҆ нꙋ́жды, гдꙋ помо́лимсѧ.

Choir: Lord, have mercy.

Deacon: That He may deliver His people from enemies visible and invisible, and confirm in us oneness of mind, brotherly love, and piety, let us pray to the Lord.

Choir: Lord, have mercy.

Deacon: For this city [or village, or holy monastery], for every city and country, and the faithful that dwell therein, let us pray to the Lord.

Choir: Lord, have mercy.

Deacon: For seasonable weather, abundance of the fruits of the earth, and peaceful times, let us pray to the Lord.

Choir: Lord, have mercy.

Deacon: For travelers by sea, land and air, for the sick, the suffering, the imprisoned, and for their salvation, let us pray to the Lord.

Choir: Lord, have mercy.

Deacon: That we may be delivered from all tribulation, wrath, and necessity, let us pray to the Lord.

Ли́къ: Гдⷭ҇и поми́лꙋй.

Дїа́конъ: Застꙋпи̑, спаси̑, поми́лꙋй, и҆ сохрани̑ на́съ, бж҃е, твое́ю блⷢ҇ода́тїю.

Ли́къ: Гдⷭ҇и поми́лꙋй.

Дїа́конъ: Прест҃ꙋю, пречⷭ҇тꙋю, пребл҃гослове́н_ нꙋю, сла́внꙋю влⷣчцꙋ на́шꙋ бцⷣꙋ и҆ приснодв҃ꙋ мр҃і́ю со все́ми ст҃ы́ми помѧнꙋвше, са́ми себѐ, и҆ дрꙋ́гъ дрꙋ́га, и҆ ве́сь живо́тъ на́шъ хрⷭ҇тꙋ̀ бг҃ꙋ предади́мъ.

Ли́къ: Тебѣ̀ гдⷭ҇и.

Моли́тва пе́рвагѡ а҆нтїфѡ́на та́йнѡ глаго́летсѧ ѿ і҆ере́а:

Гдⷭ҇и бж҃е на́шъ, є҆гѡ́же держа́ва несказа́нна, и҆ сла́ва непости́жима, є҆гѡ́же млⷭ҇ть безмѣ́рна и҆ чл҃вѣколю́бїе неизрече́нно: са́мъ, влⷣко, по блг҃оꙋтро́бїю твоемꙋ̀, при́зри на ны̀ и҆ на ст҃ы́й хра́мъ се́й, и҆ сотвори̑ съ на́ми, и҆ молѧ́щимисѧ съ на́ми, бога̑тыѧ ми́лѡсти твоѧ̑ и҆ ще́дрѡты твоѧ̑.

Choir: Lord, have mercy.

Deacon: Help us, save us, have mercy on us, and keep us, O God, by Thy grace.

Choir: Lord, have mercy.

Deacon: Calling to remembrance our most holy, most pure, most blessed, glorious Lady Theotokos and Ever-Virgin Mary with all the saints, let us commit ourselves and one another and all our life unto Christ, our God.

Choir: To Thee, O Lord.

The priest secretly says the prayer of the first antiphon:

O Lord our God, Whose dominion is indescribable, and Whose glory is incomprehensible, Whose mercy is infinite, and Whose love for mankind is ineffable: Do Thou Thyself, O Master, according to Thy tender compassion, look upon us, and upon this holy temple, and deal with us, and them that pray with us, according to Thine abundant mercies and compassion.

Возглаше́нїе: Ꙗ҆́кѡ подоба́етъ тебѣ̀ всѧ́каѧ сла́ва, че́сть и҆ поклоне́нїе, Ѻ҆ц҃ꙋ̀, и҆ сн҃ꙋ, и҆ ст҃о́мꙋ дх҃ꙋ, ны́нѣ и҆ при́снѡ, и҆ во вѣ́ки вѣкѡ́въ.

Ли́къ: А҆ми́нь.

Дїа́конъ поклони́всѧ ѡ҆устꙋпа́етъ ѿ мѣ́ста своегѡ̀, и҆ ѡ҆ше́дъ стои́тъ пред̾ і҆кѡ́ною хрⷭ҇то́вою, держа̀ и҆ ѡ҆ра́рь тремѝ пе́рсты десны́ѧ рꙋкѝ.

И҆ пое́тсѧ пе́рвый а҆нтїфѡ́нъ ѿ пѣвце́въ:

Бл҃гословѝ дꙋшѐ моѧ̀ гдⷭ҇а, бл҃гослове́нъ е҆сѝ гдⷭ҇и. Бл҃гословѝ дꙋшѐ моѧ̀ гдⷭ҇а, и҆ всѧ̑ внꙋ́треннѧѧ моѧ̑, и҆́мѧ ст҃о́е є҆гѡ̀. Бл҃гословѝ дꙋшѐ моѧ̀ гдⷭ҇а, и҆ не забыва́й всѣ́хъ воздаѧ́нїй є҆гѡ̀: Ѡ҆чища́ющагѡ всѧ̑ беззакѡ́нїѧ твоѧ̑, и҆сцѣлѧ́ющагѡ всѧ̑ недꙋ́ги твоѧ̑: И҆збавлѧ́ющагѡ ѿ и҆стлѣ́нїѧ живо́тъ тво́й, вѣнча́ющаго тѧ̀ ми́лостїю и҆ щедро́тами: И҆сполнѧ́ющаго во бл҃ги́хъ жела́нїе твоѐ: ѡ҆бнови́тсѧ ꙗ҆́кѡ ѻ҆рла̀ ю҆́ность твоѧ̀. Творѧ́й ми́лѡстыни гдⷭ҇ь, и҆ сꙋдьбꙋ̀ всѣ̑мъ ѡ҆би́димымъ. Сказа̀ пꙋти̑ своѧ̑ мѡѷсе́ови, сыновѡ́мъ і҆и҃левымъ хотѣ́нїѧ

Exclamation: For unto Thee is due all glory, honor and worship, to the Father, and to the Son, and to the Holy Spirit, now and ever, and unto the ages of ages.

Choir: Amen.

The deacon, bowing, steps aside from his place and stands before the icon of Christ, holding his orarion with three fingers of his right hand.

And the first antiphon is sung by the choir:

Bless the Lord, O my soul, and all that is within me bless His holy Name. Bless the Lord, O my soul, and forget not all His benefits; Who forgiveth all thine iniquities, and healeth all thy diseases; Who redeemeth thy life from corruption, and crowneth thee with mercy and compassion; Who satisfieth thy desire with good things; thy youth shall be renewed like the eagle's. The Lord performeth deeds of mercy, and judgment for all them that are wronged. He made known His ways unto Moses, His will unto the children

своѧ̀. Ще́дръ и҆ мⷧ҇тивъ гдⷭ҇ь, долготерпѣли́въ и҆ многомⷧ҇тивъ.

Бл҃гослови́ дꙋше́ моѧ̀ гдⷭ҇а, и҆ всѧ̀ внꙋ́треннѧѧ моѧ̀, и҆́мѧ ст҃о́е є҆гѡ̀.

Бл҃гослове́нъ є҆сѝ гдⷭ҇и.

По и҆сполне́нїи же а҆нтїфѡ́на, прише́дъ дїа́конъ и҆ ста́въ на ѻ҆бы́чнѣмъ мѣ́стѣ и҆ поклони́всѧ, глаго́летъ:

Па́ки и҆ па́ки ми́ромъ гдⷭ҇ꙋ помо́лимсѧ.

Ли́къ: Гдⷭ҇и поми́лꙋй.

Дїа́конъ: Застꙋпѝ, спасѝ, поми́лꙋй и҆ сохранѝ на́съ бж҃е, твое́ю бл҃года́тїю.

Ли́къ: Гдⷭ҇и поми́лꙋй.

Дїа́конъ: Прест҃ꙋ́ю, пречⷭ҇тꙋ́ю, пребл҃гослове́н_ нꙋ́ю, сла́внꙋю вл҃чцꙋ на́шꙋ бцⷣꙋ и҆ приснодв҃ꙋ мр҃і́ю со всѣ́ми ст҃ы́ми помѧнꙋ́вше, са́ми себѐ, и҆ дрꙋ́гъ дрꙋ́га, и҆ ве́сь живо́тъ на́шъ хрⷭ҇тꙋ̀ бг҃ꙋ предади́мъ.

Ли́къ: Тебѣ̀ гдⷭ҇и.

of Israel. The Lord is compassionate and merciful, long-suffering, and of great kindness.

Bless the Lord, O my soul, and all that is within me bless His holy Name.

Blessed art Thou, O Lord.

At the conclusion of the antiphon, the deacon, having returned to his usual place and bowed, says:

Again and again, in peace let us pray to the Lord.

Choir: Lord, have mercy.

Deacon: Help us, save us, have mercy on us, and keep us, O God, by Thy grace.

Choir: Lord, have mercy.

Deacon: Calling to remembrance our most holy, most pure, most blessed, glorious Lady Theotokos and Ever-Virgin Mary, with all the saints, let us commit ourselves and one another and all our life unto Christ, our God.

Choir: To Thee, O Lord.

Моли́тва втора́гѡ антїфѡ́на та́йнѡ
глаго́летсѧ ѿ і҆ере́а:

Г҃ди бж҃е на́шъ, спаси́ лю́ди твоѧ̑ и҆ бл҃гослови́
досто́ѧніе твоѐ, и҆сполне́ніе це́ркве
твоеѧ̀ сохрани́, ѡ҆сти́ лю́бѧщыѧ бл҃голѣ́піе
до́мꙋ твоегѡ̀: ты̀ тѣ́хъ возпросла́ви
бж҃е́ственною твое́ю си́лою, и҆ не ѡ҆ста́ви
на́съ ѹ҆пова́ющихъ на тѧ̀.

Возглаше́ніе: Ꙗ҆́кѡ твоѧ̀ держа́ва, и҆ твоѐ
є҆́сть ц҃рство и҆ си́ла и҆ сла́ва, ѻ҆ц҃а̀, и҆ сн҃а,
и҆ ст҃а́гѡ дх҃а, ны́нѣ и҆ при́снѡ, и҆ во вѣ́ки
вѣкѡ́въ.

Ли́къ: А҆ми́нь.

И҆ пое́тсѧ подо́бнѣ ѿ пѣвце́въ вторы́й
антїфѡ́нъ: дїа́конъ же подо́бнѣ твори́тъ,
ꙗ҆́коже и҆ въ пе́рвой моли́твѣ.

Сла́ва ѻ҆ц҃ꙋ̀, и҆ сн҃ꙋ, и҆ ст҃о́мꙋ дх҃ꙋ.

Хвали́ дꙋшѐ моѧ̀ гдⷭ҇а. Восхвалю̀ гдⷭ҇а въ
животѣ̀ мое́мъ, пою̀ бг҃ꙋ мое́мꙋ, до́ндеже
є҆́смь. Не надѣ́йтесѧ на кнѧ́зи, на сы́ны

The priest secretly says the prayer of the second antiphon:

O Lord our God, save Thy people and bless Thine inheritance, preserve the fullness of Thy Church, sanctify them that love the beauty of Thy house; do Thou glorify them by Thy divine power, and forsake not us that hope in Thee.

Exclamation: For Thine is the dominion, and Thine is the kingdom, and the power, and the glory, of the Father, and of the Son, and of the Holy Spirit, now and ever, and unto the ages of ages.

Choir: Amen.

And the second antiphon is sung by the choir in like manner to the first. The deacon does also as during the first prayer.

Glory to the Father, and to the Son, and to the Holy Spirit.

Praise the Lord, O my soul. While I live will I praise the Lord, I will sing unto my

человѣ́ческіѧ, въ ни́хже нѣ́сть сп҃сенїѧ. Изы́детъ
дꙋ́хъ є҆гѡ̀, и҆ возврати́тсѧ въ зе́млю свою̀: въ
то́й де́нь поги́бнꙋтъ всѧ̑ помышлє́нїѧ є҆гѡ̀.
Бл҃же́нъ, є҆мꙋ́же бг҃ъ і҆а́кѡвль помо́щникъ є҆гѡ̀,
оу҆пова́нїе є҆гѡ̀ на гд҃а бг҃а своегѡ̀: Сотво́ршаго
нб҃о и҆ зе́млю, мо́ре, и҆ всѧ̑ ꙗ҆́же въ ни́хъ:
Хранѧ́щаго и҆́стинꙋ въ вѣ́къ, творѧ́щаго сꙋ́дъ
ѡ҆би́димымъ, даю́щаго пи́щꙋ а҆́лчꙋщымъ. Гд҃ь
рѣши́тъ ѡ҆кова̑нныѧ, гд҃ь оу҆мꙋдрѧ́етъ слѣпцы̀,
гд҃ь возво́дитъ низве́ржєнныѧ, гд҃ь лю́битъ
пра́ведники. Гд҃ь храни́тъ прише́льцы, си́ра и҆
вдовꙋ̀ прїи́метъ, и҆ пꙋ́ть грѣ́шныхъ погꙋби́тъ.
Воцр҃и́тсѧ гд҃ь во вѣ́къ, бг҃ъ тво́й сїѡ́не, въ
ро́дъ и҆ ро́дъ.

И҆ ны́нѣ и҆ при́снѡ, и҆ во вѣ́ки вѣкѡ́въ.
А҆ми́нь.

Є҆диноро́дный сн҃е, и҆ сло́ве бж҃їй, безсме́ртенъ
сы́й, и҆ и҆зво́ливый сп҃сенїѧ на́шегѡ ра́ди
воплоти́тисѧ ѿ ст҃ы́ѧ бц҃ы, и҆ приснодв҃ы
мр҃і́и, непрело́жнѡ вочл҃вѣ́чивыйсѧ: распны́йсѧ

God as long as I have being. O put not your trust in princes, in the sons of men, in whom there is no salvation. His spirit shall go forth, and he shall return again to his earth; in that day all his thoughts shall perish. Blessed is he that hath the God of Jacob for his helper, whose hope is in the Lord his God; Who made heaven and earth, the sea, and all that therein is, Who preserveth truth for ever; Who rendereth judgement for the wronged, Who giveth food unto the hungry; the Lord looseth the fettered; The Lord looseth the fettered; the Lord giveth wisdom to the blind; the Lord raiseth up the fallen; the Lord loveth the righteous; the Lord preserveth the proselytes; He defendeth the fatherless and the widow, but the way of sinners shall He destroy. The Lord shall reign forever; thy God, O Sion, unto generation and generation.

Both now, and ever, and unto the ages of ages. Amen.

O Only-begotten Son and Word of God, Who art immortal, yet didst deign for our salvation to become incarnate of the holy Theotokos and Ever-Virgin Mary, and without

же хрⷵтѐ бже, смертїю смерть попра́вый, є҆ди́нъ сый стꙑ́ѧ трⷪцы, спрославлѧ́емый ѻ҆ц҃ꙋ и҆ ст҃о́мꙋ дх҃ꙋ, сп҃си на́съ.

Дїа́конъ: Па́ки и҆ па́ки ми́ромъ гдꙋ помо́лимсѧ.

Ли́къ: Гдⷵи помилꙋ́й.

Дїа́конъ: Застꙋпѝ, спасѝ, помилꙋ́й и҆ сохранѝ на́съ бже, твое́ю блгода́тїю.

Ли́къ: Гдⷵи помилꙋ́й.

Дїа́конъ: Прест҃ꙋ́ю, пречтⷵꙋ́ю, пребⷵлгослове́ннꙋю, сла́внꙋю влⷣчцꙋ на́шꙋ бцⷣꙋ и҆ присноде́вꙋ мр҃і́ю со все́ми ст҃ꙑ́ми помѧнꙋ́вше, са́ми себѐ, и҆ дрꙋ́гъ дрꙋ́га, и҆ ве́сь живо́тъ на́шъ хрⷵтꙋ̀ бг҃ꙋ предади́мъ.

Ли́къ: Тебѣ̀ гдⷵи.

Моли́тва тре́тїѧгѡ а҆нтїфѡ́на та́йнѡ глаго́летсѧ ѿ і҆ере́а:

И҆́же ѻ҆́бщыѧ сїѧ̑, и҆ согла́сныѧ дарова́вый на́мъ мл҃твы, и҆́же и҆ двема̀ и҆лѝ тре́мъ соглаⷵꙋ́ющымсѧ ѡ҆ и҆́мени твое́мъ проше́нїѧ

change didst become man, and wast crucified, O Christ God, trampling down death by
death: Thou Who art one of the Holy Trinity, glorified together with the Father and the
Holy Spirit, save us.

Deacon: Again and again, in peace let us
pray to the Lord.

Choir: Lord, have mercy.

Deacon: Help us, save us, have mercy on us,
and keep us, O God, by Thy grace.

Choir: Lord, have mercy.

Deacon: Calling to remembrance our most
holy, most pure, most blessed, glorious Lady
Theotokos and Ever-Virgin Mary, with all
the saints, let us commit ourselves and one
another and all our life unto Christ, our God.

Choir: To Thee, O Lord.

The priest secretly says the prayer of the
third antiphon:

O Thou Who hast bestowed upon
us these common and concordant
prayers, and Who hast promised that when

подати ѡбѣщавый, самъ и нынѣ рабъ
твоихъ прошенїѧ къ полезномꙋ исполни,
подаждь намъ въ настоѧщемъ вѣцѣ познанїе
твоеѧ истины, и въ бꙋдꙋщемъ животъ
вѣчный дарꙋѧ.

Возглашенїе: Ꙗкѡ блгъ и чл҃вѣколюбецъ
бг҃ъ е҆сѝ, и тебѣ славꙋ возсылаемъ, ѻ҆ц҃ꙋ,
и сн҃ꙋ, и ст҃омꙋ дх҃ꙋ, нынѣ и приснѡ, и во
вѣки вѣкѡвъ.

Ли́къ: А҆минь.

Здѣ ѿверзаютсѧ двери на
малый входъ.

Во цр҃твїи твоемъ помѧни насъ, гд҃и, е҆гда
прїидеши во цр҃твїи твоемъ.

Блажени нищїи дꙋхомъ, ꙗкѡ тѣхъ е҆сть
цр҃тво нб҃ное.

Блажени плачꙋщїи, ꙗкѡ тїи оу҆тѣшатсѧ.

Блажени кротцыи, ꙗкѡ тїи наслѣдѧтъ
землю.

two or three are agreed in Thy name Thou wouldst grant their requests: Do Thou Thyself fulfill the requests of Thy servants to their profit, granting us in this present age the knowledge of Thy truth, and in that to come, life everlasting.

Exclamation: For a good God art Thou and the Lover of mankind, and unto Thee do we send up glory, to the Father, and to the Son, and to the Holy Spirit, now and ever, and unto the ages of ages.

Choir: Amen.

Here the doors are opened for the Small Entrance.

In Thy Kingdom remember us, O Lord, when Thou comest in Thy Kingdom.

Blessed are the poor in spirit, for theirs is the Kingdom of Heaven.

Blessed are they that mourn, for they shall be comforted.

Blessed are the meek, for they shall inherit the earth.

Бл҃же́нни а҆лчꙋ́щїи и҆ жа́ждꙋщїи пра́вды, ꙗ҆́кѡ ті́и насы́тѧтсѧ.

Бл҃же́нни ми́лостивїи, ꙗ҆́кѡ ті́и поми́ловани бꙋ́дꙋтъ.

Бл҃же́нни чи́стїи се́рдцемъ, ꙗ҆́кѡ ті́и бг҃а ѹ҆́зрѧтъ.

Бл҃же́нни миротво́рцы, ꙗ҆́кѡ ті́и сы́нове бж҃їи нарекꙋ́тсѧ.

Бл҃же́нни и҆згна́нни пра́вды ра́ди, ꙗ҆́кѡ тѣ́хъ є҆́сть ца́рство нб҃ное.

Бл҃же́нни є҆стѐ, є҆гда̀ поно́сѧтъ ва́мъ, и҆ и҆зжен́тъ, и҆ реку́тъ всѧ́къ ѕо́лъ глаго́лъ, на вы̀ лжꙋ́ще менѐ ра́ди.

Ра́дꙋйтесѧ и҆ весели́тесѧ, ꙗ҆́кѡ мзда̀ ва́ша мно́га на нб҃сѣ́хъ.

Сла́ва ѻ҆ц҃ꙋ̀, и҆ сн҃ꙋ, и҆ ст҃о́мꙋ дх҃ꙋ.

И҆ ны́нѣ и҆ при́снѡ, и҆ во вѣ́ки вѣкѡ́въ, а҆ми́нь.

Пѣва́емꙋ же тре́тїемꙋ а҆нтїфѡ́нꙋ ѿ пѣвце́въ, и҆ли бл҃же́ннамъ, а҆́ще є҆́сть недѣ́лѧ, є҆гда̀ прїи́дꙋтъ на Сла́ва: сщ҃е́нникъ и҆ дїа́конъ, ста́вше пред̾ ст҃о́ю трапе́зою, творѧ́тъ покло́ны трѝ. Та́же прїе́мь

Blessed are those who hunger and thirst for righteousness, for they shall be filled.

Blessed are the merciful, for they shall obtain mercy.

Blessed are the pure in heart, for they shall see God.

Blessed are the peacemakers, for they shall be called sons of God.

Blessed are they that are persecuted for righteousness' sake, for theirs is the Kingdom of Heaven.

Blessed are ye when men shall revile and persecute you and say all manner of evil against you falsely for My sake.

Rejoice and be exceeding glad, for your reward is great in the Heavens.

Glory to the Father, and to the Son, and to the Holy Spirit, both now and ever, and unto the ages of ages. Amen.

As the Beatitudes (if it be Sunday) or the third antiphon is sung by the choir, when they come to the Glory, the priest and the deacon, standing before the Holy Table, make three bows from the waist. Then

сщ҃е́нникъ ст҃о́е є҆ѵⷢ҇лїе, дае́тъ дїа́конꙋ, и҆ и҆дꙋ́тъ ѿ десны́ѧ страны̀ созадѝ прⷭ҇то́ла, и҆ та́кѡ и҆зше́дше сѣ́верною страно́ю, предидꙋ́щымъ и҆̀мъ лампа́дамъ, творѧ́тъ ма́лый вхо́дъ, и҆ ста́вше на ѻ҆бы́чнѣмъ мѣ́стѣ, приклонѧ́ютъ ѻ҆́ба главы̑, и҆ дїа́конꙋ ре́кшꙋ: Гдⷭ҇ꙋ помо́лимсѧ, глаго́летъ сщ҃е́нникъ моли́твꙋ вхо́да та́йнѡ.

Мл҃тва вхо́да:

Вл҃ко гдⷭ҇и бж҃е на́шъ, ᲂу҆ста́вивый на нб҃сѣ́хъ чи́ны и҆ вѡ́инства а҆́гг҃лъ и҆ а҆рха́гг҃лъ въ слꙋже́нїе твоеѧ̀ сла́вы, сотворѝ со вхо́домъ на́шимъ вхо́дꙋ ст҃ы́хъ а҆́гг҃лѡвъ бы́ти, сослꙋжа́щихъ на́мъ, и҆ сославосло́вѧщихъ твою̀ бл҃гость.

Ꙗ҆́кѡ подоба́етъ тебѣ̀ всѧ́каѧ сла́ва, че́сть и҆ поклоне́нїе, ѻ҆ц҃ꙋ̀, и҆ сн҃ꙋ, и҆ ст҃о́мꙋ дх҃ꙋ, ны́нѣ и҆ при́снѡ, и҆ во вѣ́ки вѣкѡ́въ. А҆ми́нь.

the priest, taking the Holy Gospel, gives it to the deacon, and they go to the right, behind the Holy Table. Thus coming out of the north side, with candles going before them, they make the Small Entrance; and standing in the usual place, both of them bow their heads, and the deacon, having said: Let us pray to the Lord, the priest says the prayer of the Entrance secretly:

OMaster Lord our God, Who hast appointed in the heavens the ranks and hosts of angels and archangels unto the service of Thy glory: With our entry do Thou cause the entry of the holy angels, serving and glorifying Thy goodness with us.

For unto Thee is due all glory, honor, and worship: to the Father, and to the Son, and to the Holy Spirit, now and ever, and unto ages of ages. Amen.

Моли́твѣ же скончавшейсѧ, глаго́летъ
дїа́конъ ко сще́нникꙋ, показꙋ́ѧй къ восто́кꙋ
десни́цею, держа̀ вкꙋ́пѣ и ѡра́рь тремѝ
пе́рсты:

Блгословѝ, влады́ко, сты́й вхо́дъ.

И сще́нникъ, блгословлѧ́ѧ, глаго́летъ:

Блгослове́нъ вхо́дъ сты́хъ твои́хъ, всегда̀,
ны́нѣ и при́снѡ, и во вѣ́ки вѣкѡ́въ.

Посе́мъ ѿхо́дитъ ко сти́телю, и҆лѝ и҆гꙋ́менꙋ,
дїа́конъ, и цѣлꙋ́етъ є҆ѵⷢлїе, а҆́ще предстои́тъ:
а҆́ще же нѝ, цѣлꙋ́етъ сїѐ сще́нникъ.

Испо́лньшꙋсѧ же коне́чномꙋ тропарю̀,
вхо́дитъ дїа́конъ посредѣ̀, и ста́въ пред
и҆ере́емъ возвыша́етъ ма́лѡ рꙋ́цѣ, и
показꙋ́ѧй сто́е є҆ѵⷢлїе, глаго́летъ велегла́снѡ:

Премꙋ́дрость, про́сти.

Та́же поклони́всѧ, са́мъ же и сще́нникъ
созадѝ є҆гѡ̀, вхо́дитъ во сты́й ѻ҆лта́рь: и

When the prayer is ended, the deacon says
to the priest, pointing toward the east with
his right hand, holding therein his orarion
with three fingers:

Bless, master, the holy entrance.

And the priest, blessing, says:

**Blessed is the entrance of Thy saints, always,
now and ever, and unto the ages of ages.**

After that, the deacon goes to the bishop,
or to the abbot (if either is present), and he
kisses the Gospel; if not, the priest kisses it.

When the prayer has been finished, the
deacon goes to the center, and standing in
front of the priest, lifts the Holy Gospel up
to be seen by all, and says in a loud voice:

Wisdom, aright!

Then, having bowed, as does the priest
behind him, the deacon and the priest
enter into the holy altar; and the deacon

діа́конъ оу҆́бѡ полага́етъ ст҃о́е є҆ѵⷢ҇лїе на ст҃є́й
трапе́зѣ.

Пѣвцы́ же пою́тъ:

Прїиди́те, поклони́мсѧ и҆ припаде́мъ ко хрⷭ҇тꙋ̀.
Сп҃си́ ны сн҃е бж҃їй, во ст҃ы́хъ ди́венъ сы́й,
пою́щыѧ тѝ: а҆ллилꙋ́їа. [є҆ди́ножды]
А҆́ще же недѣ́лѧ: Воскрⷭ҇ы́й и҆з̾ ме́ртвыхъ,
пою́щыѧ тѝ: а҆ллилꙋ́їа. [є҆ди́ножды]

Та́же, ѻ҆бы́чныѧ тропарѝ.

Глаго́летъ і҆ере́й моли́твꙋ сїю̀ та́йнѡ:

Мл҃тва трист҃а́гѡ пѣ́нїѧ:

Бж҃е ст҃ы́й, и҆́же во ст҃ы́хъ почива́ѧй,
трист҃ы́мъ гла́сомъ ѿ серафі́мѡвъ вос-
пѣва́емый и҆ ѿ херꙋві́мѡвъ славосло́вимый,
и҆ ѿ всѧ́кїѧ нбⷭ҇ныѧ си́лы покланѧ́емый,
и҆́же ѿ небытїѧ̀ во є҆́же бы́ти приведы́й
всѧ́ческаѧ, созда́вый человѣ́ка по ѡ҆́бразꙋ
твоемꙋ̀ и҆ по подо́бїю, и҆ всѧ́кимъ твои́мъ

immediately lays the Holy Gospel on the
Holy Table.

And the choir sings:

O come, let us worship and fall down before
Christ; O Son of God Who art wondrous in
the saints, save us who chant unto Thee: Alleluia. [once]

On Sundays: Who didst rise from the dead,
save us who chant unto Thee: Alleluia. [once]

Then the usual troparia and kontakia are
sung by the choir whilst the priest says
prayer secretly:

The Prayer of the Trisagion Hymn:

O Holy God, Who restest in the saints,
Who art praised with the thrice-holy
hymn by the Seraphim, and art glorified by
the Cherubim, and art worshipped by all the
heavenly hosts, Who from non-existence
hast brought all things into being, Who
hast created man according to Thine image
and likeness, and hast adorned him with

дарова́нїемъ ᲂу҆краси́вый, да́й проша́щемꙋ
премꙋ́дрость и҆ ра́зꙋмъ, и҆ не презира́й
согрѣша́ющагѡ, но полага́й на спⷭ҇е́нїе
покаѧ́нїе, сподо́бивый на́съ, смире́нныхъ
и҆ недосто́йныхъ ра̑бъ твои́хъ, и҆ въ ча́съ
се́й ста́ти пред̾ сла́вою ст҃а́гѡ твоегѡ̀
же́ртвенника, и҆ до́лжное тебѣ̀ поклоне́нїе
и҆ славосло́вїе приноси́ти: са́мъ, влⷣко, прїими́
и҆ ѿ ᲂу҆́стъ на́съ грѣ́шныхъ трист҃ꙋ́ю пѣ́снь,
и҆ посѣти́ ны бл҃гостїю твое́ю, прости́
на́мъ вся́кое согрѣше́нїе во́льное же и҆
нево́льное, ѡ҆ст҃и́ на́ша дꙋ́шы и҆ тѣлеса̀,
и҆ да́ждь на́мъ въ преподо́бїи слꙋжи́ти
тебѣ̀ вся̑ дни̑ живота̀ на́шегѡ, мл҃твами
ст҃ы́а бцⷣы, и҆ всѣ́хъ ст҃ы́хъ, ѿ вѣ́ка тебѣ̀
бл҃гоꙋгоди́вшихъ.

Є҆гда̀ же пѣвцы̀ прїидꙋ́тъ въ послѣ́днїй
тропа́рь, гл҃етъ дїа́конъ ко і҆ере́ю, приклонѧ̀
вкꙋ́пѣ главꙋ̀, и҆ ѡ҆ра́рь въ рꙋцѣ̀ держа̀
тремѝ пе́рсты:

Thine every gift; Who givest wisdom and understanding to him that asketh, and Who disdainest not him that sinneth, but hast appointed repentance unto salvation; Who hast vouchsafed us, Thy lowly and unworthy servants, to stand even in this hour before the glory of Thy holy altar, and to offer the worship and glory due unto Thee: Do Thou Thyself, O Master, accept even from the lips of us sinners the thrice-holy hymn, and visit us in Thy goodness. Pardon us every sin, voluntary and involuntary; sanctify our souls and bodies, and grant us to serve Thee in holiness all the days of our life, through the intercessions of the holy Theotokos, and of all the saints, who from ages past have been pleasing unto Thee.

And when the singers come to the last kontakion, the deacon says to the priest, while bowing his head and holding his orarion with three fingers of his right hand:

Блгослови̂, влады́ко, вре́мѧ трист҃а́гw.

Іере́й же, зна́менꙋѧ є҆го̀, глаго́летъ:

Ꙗ҆кw ст҃ъ є҆сѝ бж҃е на́шъ, и҆ тебѣ̀ сла́вꙋ возсыла́емъ, ѻ҆ц҃ꙋ, и҆ сн҃ꙋ, и҆ ст҃о́мꙋ дх҃ꙋ, ны́нѣ и҆ при́снw.

Скончавшꙋ́сѧ же кондакꙋ̀, прихо́дитъ діа́конъ бли́зъ ст҃ы́хъ двере́й, и҆ показꙋ́ѧй ѡ҆раре́мъ, пе́рвѣе ᲂу҆̀бо ко і҆кѡ́нѣ хрⷭ҇то́вѣ глаго́летъ:

Гдⷭ҇и, спⷭ҇ѝ блгочести́выѧ, и҆ ᲂу҆слы́ши ны̀.

Та́же наво́дитъ, глаго́лѧ ко внѣ̀ стоѧ́щымъ велегла́снw:

Й во вѣ́ки вѣкѡ́въ.

Ли́къ: А҆ми́нь и҆ Трист҃о́е.

Пѣва́емꙋ же трист҃о́мꙋ, глаго́лютъ и҆ са́ми, і҆ере́й же и҆ діа́конъ, трист҃о́е: творѧ́ще вкꙋ́пѣ и҆ покло́ны трѝ пред ст҃о́ю трапе́зою.

Bless, master, the time of the Thrice-holy.

And the priest, signing him with the sign of
the Cross, exclaims:

For holy art Thou, our God, and unto Thee
do we send up glory, to the Father, and to the
Son, and to the Holy Spirit, now and ever.

And the kontakion having ended, the
deacon comes out through the holy doors,
and standing on the ambo and pointing with
his orarion, first to the icon of Christ, says:

O Lord, save the pious, and hearken unto us.

Then he points to all the people, saying in a
loud voice:

And unto the ages of ages.

Choir: **Amen** and the Trisagion.

While the Trisagion is sung, both the
priest and the deacon themselves say the
Trisagion Hymn, together making three
bows before the Holy Table.

Та́же глаго́летъ дїа́конъ ко і҆ере́ю:

Повели̑, влады́ко.

И҆ ѿхо́дѧтъ къ го́рнемꙋ мѣ́стꙋ: и҆ сщ҃е́нникъ
ѿходѧ̀ глаго́летъ:

Бл҃гослове́нъ грѧды́й во и҆́мѧ гдⷭ҇не.

Дїа́конъ: Бл҃гослови̑, влады́ко, го́рнїй прⷭ҇то́лъ.
Їере́й же: Бл҃гослове́нъ є҆сѝ на прⷭ҇то́лѣ сла́вы
црⷭ҇тві́ѧ твоегѡ̀, сѣдѧ́й на херꙋві́мѣхъ,
всегда̀, ны́нѣ и҆ при́снѡ, и҆ во вѣ́ки вѣкѡ́въ.

[Вѣ́дательно, ꙗ҆́кѡ сщ҃е́нникꙋ не подоба́етъ
на го́рнее мѣ́сто восходи́ти, нижѐ сѣдѣ́ти
на не́мъ: но сѣдѣ́ти во странѣ̀ го́рнѧгѡ
прⷭ҇то́ла, и҆з̀ ю́жныѧ страны̀.]

И҆ по и҆сполне́нїи трист҃а́гѡ, дїа́конъ,
прише́дъ пред̀ ст҃ы́ѧ две́ри,
глаго́летъ:

Во́нмемъ.

Then the deacon says to the priest:

Command, master.

And they proceed to the high place; and the priest, as he goes, says:

Blessed is He that cometh in the name of the Lord.
Deacon: Bless, master, the high throne.
Priest: Blessed art Thou on the throne of the glory of Thy kingdom, Thou that sittest upon the Cherubim, always, now and ever, and unto the ages of ages.

[It is to be noted that it is not proper for the priest to go up onto the high place, nor to sit thereon, but to sit on the south side of the high throne.]

And upon the conclusion of the Trisagion, the deacon, having come toward the holy doors, says:

Let us attend.

Їере́й же возглаша́етъ: **Ми́ръ всѣ́мъ.**

И҆ чте́цъ глаго́летъ: **И҆ дꙋ́хови твоемꙋ̀.**

И҆ дїа́конъ па́ки: **Премꙋ́дрость.**

И҆ чте́цъ: проки́менъ,
ѱало́мъ дв҃довъ.

Посе́мъ дїа́конъ: **Премꙋ́дрость.**

И҆ чте́цъ надписа́нїе а҆пⷭ҇ла: **Дѣѧ́нїй**
ст҃ыхъ а҆пⷭ҇лъ чте́нїе, и҆лѝ: **Собо́рнагѡ**
посла́нїѧ і҆а́ковлѧ, и҆лѝ **петро́ва чте́нїе,**
и҆лѝ **Къ ри́млѧнѡмъ,** и҆лѝ **Къ**
кори́нѳѧнѡмъ, и҆лѝ **Къ гала́тѡмъ**
посла́нїѧ ст҃а́гѡ а҆пⷭ҇ла па́ѵла
чте́нїе.

И҆ па́ки дїа́конъ: **Во́нмемъ.**

А҆пⷭ҇лъ же и҆спо́лньшꙋсѧ,
глаго́летъ сщ҃е́нникъ:

Ми́ръ тѝ.

И҆ чте́цъ: **И҆ дꙋ́хови твоемꙋ̀.**

Дїа́конъ: **Премꙋ́дрость.**

Priest: **Peace be unto all.**

Reader: **And to thy spirit.**

Deacon: **Wisdom.**

And the reader says the prokeimenon from the Psalms of David.

And then the deacon: **Wisdom!**

And the reader, the title of the Epistle: **The Reading is from the Acts of the holy Apostles,** or **from the Catholic Epistle of the holy Apostle James,** or **of Peter,** or **from the Epistle of the holy Apostle Paul to the Romans,** or **to the Corinthians,** or **to the Galatians,** etc.

And again the deacon: **Let us attend.**

And when the Epistle is concluded, the priest says:

Peace be unto thee.

Reader: **And to thy spirit.**

Deacon: **Wisdom.**

И҆ чте́цъ: А҆ллилꙋ́їа со стихи̑.

А҆ллилꙋ́їа же пѣва́емꙋ, и҆ прїе́мъ дїа́конъ
кади́льницꙋ и҆ ѳѷмїа́мъ, прихо́дитъ къ
сщ҃е́нникꙋ, и҆ прїе́мъ бл҃гослове́нїе ѿ негѡ̀,
кади́тъ ст҃ꙋ́ю трапе́зꙋ ѡ҆́крестъ, и҆ ѻ҆лта́рь
ве́сь, и҆ сщ҃е́нника.

Сщ҃е́нникъ же глаго́летъ мл҃твꙋ сїю̀ та́йнѡ:

Мл҃тва пре́жде є҆ѵⷢ҇лі́а:

Ѡ҆зїѧ́й въ сердца́хъ на́шихъ. чл҃вѣколю́бче
вⷧ҇дко, твоегѡ̀ бг҃оразꙋ́мїа нетлѣ́нный
свѣ́тъ, и҆ мы́сленныѧ на́ши ѿве́рзи ѻ҆́чи, во
є҆ѵⷢ҇льскихъ твои́хъ проповѣ́данїй разꙋмѣ́нїе:
вложѝ въ на́съ и҆ стра́хъ бл҃же́нныхъ
твои́хъ за́повѣдей, да плотскі̑ѧ по́хѡти
всѧ̑ попра́вше, дꙋхо́вное жи́тельство
про́йдемъ, всѧ̑, ꙗ҆́же ко бл҃гоꙋгожде́нїю
твоемꙋ̀, и҆ мꙋ́дрствꙋюще и҆ дѣ́юще. Ты̀ бо
є҆сѝ просвѣще́нїе дꙋ́шъ и҆ тѣле́съ на́шихъ,
хрⷭ҇тѐ бж҃е: и҆ тебѣ̀ сла́вꙋ возсыла́емъ,
со безнача́льнымъ твои́мъ ѻ҆ц҃е́мъ, и҆

Reader: **Alleluia** and its verses.

While the Alleluia is being chanted, the deacon, taking the censer and incense, approaches the priest, and taking a blessing from him, censes the Holy Table round about, and the whole altar, and the priest.

And the priest says this prayer silently:

The Prayer Before the Gospel.

Shine forth within our hearts the incorruptible light of Thy knowledge, O Master, Lover of mankind, and open the eyes of our mind to the understanding of the preaching of Thy Gospel. Instill in us also the fear of Thy blessed commandments, that, trampling down all lusts of the flesh, we may pursue a spiritual way of life, being mindful of and doing all that is well-pleasing unto Thee. For Thou art the enlightenment of our souls and bodies, O Christ our God, and unto Thee do we send up glory,

преста҃ы́мъ и҆ бл҃ги́мъ и҆ животворѧ́щимъ
твои́мъ дх҃омъ, ны́нѣ и҆ при́снѡ, и҆ во вѣ́ки
вѣкѡ́въ. А҆ми́нь.

Дїа́конъ же, кади́льницꙋ ѿложи́въ на
ѻ҆бы́чное мѣ́сто, прихо́дитъ къ сщ҃е́нникꙋ,
и҆ подклони́въ є҆мꙋ̀ главꙋ̀ свою̀, держа̀ и҆
ѡ҆ра́рь со ст҃ы́мъ є҆ѵⷢлїемъ кра́йними пе́рсты,
си́рѣчь, во ѻ҆́номъ мѣ́стѣ ст҃ы́ѧ трапе́зы,
глаго́летъ:

Бл҃гословѝ, влады́ко, бл҃говѣ́стителѧ ст҃а́гѡ
а҆п҃ла и҆ є҆ѵⷢлі́ста и҆́мⷦ҇.

Сщ҃е́нникъ, зна́менꙋѧ є҆го̀, глаго́летъ:

Бг҃ъ, мл҃твами ст҃а́гѡ, сла́внагѡ, всехва́ль_
нагѡ а҆п҃ла и҆ є҆ѵⷢлі́ста и҆́мⷦ҇, да да́стъ тебѣ̀
глаго́лъ бл҃говѣ́ствꙋющемꙋ си́лою мно́гою,
во и҆сполне́нїе є҆ѵⷢлїа возлю́бленнагѡ сн҃а
своегѡ̀, гд҃а на́шегѡ і҆и҃са хрⷭ҇та̀.

together with Thine unoriginate Father, and Thy Most-holy and good and life-creating Spirit, now and ever, and unto the ages of ages. Amen.

The deacon, having put away the censer in the usual place, approaches the priest, and bowing his head to him, holding the Holy Gospel with his orarion in the tips of his fingers, i.e., on that place of the Holy Table says:

Bless, master, him that proclaimeth the Good Tidings of the holy Apostle and Evangelist N..

The priest, signing him with the sign of the Cross, says:

May God, through the prayers of the holy, glorious, all-praised Apostle and Evangelist N., give speech with great power unto thee that bringest good tidings, unto the fulfillment of the Gospel of His beloved Son, our Lord Jesus Christ.

Дїа́конъ же ре́къ: А҆ми́нь,
и҆ поклони́всѧ стⷭ҇о́мꙋ є҆ѵⷢ҇лїю, во́зметъ
є҆̀, и҆ и҆зше́дъ ст҃ыми две́рьми,
предходѧ́щымъ є҆мꙋ̀ лампа́дамъ,
прихо́дитъ и҆ стои́тъ на а҆мвѡ́нѣ,
и҆лѝ на оу҆чине́ннѣмъ мѣ́стѣ.

Їере́й же, стоѧ̀ пред стⷭ҇о́ю трапе́зою и҆ зрѧ̀
къ за́падꙋ, возглаша́етъ:

Премꙋ́дрость, прости́, оу҆слы́шимъ стⷢ҇а́гѡ
є҆ѵⷢ҇лїа. Та́же: Ми́ръ всѣ̑мъ.

Лю́дїе: И҆ дꙋ́хови твоемꙋ̀.

Дїа́конъ: Ѿ и҆́мк ст҃а́гѡ є҆ѵⷢ҇лїа чте́нїе.

Ли́къ: Сла́ва тебѣ̀, гдⷭ҇и, сла́ва тебѣ̀.

Сщ҃е́нникъ: Во́нмемъ.

А҆́ще же сꙋ́ть два̀ дїа́кона, то є҆ди́нъ да
глаго́летъ: Премꙋ́дрость, прости́. Та́же, и҆:
Во́нмемъ.

И҆ и҆спо́лнившꙋсѧ є҆ѵⷢ҇лїю,
глаго́летъ сщ҃е́нникъ:

And the deacon having said: **Amen**,
and having venerated the Holy Gospel,
takes it, and goes out through the holy
doors, candles preceding him, and goes
forth and stands on the ambo, or on the
appointed place.

And the priest, standing before the Holy
Table and looking toward the west,
exclaims:

Wisdom. Aright! Let us hear the holy Gospel. Then: **Peace be unto all.**

People: **And to thy spirit.**

Deacon: **The reading is from the holy Gospel according to N..**

Choir: **Glory to Thee, O Lord, glory to Thee.**

Priest: **Let us attend.**

If there be two deacons, one may say:
Wisdom. Aright! then also **Let us attend.**

When the Gospel is concluded,
the priest says:

Миръ ти блговѣствꙋющемꙋ.

Ли́къ: Сла́ва тебѣ̀, гдⷭ҇и, сла́ва тебѣ̀.

И̑ ѿше́дъ діа́конъ да́же до ст҃ы́хъ
двере́й, ѿдае́тъ ст҃о́е є̑ѵⷢ҇ліе сщ҃е́нникꙋ, и̑
затворѧ́ютсѧ па́ки свѧты́ѧ две́ри.

Діа́конъ, ста́въ на ѡ̑бы́чнѣмъ мѣ́стѣ,
начина́етъ си́це:

Рце́мъ вси ѿ всеѧ̀ дꙋшѝ, и̑ ѿ всегѡ̀
помышле́нїѧ на́шегѡ рце́мъ.

Ли́къ: Гдⷭ҇и поми́лꙋй.

Діа́конъ: Гдⷭ҇и вседержи́телю, бж҃е ѻ̑ц҃ъ
на́шихъ, мо́лимъ ти сѧ, ѹ̑слы́ши и̑
поми́лꙋй.

Ли́къ: Гдⷭ҇и поми́лꙋй.

Діа́конъ: Поми́лꙋй на́съ бж҃е, по вели́цѣй
ми́лости твое́й, мо́лимъ ти сѧ, ѹ̑слы́ши
и̑ поми́лꙋй.

Ли́къ: Гдⷭ҇и поми́лꙋй, три́жды.

Діа́конъ: Є̑щѐ мо́лимсѧ ѡ̑ вели́комъ гос-
поди́нѣ и̑ ѻ̑тцѣ̀ на́шемъ свѧтѣ́йшемъ

Peace be unto thee that bringest Good Tidings.

Choir: Glory to Thee, O Lord, glory to Thee.

And the deacon goes to the holy doors, and gives the Holy Gospel to the priest, and the holy doors are closed again.

The deacon, standing in the usual place, begins thus:

Let us all say with our whole soul and with our whole mind, let us say:

Choir: Lord, have mercy.

Deacon: O Lord Almighty, the God of our Fathers, we pray Thee, hearken and have mercy.

Choir: Lord, have mercy.

Deacon: Have mercy on us, O God, according to Thy great mercy, we pray Thee, hearken and have mercy.

Choir: Lord, have mercy (thrice).

Deacon: Again we pray for our great lord

патрїа́рсѣ и҆м҃къ, и҆ ѡ҆ господи́нѣ на́шемъ
высокопрешсⷳе́ннѣйшемъ мнтрополі́тѣ
и҆м҃къ, первоїера́рсѣ рꙋ́сскїѧ зарꙋбе́жныѧ
цр҃кве, ѡ҆ господи́нѣ на́шемъ высоко-
прешсⷳе́ннѣйшемъ а҆рхїепі́скопѣ [и҆лѝ
прешсⷳе́ннѣйшемъ е҆пі́скопѣ] и҆м҃къ, и҆ ѡ҆
всѣ́й во хрⷭ҇тѣ̀ бра́тїи на́шей.

Ли́къ: Гдⷭ҇и поми́лꙋй, три́жды.

С҃щенникъ же глаго́летъ
мл҃твꙋ прилѣ́жнагѡ моле́нїѧ та́йнѡ:

Гдⷭ҇и бж҃е на́шъ, прилѣ́жное сїѐ моле́нїе
прїимѝ ѿ твои́хъ ра́бъ, и҆ поми́лꙋй на́съ по
мно́жествꙋ ми́лости твоеѧ̀, и҆ щедрѡ́ты
твоѧ̀ низпослѝ на ны̀, и҆ на всѧ̀ лю́ди твоѧ̀,
ча́ющыѧ ѿ тебѐ бога́тыѧ ми́лти.

Дїа́конъ: Е҆щѐ мо́лимсѧ ѡ҆ странѣ̀ сей,
власте́хъ и҆ во́инствѣ е҆ѧ̀, и҆ всѣ́хъ вѣ́рою
и҆ бл҃гоче́стїемъ живꙋ́щихъ въ ней.

Ли́къ: Гдⷭ҇и поми́лꙋй, три́жды.

and father, the Most Holy Patriarch N.; for our lord the Very Most Reverend Metropolitan N., First Hierarch of the Russian Church Abroad, for our lord the Most [or Right] Reverend Archbishop [or Bishop] N.; and for all our brethren in Christ.

Choir: Lord, have mercy (thrice).

The priest says secretly the
Prayer of Fervent Supplication:

O Lord our God, accept this fervent supplication from Thy servants, and have mercy on us according to the multitude of Thy mercies, and send down Thy compassion upon us, and upon all Thy people that await of Thee abundant mercy.

Deacon: Again we pray for this land, its authorities and armed forces, and all who with faith and piety dwell therein.

Choir: Lord, have mercy (thrice).

Дїаконъ: Е̂щѐ мо́лимсѧ ѡ҆ бг҃охрани́мѣй странѣ̀ рѡссі́йстѣй и҆ правосла́вныхъ лю́дехъ є҆ѧ̀ во ѻ҆те́чествїи и҆ разсѣѧ́нїи сꙋ́щихъ и҆ ѡ҆ сп҃се́нїи и҆́хъ.

Ли́къ: Гд҃и поми́лꙋй, три́жды.

Дїаконъ: Е̂щѐ мо́лимсѧ гдꙋ бг҃ꙋ на́шемꙋ ѡ҆ є҆́же и҆зба́вити лю́ди своѧ̀ ѿ вра̑гъ ви́димыхъ и҆ неви́димыхъ, въ на́съ же оу҆тверди́ти є҆диномы́слїе, братолю́бїе и҆ бл҃гоче́стїе.

Ли́къ: Гд҃и поми́лꙋй, три́жды.

Дїаконъ: Е̂щѐ мо́лимсѧ ѡ҆ бра́тїахъ на́шихъ, сщ҃е́нницѣхъ, сщ҃енномона́сѣхъ, и҆ всѣ́мъ во хрⷵтѣ̀ бра́тствѣ на́шемъ.

Ли́къ: Гд҃и поми́лꙋй, три́жды.

Дїаконъ: Е̂щѐ мо́лимсѧ ѡ҆ бл҃же́нныхъ и҆ приснопа́мѧтныхъ ст҃ѣ́йшихъ патрїа́рсѣхъ правосла́вныхъ, и҆ бл҃гочести́выхъ цр҃е́хъ, и҆ бл҃говѣ́рныхъ цр҃и́цахъ, и҆ созда́телехъ ст҃а́го хра́ма сегѡ̀ [а҆́ще во ѡ҆би́тели: ст҃ы́ѧ ѡ҆би́тели сеѧ̀], и҆ ѡ҆ всѣ́хъ преждепочи́вшихъ ѻ҆тцѣ́хъ и҆ бра́тїахъ, здѣ̀ лежа́щихъ и҆ повсю́дꙋ, правосла́вныхъ.

Deacon: Again we pray for the God-preserved Russian land and its Orthodox people both in the homeland and the diaspora, and for their salvation.

Choir: Lord, have mercy (thrice).

Deacon: Again we pray to the Lord our God that He may deliver His people from enemies, visible and invisible, and confirm in us oneness of mind, brotherly love, and piety.

Choir: Lord, have mercy (thrice).

Deacon: Again we pray for our brethren, the priests, the priestmonks, and all our brethren in Christ.

Choir: Lord, have mercy (thrice).

Deacon: Again we pray for the blessed and ever-memorable holy Orthodox patriarchs, and for pious kings and right-believing queens, and for the founders of this holy temple [if it be a monastery: this holy monastery], and for our fathers and brethren gone to their rest before us, and for all the Orthodox here and everywhere laid to rest.

Ли́къ: Гдⷭ҇и поми́лꙋй, три́жды.

[Здѣ̀ прилага́ютсѧ проше́нїѧ ѡ҆ болѧ́щихъ,
ѡ҆ пꙋтеше́ствꙋющихъ, и҆ дрꙋгі́ѧ.]

Дїа́конъ: Є҆щѐ мо́лимсѧ ѡ҆ плодоносѧ́щихъ
и҆ добродѣ́ющихъ во ст҃е́мъ и҆ всечестнѣ́мъ
хра́мѣ се́мъ, трꙋжда́ющихсѧ, пою́щихъ и҆
предстоѧ́щихъ лю́дехъ, ѡ҆жида́ющихъ ѿ
тебѐ вели́кїѧ и҆ бога́тыѧ млⷭ҇ти.

Ли́къ: Гдⷭ҇и поми́лꙋй, три́жды.

Возглаше́нїе: Ꙗ҆́кѡ ми́лтивъ и҆ чл҃вѣколю́бецъ
бг҃ъ є҆сѝ, и҆ тебѣ̀ сла́вꙋ возсыла́емъ, ѻ҆ц҃ꙋ,
и҆ сн҃ꙋ, и҆ ст҃о́мꙋ дх҃ꙋ, ны́нѣ и҆ прⷭ҇нѡ, и҆ во
вѣ́ки вѣкѡ́въ.

Ли́къ: А҆ми́нь.

Дїа́конъ: Помоли́тесѧ, ѡ҆глаше́ннїи гдⷭ҇ви.

Ли́къ: Гдⷭ҇и поми́лꙋй.

Дїа́конъ: Вѣ́рнїи, ѡ҆ ѡ҆глаше́нныхъ
помо́лимсѧ, да гдⷭ҇ь поми́лꙋетъ и҆́хъ.

Choir: Lord, have mercy (thrice).

[Here may be inserted various petitions as desired: see Special Petitions, page 282.]

Deacon: Again we pray for them that bring offerings and do good works in this holy and all-venerable temple; for them that minister and them that chant, and for all the people here present that await of Thee great and abundant mercy.

Choir: Lord, have mercy (thrice).

Exclamation: For a merciful God art Thou and the Lover of mankind, and unto Thee do we send up glory, to the Father, and to the Son, and to the Holy Spirit, now and ever, and unto the ages of ages.

Choir: Amen.

Then the deacon: Pray, ye catechumens, to the Lord.

Choir: Lord, have mercy.

Deacon: Ye faithful, let us pray for the catechumens that the Lord will have mercy on them.

Ли́къ: Гдⷭ҇и поми́лꙋй.

Дїа́конъ: Ѿгласи́тъ и҆́хъ сло́вомъ и҆́стины.

Ли́къ: Гдⷭ҇и поми́лꙋй.

Дїа́конъ: Ѿкры́етъ и҆̀мъ є҆ѵⷢ҇лїе пра́вды.

Ли́къ: Гдⷭ҇и поми́лꙋй.

Дїа́конъ: Соедини́тъ и҆́хъ ст҃е́й свое́й собо́рнѣй и҆ а҆пⷭ҇льстѣй цр҃кви.

Ли́къ: Гдⷭ҇и поми́лꙋй.

Дїа́конъ: Спⷭ҇и́, поми́лꙋй, застꙋпѝ и҆ сохранѝ и҆́хъ, бж҃е, твое́ю бл҃года́тїю.

Ли́къ: Гдⷭ҇и поми́лꙋй.

Дїа́конъ: Ѡ҆глаше́ннїи, главы̑ ва́шѧ гдⷭ҇ви приклони́те.

Ли́къ: Тебѣ̀ гдⷭ҇и.

Мл҃тва ѡ҆ ѡ҆глаше́нныхъ та́йнѡ глаго́летсѧ ѿ і҆ере́а:

Гдⷭ҇и бж҃е на́шъ, и҆́же на нб҃сѣ́хъ живы́й, и҆ призира́ѧй на всѧ̑ дѣла̀ твоѧ̑, при́зри

Choir: Lord, have mercy.

Deacon: That He will catechize them with the word of truth.

Choir: Lord, have mercy.

Deacon: That He will reveal unto them the Gospel of righteousness.

Choir: Lord, have mercy.

Deacon: That He will unite them to His Holy, Catholic and Apostolic Church.

Choir: Lord, have mercy.

Deacon: Save them, have mercy on them, help them, and keep them, O God, by Thy grace.

Choir: Lord, have mercy.

Deacon: Ye catechumens, bow your heads unto the Lord.

Choir: To Thee, O Lord.

The priest secretly says the
Prayer for the Catechumens:

O Lord our God, Who dwellest in the heavens and lookest down upon all

на рабы̑ твоѧ̑ ѡⷢлашє́нныѧ, прикло́ншыѧ
своѧ̑ вы̑ѧ преⷣ тобо́ю: и да́ждь и҆̀мъ ле́гкїй
ꙗ҆ре́мъ, сотворѝ и҆́хъ оу҆́ды чⷭтны ст҃ы̑ѧ твоеѧ̀
цр҃кве, и҆ сподо́би и҆́хъ ба́ни пакибытїѧ̀,
ѡ҆ставле́нїѧ грѣхѡ́въ, и҆ ѻ҆де́жди нетлѣ́нїѧ,
въ позна́нїе тебѐ и҆́стиннагѡ бг҃а на́шегѡ.

Возглаше́нїе: Да и҆ ті́и съ на́ми сла́вѧтъ
пречⷭтно́е и҆ великолѣ́пое и҆́мѧ твоѐ, ѻ҆ц҃а̀,
и҆ сн҃а, и҆ ст҃а́гѡ дх҃а, нынѣ и҆ прⷭнѡ, и҆ во
вѣ́ки вѣкѡ́въ.

Ли́къ: А҆ми́нь.

И҆ простира́етъ
а҆нтїмінсъ сщ҃е́нникъ.

Дїа́конъ глаго́летъ: Е҆ли́цы ѡ҆глаше́ннїи,
и҆зыди́те.

А҆́ще ли є҆́сть вторы́й дїа́конъ,
возглаша́етъ и҆ то́й:

Thy works: Look upon Thy servants the Catechumens, who have bowed their necks before Thee, and grant them the easy yoke, make them honorable members of Thy holy Church, and vouchsafe unto them the laver of regeneration, the remission of sins, and the garment of incorruption, unto the knowledge of Thee our true God.

Exclamation: That they also with us may glorify Thine most honorable and majestic name: of the Father, and of the Son, and of the Holy Spirit, now and ever, and unto the ages of ages.

Choir: Amen.

And the priest spreads out
the antimension.

Deacon: As many as are catechumens, depart.

If there be a second deacon,
he exclaims this:

Ѡглашеннїи, изыдите.

Та́же па́ки пе́рвый:

Ели́цы ѡглаше́ннїи, изыди́те. Да никто̀ ѿ ѡглаше́нныхъ: ели́цы вѣ́рнїи, па́ки и па́ки ми́ромъ гдꙋ̀ помо́лимсѧ.

Ли́къ: Гдⷵи поми́лꙋй.

Аще ли же еди́нъ то́чїю їере́й, тогда̀ глаго́летъ си́це:

Ели́цы ѡглаше́ннїи, изыди́те, ѡглаше́ннїи изыди́те, ели́цы ѡглаше́ннїи изыди́те: да никто̀ ѿ ѡглаше́нныхъ, ели́цы вѣ́рнїи, па́ки и па́ки ми́ромъ гдꙋ̀ помо́лимсѧ.

Ли́къ: Гдⷵи поми́лꙋй.

Мл҃тва вѣ́рныхъ, пе́рваѧ, та́йнѡ глаго́летсѧ ѿ їере́а:

Ты̀, гдⷵи, показа́лъ есѝ на́мъ вели́кое сїѐ, спасе́нїѧ та́инство. Ты сподо́билъ

Catechumens, depart.

Then again the first deacon:

As many as are catechumens, depart. Let none of the catechumens remain. As many as are of the faithful: again and again, in peace let us pray to the Lord.

Choir: Lord, have mercy.

But if there be only a priest alone, then he says this:

As many as are catechumens, depart. Catechumens, depart. As many as are catechumens, depart: let none of the catechumens remain. As many as are of the faithful, again and again, in peace let us pray to the Lord.

Choir: Lord, have mercy.

The priest says secretly the First Prayer of the Faithful:

Thou, O Lord, hast shown us this great mystery of salvation. Thou hast

є҆сѝ на́съ смире́нныхъ и҆ недосто́йныхъ рабъ
твои́хъ, бы́ти слꙋжи́телємъ свѧта́гѡ
твоегѡ̀ же́ртвенника. Ты̀ оу҆довлѝ на́съ
си́лою ст҃а́гѡ твоегѡ̀ дх҃а въ слꙋжбꙋ̀ сїю̀,
да неѡсꙋжде́ннѡ ста́вше пред̾ ст҃о́ю сла́вою
твое́ю, принесе́мъ тѝ же́ртвꙋ хвале́нїѧ: ты̀
бо̀ є҆сѝ дѣ́йствꙋѧй всѧ̑ во всѣ́хъ. Да́ждь,
гдⷭи, и҆ ѡ҆ на́шихъ грѣсѣ́хъ, и҆ ѡ҆ людски́хъ
невѣ́дѣнїихъ, прїѧ́тнѣй бы́ти же́ртвѣ
на́шей, и҆ бл҃гопрїѧ́тнѣй пред̾ тобо́ю.

Дїа́конъ: Застꙋпѝ, сп҃сѝ, поми́лꙋй и҆ сохранѝ
на́съ бж҃е, твое́ю бл҃года́тїю.

Ли́къ: Гдⷭи поми́лꙋй.

Дїа́конъ: Премꙋ́дрость.

Возглаше́нїе: Ꙗ҆́кѡ подоба́етъ тебѣ̀ всѧ́каѧ
сла́ва, че́сть и҆ поклоне́нїе, ѻ҆ц҃ꙋ̀, и҆ сн҃ꙋ, и҆
ст҃о́мꙋ дх҃ꙋ, ны́нѣ и҆ при́снѡ, и҆ во вѣ́ки
вѣкѡ́въ.

Ли́къ: А҆ми́нь.

Дїа́конъ: Па́ки и҆ па́ки ми́ромъ гдⷭꙋ
помо́лимсѧ.

vouchsafed us, Thy lowly and unworthy servants, to be ministers of Thy holy altar. Do Thou enable us by the power of Thy Holy Spirit for this liturgy, that, standing uncondemned before Thy holy glory, we may offer unto Thee a sacrifice of praise: for Thou art He Who worketh all things in all. Grant, O Lord, that our sacrifice may be acceptable both for our sins and for the errors of the people and well-pleasing before Thee.

Deacon: Help us, save us, have mercy on us, and keep us, O God, by Thy grace.

Choir: Lord, have mercy.

Deacon: Wisdom.

Exclamation: For unto Thee is due all glory, honor, and worship, to the Father, and to the Son, and to the Holy Spirit, now and ever, and unto the ages of ages.

Choir: Amen.

Deacon: Again and again, in peace let us pray to the Lord.

Ли́къ: Гд҃и поми́лꙋй.

Є҆гда̀ сщ҃е́нникъ є҆ди́нъ слꙋ́житъ,
сїѧ̀ не глаго́летъ:

Дїа́конъ: Ѡ҆ свы́шнѣмъ ми́рѣ, и҆ спасе́нїи
дꙋ́шъ на́шихъ, гдꙋ помо́лимсѧ.

Ли́къ: Гд҃и поми́лꙋй.

Дїа́конъ: Ѡ҆ ми́рѣ всегѡ̀ мі́ра, блгостоѧ́нїи
ст҃ы́хъ бж҃їихъ цр҃кве́й и҆ соедине́нїи всѣ́хъ,
гдꙋ помо́лимсѧ.

Ли́къ: Гд҃и поми́лꙋй.

Дїа́конъ: Ѡ҆ ст҃ѣ́мъ хра́мѣ се́мъ, и҆ съ
вѣ́рою, блгоговѣ́нїемъ и҆ стра́хомъ бж҃їимъ
входѧ́щихъ во́нь, гдꙋ помо́лимсѧ.

Ли́къ: Гд҃и поми́лꙋй.

Дїа́конъ: Ѡ҆ и҆зба́витисѧ на́мъ ѿ всѧ́кїѧ
ско́рби, гнѣ́ва и҆ нꙋ́жды, гдꙋ помо́лимсѧ.

Ли́къ: Гд҃и поми́лꙋй.

Мл҃тва вѣ́рныхъ, втора́ѧ,
та́йнѡ глаго́летсѧ ѿ і҆ере́а:

Choir: Lord, have mercy.

When a priest serves alone,
these are not said:

Deacon: For the peace from above, and the salvation of our souls, let us pray to the Lord.

Choir: Lord, have mercy.

Deacon: For the peace of the whole world, the good estate of the holy churches of God, and the union of all, let us pray to the Lord.

Choir: Lord, have mercy.

Deacon: For this holy temple, and for them that with faith, reverence, and fear of God enter herein, let us pray to the Lord.

Choir: Lord, have mercy.

Deacon: That we may be delivered from all tribulation, wrath, and necessity, let us pray to the Lord.

Choir: Lord, have mercy.

The priest says secretly the
Second Prayer of the Faithful:

Бже, посѣтивый въ млⷵти и щедротахъ смиреніе наше, поставивый насъ, смиренныхъ и грѣшныхъ и недостойныхъ рабъ твоихъ, предъ стꙋю славою твоею, слꙋжити стꙋмꙋ жертвенникꙋ твоемꙋ: ты оукрѣпи насъ силою стагѡ твоегѡ дхⷶа въ слꙋжбꙋ сію, и даждь намъ слово во ѿверзеніе оустъ нашихъ, во еже призывати бл҃годать стагѡ твоегѡ дхⷶа на хотѧщыѧ предложитисѧ дары.

Дїаконъ [без негꙋже іерей глаголетъ]: Застꙋпи, спси, помилꙋй и сохрани насъ бже, твоею бл҃годатїю.

Ликъ: Гдⷵи помилꙋй.

Дїаконъ: Премꙋдрость.

Входитъ дїаконъ сѣверными дверьми.

Возглашеніе: Ꙗкѡ да под державою твоею всегда хранⷨими, тебѣ славꙋ возсылаемъ, оц҃ꙋ, и сн҃ꙋ, и стꙋмꙋ дхⷶꙋ, нынѣ и присно, и во вѣки вѣкѡвъ.

Ликъ: Аминь.

O God, Who hast visited our lowliness in mercy and compassion; Who hast appointed us, Thy lowly, and sinful, and unworthy servants, to minister at Thy holy altar in the presence of Thy holy glory: Do Thou strengthen us by Thy Holy Spirit for this liturgy, and grant us speech in the opening of our mouth with which to invoke the grace of Thy Holy Spirit upon the Gifts to be offered.

Deacon [or priest if there is no deacon present]: Help us, save us, have mercy on us, and keep us, O God, by Thy grace.

Choir: Lord, have mercy.

Deacon: Wisdom.

The deacon enters through the north door.

Exclamation: That always being guarded under Thy dominion, we may send up glory unto Thee, to the Father, and to the Son, and to the Holy Spirit, now and ever, and unto the ages of ages.

Choir: Amen.

И ѿверза́ютсѧ ст҃ы́ѧ две́ри.

Та́же прїе́мь дїа́конъ кади́льницꙋ, и
дꙋ́ѵмїа́мъ вложи́въ, прихо́дитъ ко сщ҃е́нникꙋ,
и прїе́мь блгослове́нїе ѿ негѡ̀, кади́тъ
ст҃ꙋ́ю трапе́зꙋ ѡ҆кре́стъ и ѻ҆лта́рь ве́сь,
и і҆кѡноста́съ, и сщ҃е́нника, ли́ки, и лю́ди:
глаго́летъ же и н҃-й ѱало́мъ, та́же тропари̑
ꙋ҆мили́тельныѧ, е҆ли́кѡ и҆зво́литъ.

Мл҃тва ю҆́же тво́ритъ сщ҃е́нникъ въ себѣ̀,
херꙋві́мской пѣ́сни пѣва́емѣй:

Н҃иктѡ́же досто́инъ ѿ свѧза́вшихсѧ
плотски́ми похотьми́ и сластьми́
приходи́ти, и҆лѝ приближи́тисѧ, и҆лѝ слꙋжи́ти
тебѣ̀, цр҃ю̀ сла́вы: е҆́же бо слꙋжи́ти тебѣ̀,
вели́ко и стра́шно и самѣ́мъ нбⷭными
си́ламъ. Но ѻ҆ба́че неизрече́ннагѡ ра́ди
и безмѣ́рнагѡ твоегѡ̀ чл҃вѣколю́бїѧ,
непрело́жнѡ и неизмѣ́ннѡ бы́лъ е҆сѝ
чл҃вѣ́къ, и а҆рхїере́й на́мъ бы́лъ е҆сѝ: и
слꙋже́бныѧ сеѧ̀ и безкро́вныѧ же́ртвы

And the holy doors are opened.

Then the deacon, taking the censer and placing incense in it, approaches the priest, and, taking a blessing from him, censes around the Holy Table, and the whole altar, and the icons, and the priest, and the choir, and the people, saying Psalm 50 to himself, and the troparia of compunction, as many as he may wish.

Whilst the Cherubic Hymn is being sung, the priest reads within himself this prayer:

None is worthy among them that are bound with carnal lusts and pleasures, to approach or to draw nigh, or to minister unto Thee, O King of glory, for to serve Thee is a great and fearful thing even unto the heavenly hosts themselves. Yet because of Thine ineffable and immeasurable love for mankind, without change or alteration Thou didst become man, and didst become our High Priest, and didst deliver unto us

сщеннодѣ́йствїе преда́лъ є҆сѝ на́мъ, ꙗ҆́кѡ
влⷣка всѣ́хъ: ты́ бо є҆ди́нъ, гдⷭ҇и бж҃е на́шъ,
влⷣчествꙋеши нбⷭ҇ными и҆ земны́ми, и҆́же
на прⷭ҇то́лѣ херꙋві́мстѣ носи́мый, и҆́же
серафі́мѡвъ гдⷭ҇ь, и҆ цр҃ь і҆и҃левъ, и҆́же є҆ди́нъ
ст҃ъ, и҆ во ст҃ы́хъ почива́ѧй. Та̀ оу҆́бо молю̀
є҆ди́наго бл҃га́го и҆ благопослꙋшли́ваго:
при́зри на мѧ̀ грѣ́шнаго и҆ непотре́бнаго
раба̀ твоего̀, и҆ ѡ҆чи́сти мою̀ дꙋ́шꙋ и҆ се́рдце
ѿ со́вѣсти лꙋка́выѧ, и҆ оу҆дово́ли мѧ̀, си́лою
ст҃а́гѡ твоегѡ̀ дх҃а, ѡ҆блече́нна бл҃года́тїю
сщ҃е́нства, предста́ти ст҃ѣ́й твое́й се́й
трапе́зѣ, и҆ сщеннодѣ́йствовати ст҃о́е и҆
пречⷭ҇то́е твоѐ тѣ́ло и҆ честнꙋ́ю кро́вь: къ
тебѣ́ бо прихождꙋ̀ приклонь мою̀ вы́ю, и҆
молю́ ти сѧ, да не ѿврати́ши лица̀ твоегѡ̀
ѿ менѐ, нижѐ ѿри́неши менѐ ѿ ѻ҆́трѡкъ
твои́хъ: но спосо́бенъ принесе́ннымъ тебѣ̀
бы́ти, мно́ю грѣ́шнымъ и҆ недосто́йнымъ
рабо́мъ твои́мъ, дарѡ́мъ си́мъ: ты́ бо
є҆сѝ приносѧ́й и҆ приноси́мый, и҆ прїе́млѧй
и҆ раздава́емый хрⷭ҇тѐ бж҃е на́шъ, и҆ тебѣ̀

the ministry of this liturgical and bloodless sacrifice, for Thou art the Master of all. Thou alone, O Lord our God, dost rule over those in heaven and those on earth, art borne upon the throne of the Cherubim, art Lord of the Seraphim and King of Israel, Thou alone art holy and restest in the saints. I implore Thee, therefore, Who alone art good and inclined to listen: Look upon me Thy sinful and unprofitable servant, and purge my soul and heart of a wicked conscience, and by the power of Thy Holy Spirit, enable me, who am clothed with the grace of the priesthood, to stand before this Thy Holy Table, and to perform the sacred Mystery of Thy holy and immaculate Body and precious Blood. For unto Thee do I draw nigh, bowing my neck, and I pray Thee: Turn not Thy countenance away from me, neither cast me out from among Thy children, but vouchsafe that these gifts be offered unto Thee by me, Thy sinful and unworthy servant: for

слáвꙋ возсылáемъ, со безначáльнымъ
твои́мъ Ѻ҆ц҃éмъ, и҆ прест҃ы́мъ, и҆ бл҃ги́мъ,
и҆ животворѧ́щимъ твои́мъ дх҃омъ, ны́нѣ
и҆ при́снѡ, и҆ во вѣ́ки вѣкѡ́въ. А҆ми́нь.

И҆спо́лнившейсѧ же мл҃твѣ, глаго́лютъ и҆ ті́и
херꙋві́мскꙋю пѣ́снь, три́жды: по ко́емждо
же скончáнїи, покланѧ́ютсѧ по є҆ди́нощи.

Сщ҃éнникъ: И҆́же херꙋві́мы тáйнѡ ѡ҆бразꙋ́юще,
и҆ животворѧ́щей Трⷪ҇цѣ трист҃ꙋ́ю пѣ́снь
припѣвáюще, всѧ́кое ны́нѣ жите́йское
ѿложи́мъ попече́нїе.
Дїáконъ: Ꙗ҆́кѡ да цр҃ѧ̀ всѣ́хъ поди́мемъ,
а҆́гг҃льскими неви́димѡ дорꙋноси́ма чи́нми.
А҆ллилꙋ́їа, а҆ллилꙋ́їа, а҆ллилꙋ́їа.

А҆ сїѐ въ вели́кїй четверто́къ
то́чїю пое́тсѧ:

Thou art He that offereth and is offered, that accepteth and is distributed, O Christ our God, and unto Thee do we send up glory, together with Thine unoriginate Father, and Thy Most-holy, good and life-creating Spirit, now and ever, and unto the ages of ages. Amen.

When the prayer is completed, the priest and the deacon say also the Cherubic Hymn, thrice; and bowing once at the conclusion of each repetition.

Priest: Let us, who mystically represent the Cherubim and chant the thrice-holy hymn to the life-creating Trinity, now lay aside all earthly care.

Deacon: That we may receive the King of all, Who cometh invisibly upborne by the ranks of angels. Alleluia, alleluia, alleluia.

But on Great Thursday
only this is chanted:

Ве́чери твоеѧ̀ та́йныѧ дне́сь, сн҃е бж҃їй, прича́стника мѧ̀ прїимѝ. Не бо̀ врагѡ́мъ твои́мъ та́йнꙋ пове́мъ, ни лобза́нїѧ ти да́мъ ꙗ҆́кѡ і҆ꙋ́да, но ꙗ҆́кѡ разбо́йникъ и҆сповѣ́даю тѧ̀: помѧнѝ мѧ̀, гд҃и, во цр҃тви твое́мъ. А҆ллилꙋ́їа, а҆ллилꙋ́їа, а҆ллилꙋ́їа.

Въ вели́кꙋю же сꙋббѡ́тꙋ пою́тъ сі́е:

Да молчи́тъ всѧ́каѧ пло́ть человѣ́ча, и҆ да стои́тъ со стра́хомъ и҆ тре́петомъ, и҆ ничто́же земно́е въ себѣ̀ да помышлѧ́етъ: цр҃ь бо ца́рствꙋющихъ, и҆ гд҃ь госпо́дствꙋющихъ прихо́дитъ закла́тисѧ и҆ да́тисѧ въ снѣ́дь вѣ́рнымъ.

Предхо́дѧтъ же семꙋ̀ ли́цы а҆́гг҃льстїи со всѧ́кимъ нача́ломъ и҆ вла́стїю, многоѻчи́тїи херꙋві́ми и҆ шестокрила́тїи серафі́ми, ли́ца закрыва́юще и҆ вопїю́ще пѣ́снь: А҆ллилꙋ́їа, а҆ллилꙋ́їа, а҆ллилꙋ́їа.

Of Thy Mystical Supper, O Son of God, receive me today as a communicant; for I will not speak of the Mystery to Thine enemies, nor will I give Thee a kiss as did Judas, but like the thief do I confess Thee: Remember me, O Lord, in Thy kingdom. Alleluia, alleluia, alleluia.

On Great Saturday, this is chanted:

Let all mortal flesh keep silence, and stand with fear and trembling; and let it take no thought for any earthly thing. For the King of kings and Lord of lords draweth nigh to be sacrificed and given as food to the faithful.

Before Him go the choirs of angels with all the principalities and powers, the many-eyed cherubim and the six winged seraphim, covering their faces and crying aloud the hymn: Alleluia, alleluia, alleluia.

Та́же ѿхо́дѧтъ въ предложе́нїе, предходѧ́щꙋ дїа́конꙋ, и҆ кади́тъ і҆ере́й ст҃а́ѧ, въ себѣ̀ молѧ́сѧ:

Бж҃е, ѡ҆чⷭ҇ти мѧ̀ грѣ́шнаго, три́жды.

Дїа́конъ глаго́летъ ко сщⷷе́нникꙋ:

Возмѝ, влады́ко.

И҆ сщⷷе́нникъ, взе́мъ возд꙼ꙋхъ, возлага́етъ на лѣ́вое ра́мо є҆гѡ̀, глаго́лѧ:

Возми́те рꙋ́ки ва́ша во ст҃а́ѧ, и҆ бл҃гослови́те гдⷭ҇а.

Та́же ст҃ы́й ді́скосъ прїе́мь, возлага́етъ на главꙋ̀ дїа́кона, со всѧ́кимъ внима́нїемъ и҆ бл҃гоговѣ́нїемъ, и҆мѣ́ѧй вкꙋ́пѣ дїа́конъ и҆ кади́льницꙋ на є҆ди́номъ ѿ пе́рстовъ десны́ѧ рꙋки̑. Са́мъ же ст҃ы́й поти́ръ въ рꙋцѣ̀ прїе́млетъ: и҆ и҆схо́дѧтъ ѻ҆́ба сѣ́верною страно́ю молѧ́щесѧ, предходѧ́щымъ и҆̀мъ лампа́дамъ.

And the priest goes to the table of oblation
after the deacon, and censes the holy
things, praying quietly:

O God, cleanse me, a sinner. Thrice.

The deacon says to the priest:

Lift up, master.

And the priest, taking the aer, lays it upon
the deacon's left shoulder, saying:

**Lift up your hands in the sanctuary, and
bless the Lord.**

And taking the holy discos, he places
it upon the deacon's head, with all
attentiveness and reverence, the deacon
having also the censer on one of his fingers
of his right hand. The priest himself takes
the holy chalice in his hands. They come
out by the north door, preceded by the
candle-bearers.

Дїа́конъ глаго́летъ: Вели́каго господи́на и
Отца̀ на́шегѡ и҆м҃къ, ст҃ѣ́йшагѡ патрїа́рха
моско́вскагѡ и҆ всеѧ̀ рꙋси́, и҆ господи́на
на́шегѡ высокопрешсщ҃е́ннѣйшагѡ и҆м҃къ,
митрополі́та восто́чно-америка́нскагѡ и҆
нью-йо́ркскагѡ, первоїера́рха рꙋсскі́ѧ зарꙋбѣ́-
жныѧ цр҃кве, и҆ господи́на на́шегѡ высоко-
прешсщ҃е́ннѣйшагѡ и҆м҃къ, а҆рхїепі́скопа [и҆лѝ
прешсщ҃е́ннѣйшагѡ є҆пі́скопа, є҆гѡ́же є҆́сть
Ѻбласть], да помѧне́тъ гд҃ь бг҃ъ во цр҃твїи
свое́мъ, всегда̀, ны́нѣ и҆ при́снѡ, и҆ во вѣ́ки
вѣкѡ́въ.

Та́же сщ҃е́нникъ: Бг҃охрани́мꙋю странꙋ̀
рѡссі́йскꙋю и҆ правосла́вныѧ лю́ди є҆ѧ̀
во Ѻте́чествїи и҆ разсѣ́ѧнїи сꙋ́щїѧ, да
помѧне́тъ гд҃ь бг҃ъ во цр҃твїи свое́мъ, всегда̀,
ны́нѣ и҆ при́снѡ, и҆ во вѣ́ки вѣкѡ́въ.

Странꙋ̀ сїю̀, вла́сти и҆ во́инство є҆ѧ̀, и҆
всѣ́хъ вѣ́рою и҆ бл҃гоче́стїемъ живꙋ́щихъ
въ не́й, да помѧне́тъ гд҃ь бг҃ъ во цр҃твїи
свое́мъ, всегда̀, ны́нѣ и҆ при́снѡ, и҆ во вѣ́ки
вѣкѡ́въ.

The deacon says: Our great lord and father N., the Most Holy Patriarch of Moscow and all Russia; our lord the Very Most Reverend N., Metropolitan of Eastern America and New York, and First Hierarch of the Russian Church Abroad; our lord the Most [or Right] Reverend N., Archbishop [or Bishop] of [name of diocese], may the Lord God remember in His Kingdom, always, now and ever, and unto the ages of ages.

Priest: The God-preserved Russian land and its Orthodox people both in the homeland and in the diaspora, may the Lord God remember in His kingdom, always, now and ever, and unto the ages of ages.

This land, its authorities and armed forces, and all who with faith and piety dwell therein, may the Lord God remember in His kingdom, always, now and ever, and unto the ages of ages.

Сщенство, мона́шество, всѣ́хъ гони́мыхъ и стра́ждꙋщихъ за вѣ́рꙋ правосла́внꙋю, созда́телей, блготвори́телей и бра́тїю ста́гѡ хра́ма сегѡ̀ [и҆лѝ ста́ѧ ѻ҆би́тели сеѧ̀], и всѣ́хъ ва́съ правосла́вныхъ хрⷭ҇тїа́нъ, да помѧне́тъ гдⷭ҇ь бгъ во црⷭ҇твїи своёмъ, всегда̀, нынѣ и при́снѡ, и во вѣ́ки вѣкѡ́въ.

Ли́къ: А҆ми́нь.

Вше́дъ же дїа́конъ внꙋ́трь ста́ыхъ двере́й, стои́тъ ѡ҆десну́ю, и҆ хотѧ́щꙋ сщенникꙋ вни́ти, глаго́летъ къ немꙋ̀ дїа́конъ:

Да помѧне́тъ гдⷭ҇ь бгъ сщенство твоѐ во црⷭ҇твїи своёмъ.

И҆ сщенникъ къ немꙋ̀:

Да помѧне́тъ гдⷭ҇ь бгъ сщеннодїа́конство твоѐ во црⷭ҇твїи своёмъ, всегда̀, нынѣ и при́снѡ, и҆ во вѣ́ки вѣкѡ́въ.

И҆ сщенникъ ѹ҆́бѡ поставлѧ́етъ ста́ый поти́ръ на ста́ю трапе́зꙋ: ста́ый же ді́скосъ

The clergy, the monastics, all that are persecuted and suffer for the Orthodox Faith, the founders, benefactors, and the brotherhood of this holy temple (or holy monastery), and all of you Orthodox Christians, may the Lord God remember in His kingdom, always, now and ever, and unto the ages of ages.

Choir: Amen.

Having passed through the holy doors, the deacon stands to the right; and as the priest enters, the deacon says to him:

May the Lord God remember thy priesthood in His kingdom.

And the priest says to him:

May the Lord God remember thy sacred diaconate in His kingdom, always, now and ever, and unto the ages of ages.

And the priest places the holy chalice on the Holy Table; and taking the holy diskos

взе́мъ со главы̀ дїа́кона, поставлѧ́етъ и̑
то́й на ст҃ꙋю трапе́зꙋ, глаго́лѧ:

Бл҃гоѻбра́зный і̑ѡ́сифъ, съ дре́ва сне́мъ
пречⷭ҇то́е твоѐ тѣ́ло, плащани́цею чи́стою
ѡ̑бви́въ, и̑ бл҃гоꙋха́ньми во гро́бѣ но́вѣ
закры́въ, положѝ.

Во гро́бѣ пло́тски, во а̑́дѣ же съ дш҃е́ю
ꙗ̑́кѡ бг҃ъ, въ раѝ же съ разбо́йникомъ, и̑
на прⷭ҇то́лѣ бы́лъ є̑сѝ хрⷭ҇тѐ, со ѻ̑ц҃е́мъ и̑
дх҃омъ, всѧ̑ и̑сполнѧ́ѧй неѡписа́нный.

Ꙗ̑́кѡ живоно́сецъ, ꙗ̑́кѡ раѧ̀ краснѣ́йшїй
вои̑́стиннꙋ, и̑ всѧ́кагѡ черто́га ца́рскагѡ
ꙗ̑ви́сѧ свѣтлѣ́йшїй хрⷭ҇тѐ гро́бъ тво́й,
и̑сто́чникъ на́шегѡ воскрⷭ҇нїѧ.

Та́же покро́вцы ѹ̑́бѡ взе́мъ ѿ сщ҃е́ннагѡ
ді́скоса, и̑ ст҃а́гѡ потира̀, полага́етъ на
є̑ди́ной странѣ̀ ст҃ы́ѧ трапе́зы: возд꙳ꙋ́хъ
же ѿ дїа́кона ра́ма взе́мъ, и̑ покади́въ
покрыва́етъ и̑́мъ ст҃а́ѧ, глаго́лѧ:

from the head of the deacon, places it on
the Holy Table, saying:

The noble Joseph, having taken Thy most
pure Body down from the Tree and wrapped
It in pure linen and covered It with spices,
laid It in a new tomb.

In the grave bodily, but in Hades with
Thy soul as God; in Paradise with the thief,
and on the throne with the Father and the
Spirit wast Thou Who fillest all things, O
Christ the Inexpressible.

Thy tomb, the source of our resurrection,
O Christ, hath appeared as life-bearing, as
more beautiful than Paradise and truly more
resplendent than any royal chamber.

Then taking the veils from the holy diskos
and the holy chalice, the priest lays them
to one side on the Holy Table; taking the
aer from the deacon's shoulder, and having
censed it, he covers the Holy Gifts with it,
saying:

Бл҃гоѡбра́зный і҆ѡ́сифъ, съ дре́ва сне́мъ
пречⷭ҇тое твоѐ тѣ́ло, плащани́цею чи́стою
ѡ҆бви́въ, и҆ бл҃гоꙋха́ньми во гро́бѣ но́вѣ
закры́въ, положѝ.

И҆ прїе́мъ кади́льницꙋ ѿ дїа́коновы
рꙋкѝ, кади́тъ ст҃а́ѧ три́жды,
глаго́лѧ:

Оу҆бл҃жѝ гдⷭ҇и, бл҃говоле́нїемъ твои́мъ сїѡ́на,
и҆ да сози́ждꙋтсѧ стѣ́ны і҆ерꙋсали́мскїѧ:
тогда̀ благоволи́ши же́ртвꙋ пра́вды, возно_
ше́нїе и҆ всесожега́ємаѧ, тогда̀ возложа́тъ
на ѻ҆лта́рь тво́й тельцы̀.

И҆ ѿда́въ кади́льницꙋ, и҆ приклони́въ же
главꙋ̀, глаго́летъ дїа́конꙋ:

Помоли́сѧ ѡ҆ мнѣ̀, бра́те и҆ сослꙋжи́телю.

И҆ дїа́конъ къ немꙋ̀:

The noble Joseph, having taken Thy most pure Body down from the Tree and wrapped It in pure linen and covered It with spices, laid It in a new tomb.

And taking the censer from the hand of the deacon, the priest censes the Holy Gifts thrice, saying:

O Lord, be favorable in Thy good will unto Sion, and let the walls of Jerusalem be builded up. Then shalt Thou be pleased with the sacrifice of righteousness, with oblation and whole-burnt offerings; then shall they offer young bullocks upon Thine altar.

And having returned the censer, and having bowed his head, the priest says to the deacon:

Pray for me, brother and concelebrant.

And the deacon says to him:

Дхъ ст҃ы́й на́йдетъ на тѧ̀, и҆ си́ла вы́шнѧгѡ ѡ҆сѣни́тъ тѧ̀.

И҆ сщ҃е́нникъ: То́йже дх҃ъ содѣ́йствꙋетъ на́мъ всѧ̑ дни̑ живота̀ на́шегѡ.

Та́же и҆ дїа́конъ, поклони́въ и҆ са́мъ главꙋ̀, держа̀ вкꙋ́пѣ и҆ ѻ҆ра́рь треми́ пе́рсты десни́цы, глаго́летъ ко сщ҃е́нникꙋ:

Помѧни́ мѧ, влⷣко ст҃ы́й.

И҆ сщ҃е́нникъ: Да помѧне́тъ тѧ̀ гдⷭ҇ь бг҃ъ во црⷭ҇твїи свое́мъ, всегда̀, ны́нѣ и҆ при́снѡ, и҆ во вѣ́ки вѣкѡ́въ.

И҆ дїа́конъ: А҆ми́нь.

И҆ цѣлова́въ десни́цꙋ сщ҃е́нника, и҆схо́дитъ дїа́конъ сѣ́верными две́рьми, и҆ ста́въ на ѻ҆бы́чнѣмъ мѣ́стѣ, глаго́летъ:

И҆спо́лнимъ моли́твꙋ на́шꙋ гдⷭ҇ви.

Ли́къ: Гдⷭ҇и поми́лꙋй.

Дїа́конъ: Ѡ҆ предложе́нныхъ честны́хъ дарѣ́хъ, гдⷭ҇ꙋ помо́лимсѧ.

The Holy Spirit shall come upon thee, and the power of the Most High shall overshadow thee.

And the priest: The same Spirit shall minister with us all the days of our life.

And the deacon, bowing his head himself and holding his orarion with the three fingers of his right hand, says to the priest:

Remember me, holy master.

And the priest: May the Lord God remember thee in His kingdom, always, now and ever, and unto the ages of ages.

Deacon: Amen.

And the deacon, having kissed the right hand of the priest, goes out the north door, and standing in the usual place, says:

Let us complete our prayer unto the Lord.

Choir: Lord, have mercy.

Deacon: For the precious Gifts set forth, let us pray to the Lord.

Ли́къ: Гдⷭи помилꙋй.

Дїа́конъ: Ѡ ст҃ѣмъ хра́мѣ се́мъ, и҆ съ вѣ́рою, блгоговѣ́нїемъ и҆ стра́хомъ бж҃їимъ входѧ́щихъ во́нь, гдꙋ помо́лимсѧ.

Ли́къ: Гдⷭи помилꙋй.

Дїа́конъ: Ѡ и҆зба́витисѧ на́мъ ѿ всѧ́кїѧ ско́рби, гнѣ́ва и҆ нꙋ́жды, гдꙋ помо́лимсѧ.

Ли́къ: Гдⷭи помилꙋй.

Мл҃тва приноше́нїѧ, по поставле́нїи на ст҃ѣмъ престо́лѣ бжⷭтвенныхъ даро́въ, ю҆́же сщ҃е́нникъ глаго́летъ та́йнѡ:

Гдⷭи бж҃е на́шъ, созда́вый на́съ и҆ введы́й въ жи́знь сїю̀, показа́вый на́мъ пꙋти̑ во спасе́нїе, дарова́вый на́мъ небе́сныхъ та̑инъ ѿкрове́нїе: ты̀ бо є҆сѝ положи́вый на́съ въ слꙋжбꙋ сїю̀ си́лою дх҃а твоегѡ̀ ст҃а́гѡ: благоволѝ ᲂу҆́бо, гдⷭи, бы́ти на́мъ слꙋжи́телемъ но́вагѡ твоегѡ̀ завѣ́та, слꙋга́мъ ст҃ы́хъ твои́хъ та́инствъ: прїимѝ на́съ, приближа́ющихсѧ ст҃о́мꙋ твоемꙋ̀

Choir: Lord, have mercy.

Deacon: For this holy temple, and for them that with faith, reverence, and fear of God enter herein, let us pray to the Lord.

Choir: Lord, have mercy.

Deacon: That we may be delivered from all tribulation, wrath, and necessity, let us pray to the Lord.

Choir: Lord, have mercy.

The priest secretly says the Prayer of the Oblation, after placing the Divine Gifts on the Holy Table:

O Lord our God, Who hast created us and brought us into this life; Who hast shown us the ways to salvation, and bestowed on us the revelation of heavenly Mysteries: it is Thou who hast appointed us to this service by the power of Thy Holy Spirit. Therefore, O Lord, enable us to be ministers of Thy New Covenant and servants of Thy Holy Mysteries. Through the greatness of Thy

же́ртвенникꙋ, по мно́жествꙋ ми́лости твоеѧ̀, да бꙋ́демъ досто́йни приноси́ти тебѣ̀ слове́снꙋю сїю̀ и҆ безкро́внꙋю же́ртвꙋ ѡ на́шихъ согрѣше́нїихъ и҆ ѡ лю́дскихъ невѣ́жествїихъ: ю҆́же прїе́мь во ст҃ы́й и҆ пренебе́сный и҆ мы́сленный тво́й же́ртвенникъ, въ воню̀ благоꙋха́нїѧ, возниспослѝ на́мъ благода́ть ст҃а́гѡ твоегѡ̀ дх҃а. При́зри на ны̀, бж҃е, и҆ ви́ждь на слꙋ́жбꙋ сїю̀ на́шꙋ, и҆ прїимѝ ю҆̀, ꙗ҆́коже прїѧ́лъ є҆сѝ а҆́велевы да́ры, нѡ́евы же́ртвы, а҆враа́мова всепло́дїѧ, мѡѷсе́ова и҆ а҆арѡ́нѡва сщ҃е́нства, самꙋ́илова ми́рнаѧ. Ꙗ҆́коже прїѧ́лъ є҆сѝ ѿ ст҃ы́хъ твои́хъ а҆пⷭ҇лъ и҆́стиннꙋю сїю̀ слꙋ́жбꙋ, си́це и҆ ѿ рꙋ́къ на́съ грѣ́шныхъ прїимѝ да́ры сїѧ̑ въ бла́гости твое́й, гдⷭ҇и: ꙗ҆́кѡ да сподо́бльшесѧ слꙋжи́ти безъ поро́ка ст҃о́мꙋ твоемꙋ̀ же́ртвеннику, ѡ҆бра́щемъ мздꙋ̀ вѣ́рныхъ и҆ мꙋ́дрыхъ строи́телей въ де́нь стра́шный воздаѧ́нїѧ твоегѡ̀ пра́веднагѡ.

Дїа́конъ: Застꙋпѝ, сп҃сѝ, поми́лꙋй и҆ сохранѝ на́съ бж҃е твое́ю бл҃года́тїю.

mercy, accept us as we draw near to Thy holy altar, so that we may be worthy to offer unto Thee this rational and bloodless sacrifice for our sins and for the errors of Thy people. Having received it upon Thy holy and noetic altar above the heavens as an odor of good fragrance, do Thou send down upon us the grace of Thy Holy Spirit. Look down on us, O God, and behold this our service. Receive it as Thou didst receive the gifts of Abel, the sacrifices of Noah, the whole-burnt offerings of Abraham, the priestly offices of Moses and Aaron, and the peace-offerings of Samuel. Even as Thou didst receive from Thy holy apostles this true worship, so now, in Thy goodness, accept these gifts from the hands of us sinners, O Lord; that having been accounted worthy to serve without offence at Thy holy altar, we may receive the reward of wise and faithful stewards on the dread day of Thy just and good retribution.

Deacon: Help us, save us, have mercy on us, and keep us, O God, by Thy grace.

Ли́къ: Гдⷭ҇и поми́лꙋй.

Дїа́конъ: Днѐ всегѡ̀ [а҆́ще лїтꙋргі́а соединѧ́етсѧ съ вече́рней, Ве́чера всегѡ̀] соверше́нна, ст҃а, ми́рна и҆ безгрѣ́шна, оу҆ гдⷭ҇а про́сим.

Ли́къ: Пода́й гдⷭ҇и.

Дїа́конъ: А҆́гг҃ла ми́рна, вѣ́рна наста́вника, храни́телѧ дꙋ́шъ и҆ тѣле́съ на́шихъ, оу҆ гдⷭ҇а про́сим.

Ли́къ: Пода́й гдⷭ҇и.

Дїа́конъ: Проще́нїѧ и҆ ѡ҆ставле́нїѧ грѣхѡ́въ и҆ прегрѣше́нїй на́шихъ, оу҆ гдⷭ҇а про́сим.

Ли́къ: Пода́й гдⷭ҇и.

Дїа́конъ: До́брыхъ и҆ поле́зныхъ дꙋша́мъ на́шымъ, и҆ ми́ра мі́рови, оу҆ гдⷭ҇а про́сим.

Ли́къ: Пода́й гдⷭ҇и.

Дїа́конъ: Про́чее вре́мѧ живота̀ на́шегѡ въ ми́рѣ и҆ покаѧ́нїи сконча́ти, оу҆ гдⷭ҇а про́сим.

Ли́къ: Пода́й гдⷭ҇и.

Choir: Lord, have mercy.

Deacon: That the whole day (but if it be a Vesperal Liturgy: whole evening) may be perfect, holy, peaceful, and sinless, let us ask of the Lord.

Choir: Grant this, O Lord.

Deacon: An angel of peace, a faithful guide, a guardian of our souls and bodies, let us ask of the Lord.

Choir: Grant this, O Lord.

Deacon: Pardon and remission of our sins and offenses, let us ask of the Lord.

Choir: Grant this, O Lord.

Deacon: Things good and profitable for our souls, and peace for the world, let us ask of the Lord.

Choir: Grant this, O Lord.

Deacon: That we may complete the remaining time of our life in peace and repentance, let us ask of the Lord.

Choir: Grant this, O Lord.

Діаконъ: Хртїанскїѧ кончины живота нашегѡ, безболѣзненны, непостыдны, мирны, и добрагѡ ѿвѣта на страшнѣмъ судищи хртовѣ просимъ.

Ликъ: Подай гди.

Діаконъ: Престую, пречту, преблгословенную, славную влчцу нашу бцу, и приснодѣву мрїю со всѣми стыми помянувше, сами себе, и другъ друга, и весь животъ нашъ хрту бгу предадимъ.

Ликъ: Тебѣ гди.

Возглашеніе: Щедротами единороднагѡ сна твоегѡ, съ нимже блгословенъ еси, со престымъ и бгимъ и животворѧщимъ твоимъ дхомъ, нынѣ и приснѡ, и во вѣки вѣкѡвъ.

Ликъ: Аминь.

Іерей: Миръ всѣмъ.

Ликъ: И дхови твоему.

Діаконъ: Возлюбимъ другъ друга, да единомыслїемъ исповѣмы.

Deacon: A Christian ending to our life, painless, blameless, peaceful, and a good defense before the dread judgment seat of Christ, let us ask.

Choir: Grant this, O Lord.

Deacon: Calling to remembrance our most holy, most pure, most blessed, glorious Lady Theotokos and Ever-Virgin Mary, with all the Saints, let us commit ourselves and one another and all our life unto Christ, our God.

Choir: To Thee, O Lord.

Exclamation: Through the compassions of Thine Only-begotten Son, with Whom Thou art blessed, together with Thine all-holy and good and life-creating Spirit, now and ever, and unto the ages of ages.

Choir: Amen.

Priest: Peace be unto all.

Choir: And to thy spirit.

Deacon: Let us love one another, that with one mind we may confess:

Ли́къ: Ѻ҆ц҃а̀, и҆ сн҃а, и҆ ст҃а́гѡ дх҃а, трⷯцꙋ є҆дино-
сꙋ́щнꙋю, и҆ нераздѣ́льнꙋю.

И҆ сщ҃е́нникъ покланѧ́етсѧ три́жды,
глаго́лѧ та́йнѡ:

Возлюблю̀ тѧ̀ гдⷭ҇и, крѣ́посте моѧ̀, гдⷭ҇ь
оу҆твержде́нїе моѐ, и҆ прибѣ́жище моѐ,
три́жды.

И҆ цѣлꙋ́етъ ст҃а̑ѧ си́це, ꙗ҆́коже сꙋ́ть
покрове́ны, пе́рвѣе верхꙋ̀ ст҃а́гѡ ді́скоса:
та́же верхꙋ̀ ст҃а́гѡ поти́ра, и҆ кра́й ст҃ы́ѧ
трапе́зы пред собо́ю. А҆́ще ли бꙋ́дꙋтъ
сщ҃е́нникѡвъ два̀, и҆лѝ мно́жае,
то и҆ ѻ҆нѝ цѣлꙋ́ютъ ст҃а̑ѧ всѧ̑,
и҆ дрꙋ́гъ дрꙋ́га въ ра́мена.

Настоѧ́тель же глаго́летъ:

Хрⷭ҇то́съ посредѣ̀ на́съ.

И҆ ѿвѣща́етъ цѣлова́вый:

И҆ є҆́сть, и҆ бꙋ́детъ.

Choir: The Father, and the Son, and the Holy Spirit: the Trinity one in essence and indivisible.

And the priest bows thrice, saying secretly:

I will love Thee, O Lord, my strength. The Lord is my firm foundation, and my fortress. Thrice.

And he kisses the Holy Things that are covered, thus: first the top of the holy diskos, then the rim of the holy chalice and the edge of the Holy Table before him. If there be two priests, or more, then they all kiss the holy things, and one another on the shoulders.

The senior celebrant says:

Christ is in our midst.

And he that kisses replies:

He is, and shall be.

Та́кожде и҆ дїа́кони, а҆́ще бꙋ́дꙋтъ два̀
и҆лѝ трѝ, цѣлꙋютъ кі́йждо ѡ҆ра́рь сво́й
и҆дѣ́же крⷭта̀ ѻ҆́бразъ, и҆ дрꙋ́гъ дрꙋ́га
въ ра́мена, то́жде глаго́люще, є҆́же и҆
сщⷭенницы.

Подо́бнѣ же и҆ дїа́конъ споклонѧ́етсѧ, на
не́мже стои́тъ мѣ́стѣ, и҆ цѣлꙋ́етъ ѡ҆ра́рь
сво́й, и҆дѣ́же є҆́сть крⷭта̀ ѻ҆́бразъ, и҆ та́кѡ
возглаша́етъ:

Две́ри, две́ри премꙋ́дростїю во́нмемъ.

Сщⷭенникъ же воздвиза́етъ воздꙋ́хъ, и҆
держи́тъ над̾ стⷮыми дара́мѝ. А҆́ще же и҆ні́и
бꙋ́дꙋтъ сщⷭенницы слꙋжа́щїи, та́кожде
воздвиза́ютъ стⷮы́й воздꙋ́хъ, и҆ держа́тъ над̾
стⷮыми дара́мѝ, потрѧса́юще, и҆ глаго́люще въ
себѣ̀, ꙗ҆́коже и҆ лю́дїе, и҆сповѣ́данїе вѣ́ры:

Вѣ́рꙋю во є҆ди́наго бга ѻ҆ц҃а̀ вседержи́телѧ,
творца̀ нбꙋ и҆ землѝ, ви́димымъ же
всѣ́мъ и҆ неви́димымъ. И҆ во є҆ди́наго гда

Likewise the deacons, if there be two, or three, kiss each his own orarion, where the figure of the Cross is, and one another on the shoulders, saying that which the priests have said.

In like manner the deacon bows, on the place where he stands, and kisses his orarion where the figure of the Cross is, and then exclaims:

The doors, the doors! In wisdom let us attend.

The priest lifts up the aer, and holds it over the Holy Gifts. If there be other priests concelebrating, they likewise lift up the holy aer, and hold it over the Holy Gifts, waving it and saying secretly, as do the people also, the Confession of faith:

I believe in one God, the Father Almighty, Maker of heaven and earth and all things visible and invisible; and in one Lord Jesus Christ, the Son of God, the Only-begotten,

і҆и҃са хрⷭта̀, си҃на бж҃їѧ, є҆диноро́днаго, и҆́же ѿ
ѻ҆ц҃а̀ рожде́ннаго пре́жде всѣ́хъ вѣ̑къ: свѣ́та
ѿ свѣ́та, бг҃а и҆́стинна ѿ бг҃а и҆́стинна,
рожде́нна, не сотворе́нна, є҆диносꙋ́щна ѻ҆ц҃ꙋ̀,
и҆́мже всѧ̑ бы́ша. На́съ ра́ди человѣ́къ, и҆
на́шегѡ ра́ди спасе́нїѧ, сше́дшаго съ нб҃съ,
и҆ воплоти́вшагосѧ ѿ дх҃а ст҃а и҆ мр҃і́и дв҃ы,
и҆ вочл҃вѣ́чшасѧ. Распѧ́таго же за ны̀
при понті́йстѣмъ пїла́тѣ, и҆ страда́вша,
и҆ погребе́нна, и҆ воскрⷭшаго въ тре́тїй де́нь
по писа́нїємъ. И҆ возше́дшаго на нб҃са, и҆
сѣдѧ́ща ѡ҆деснꙋ́ю ѻ҆ц҃а̀. И҆ па́ки грѧдꙋ́щаго
со сла́вою, сꙋди́ти живы̑мъ и҆ ме́ртвымъ,
є҆гѡ́же цр҃твїю не бꙋ́детъ конца̀. И҆ въ
дх҃а ст҃а́го, гдⷭа, животворѧ́щаго, и҆́же ѿ
ѻ҆ц҃а̀ и҆сходѧ́щаго, и҆́же со ѻ҆ц҃е́мъ и҆ сн҃омъ
спокланѧ́ема и҆ сславима, глаго́лавшаго
прⷪро́ки. Во є҆ди́нꙋ ст҃ꙋ́ю соборнꙋ́ю и҆ а҆пⷭльскꙋ́ю
цр҃ковь. И҆сповѣ́дꙋю є҆ди́но крⷭще́нїе, во
ѡ҆ставле́нїе грѣхѡ́въ. Ча́ю воскрⷭнїѧ ме́рт-
выхъ: И҆ жи́зни бꙋ́дꙋщагѡ вѣ́ка. А҆ми́нь.

begotten of the Father before all ages, Light of Light, true God of true God, begotten, not made, of one essence with the Father, by Whom all things were made; Who for us men and for our salvation came down from the Heavens, and was incarnate of the Holy Spirit and the Virgin Mary, and became man; and was crucified for us under Pontius Pilate, and suffered, and was buried; and arose on the third day according to the Scriptures; and ascended into the heavens, and sitteth at the right hand of the Father; and shall come again, with glory, to judge both the living and the dead, Whose kingdom shall have no end. And in the Holy Spirit, the Lord, the Giver of Life, Who proceedeth from the Father, Who with the Father and the Son together is worshipped and glorified, Who spake by the prophets. In one Holy, Catholic, and Apostolic Church. I confess one baptism for the remission of sins. I look for the resurrection of the dead; and the life of the age to come. Amen.

Дїа́конъ: Ста́немъ до́брѣ, ста́немъ со стра́хомъ, во́нмемъ, ст҃о́е возноше́нїе въ ми́рѣ приноси́ти.

Ли́къ: Ми́лость ми́ра, же́ртвꙋ хвале́нїѧ.

И҆ сщ҃е́нникъ оу҆́бѡ взе́мъ возд҃ꙋ́хъ ѿ ст҃ы́хъ, и҆ цѣлова́въ и҆̀, полага́етъ на є҆ди́но мѣ́сто, глаго́лѧ:

Бл҃года́ть гдⷭ҇а на́шегѡ і҆и҃са хрⷭ҇та̀, и҆ люб́ы бг҃а и҆ ѻ҆ц҃а̀, и҆ прича́стїе ст҃а́гѡ дх҃а, бꙋ́ди со всѣ́ми ва́ми.

Дїа́конъ же поклони́всѧ, вхо́дитъ во ст҃ы́й ѻ҆лта́рь. И҆ прїи́мъ рі́пі́дꙋ, вѣ́етъ ст҃а́ѧ бл҃гоговѣ́йнѡ. А҆́ще же нѣ́сть рі́пі́ды, твори́тъ сїѐ со є҆ди́нѣмъ покро́вцемъ.

Ли́къ: И҆ со дх҃омъ твои́мъ.

Сщ҃е́нникъ: Горѣ̀ и҆мѣ́имъ сердца̀.

Ли́къ: И҆́мамы ко гдꙋ҃.

Сщ҃е́нникъ: Бл҃годари́мъ гдⷭ҇а.

Ли́къ: Досто́йно и҆ пра́ведно є҆́сть, покланѧ́тисѧ ѻ҆ц҃ꙋ̀, и҆ сн҃ꙋ, и҆ ст҃о́мꙋ дх҃ꙋ, трⷪ҇цѣ є҆диносꙋ́щнѣй и҆ нераздѣ́льнѣй.

Deacon: Let us stand well. Let us stand with fear. Let us attend, that we may offer the holy oblation in peace.

Choir: A mercy of peace, a sacrifice of praise.

The priest then having taken the aer off the Holy Gifts, and kissing it, lays it to one side, saying:

The grace of our Lord Jesus Christ, and the love of God the Father, and the communion of the Holy Spirit be with you all.

And the deacon, having bowed, enters the holy altar, and taking a fan, fans the Holy Things reverently. If there be no fan, he uses one of the veils.

Choir: And with thy spirit.

Priest: Let us lift up our hearts.

Choir: We lift them up unto the Lord.

Priest: Let us give thanks unto the Lord.

Choir: It is meet and right to worship the Father, the Son, and the Holy Spirit, the Trinity one in essence and indivisible.

Сщⷵе́нникъ же мо́лнтсѧ:

Сы́й влⷣко, гдⷭ҇и бж҃е о҆ч҃е вседержи́телю покланѧ́емый! досто́йнѡ ꙗ҆́кw вои́стиннꙋ, и҆ пра́ведно, и҆ лѣ́по великолѣ́пїю ст҃ы́ни твоеѧ̀, тебѐ хвали́ти, тебѐ пѣ́ти, тебѐ бл҃гослови́ти, тебѣ̀ клⷶнѧ́тисѧ, тебѐ благодари́ти, тебѐ сла́вити є҆ди́наго вои́стиннꙋ сꙋ́щаго бг҃а, и҆ тебѣ̀ приноси́ти се́рдцемъ сокрꙋше́нными и҆ дх҃омъ смире́нїѧ слове́снꙋю сїю̀ слꙋ́жбꙋ на́шꙋ: ꙗ҆́кѡ ты̀ є҆сѝ дарова́вый на́мъ позна́нїе твоеѧ̀ и҆́стины. И҆ кто̀ дово́ленъ возглаго́лати си́лы твоѧ̀, слы́шаны сотвори́ти всѧ̑ хвалы̑ твоѧ̑, и҆лѝ повѣ́дати всѧ̑ чꙋдеса̀ твоѧ̑ во всѧ́ко вре́мѧ; влⷣко всѣ́хъ, гдⷭ҇и небесѐ и҆ землѝ, и҆ всеѧ̀ тва́ри, ви́димыѧ же и҆ неви́димыѧ, сѣдѧ́й на прⷭ҇то́лѣ сла́вы и҆ призира́ѧй бе́здны, безнача́льне, неви́диме, непостижи́ме, неѡпи́санне, неизмѣ́нне, о҆ч҃е гдⷭ҇а на́шегѡ і҆и҃са хрⷭ҇та̀, вели́кагѡ бг҃а и҆ спаси́телѧ, ѹ҆пова́нїѧ на́шегѡ, и҆́же

The priest prays:

O Master, Thou Who art, adorable Lord, God, Father Almighty! It is truly meet and right, and befitting the majesty of Thy holiness, to praise Thee, to hymn Thee, to bless Thee, to worship Thee, to thank Thee, to glorify Thee the only God that truly existeth, and to offer unto Thee this our rational service with contrite heart and humble spirit; for Thou hast Thyself bestowed upon us the knowledge of Thy truth. And who is sufficient to speak of Thy might, to make all Thy praises to be heard, or to proclaim Thy wonders at all times? O Master of all, Lord of heaven and earth, and of all creation, visible and invisible, Who sittest on the throne of glory and lookest upon the deeps, Who art without beginning, invisible, ineffable, inconceivable, immutable, the Father of our Lord Jesus Christ, the great God and Saviour, our Hope, Who is the image of Thy goodness; the

є҆́сть ѻ҆́бразъ твоеѧ̀ бла́гости: печа́ть
равноѻбра́знаѧ, въ себѣ̀ показꙋ́ѧ тѧ̀ ѻ҆ц҃а̀,
сло́во живо́е, бг҃ъ и҆́стинный, превѣ́чнаѧ
премꙋ́дрость, живо́тъ, ѡ҆сщ҃е́нїе, си́ла,
свѣ́тъ и҆́стинный, и҆́мже дх҃ъ ст҃ый ꙗ҆ви́сѧ
и҆́стины, сꙋноположе́нїѧ дарова́нїе, ѡ҆брꙋче́нїе
бꙋ́дꙋщагѡ наслѣ́дїѧ, нача́токъ вѣ́чныхъ
бла̑гъ, животворѧ́щаѧ си́ла, и҆сто́чникъ
ѡ҆сщ҃е́нїѧ, ѿ негꙋ́же всѧ̀ тва́рь слове́снаѧ
же и҆ ѹ҆́мнаѧ ѹ҆крѣплѧ́ема тебѣ̀ слꙋ́житъ и҆
тебѣ̀ присносꙋ́щное возсыла́етъ славосло́вїе,
ꙗ҆́кѡ всѧ́ческаѧ рабѡ́тна тебѣ̀: тебѐ бо
хва́лѧтъ а҆́гг҃ли, а҆рха́гг҃ли, прⷭто́ли, гдⷭтвїѧ,
нача̑ла, вла̑сти, си̑лы и҆ многоѻчи́тїи
херꙋві́ми: тебѣ̀ предстоѧ́тъ ѻ҆́крестъ
серафі́ми, ше́сть кри́лъ є҆ди́номꙋ, и҆ ше́сть
кри́лъ є҆ди́номꙋ, и҆ ше́сть кри́лъ є҆ди́номꙋ: и҆
двѣма̀ ѹ҆́бѡ покрыва́ютъ ли́ца своѧ̑, двѣма̀
же но́ги, и҆ двѣма̀ летѧ́юще, взыва́ютъ
є҆ди́нъ ко дрꙋго́мꙋ, непреста́нными ѹ҆сты̀,
немо́лчными славосло́веньми.

seal of equal kind, showing forth Thee, the Father, in Himself, the living Word, the true God, the pre-eternal Wisdom, Life, Sanctification, Power, the True Light through Whom the Holy Spirit was made manifest; the Spirit of Truth, the Gift of Adoption, the Pledge of the inheritance to come, the First-fruits of eternal good things, the life-creating Power, the Fount of sanctification, by Whom every rational and intelligent creature is strengthened to serve Thee and evermore doth send up to Thee a doxology, for all things work for Thee; the Angels, Archangels, Thrones, Dominions, Principalities, Authorities, Powers, and the many-eyed Cherubim do praise Thee; before Thee stand round about the Seraphim, six wings hast one, and six wings hast another: for with two they cover their faces, and with two their feet, and with two they fly, crying aloud one to another, with unceasing lips and never-ending doxologies.

Возглаше́нїе: Побѣ́днꙋю пѣ́снь пою́ще, вопїю́ще, взыва́юще и҆ глаго́люще.

Ли́къ: Ст҃ъ, ст҃ъ, ст҃ъ гдⷭ҇ь саваѡ́ѳъ, и҆спо́лнь нб҃о и҆ землѧ̀ сла́вы твоеѧ̀, ѡ҆са́нна въ вы́шнихъ, бл҃гослове́нъ грѧды́й во и҆́мѧ гдⷭ҇не, ѡ҆са́нна въ вы́шнихъ.

И҆ здѣ̀ па́ки дїа́конъ, прїи́мъ ст҃ꙋю ѕвѣзди́цꙋ ѿ ст҃а́гѡ ді́скоса, твори́тъ крⷭ҇та̀ ѡ҆́бразъ верхꙋ̀ є҆гѡ̀, и҆ цѣлова́въ ю҆̀, полага́етъ.

Та́же прихо́дитъ, и҆ ста́нетъ на деснѣ́й странѣ̀: и҆ взе́мъ рїпі́дꙋ въ рꙋцѣ̀, ѡ҆ма́хнⷡ҇ветъ ти́хѡ со всѧ́кимъ внима́нїемъ и҆ стра́хомъ верхꙋ̀ ст҃ы́хъ дарѡ́въ, ꙗ҆́кѡ не сѣ́сти мꙋ́хамъ, ни и҆но́мꙋ чесомꙋ̀ таково́мꙋ.

Сщ҃е́нникъ мо́литсѧ та́йнѡ:

Съ си́ми бл҃же́нными си́лами, влⷣко чл҃вѣколю́бче, и҆ мы̀ грѣ́шнїи вопїе́мъ и҆ глаго́лемъ: ст҃ъ є҆сѝ ꙗ҆́кѡ вои́стиннꙋ и҆ пресвѧ́тъ, и҆ нѣ́сть мѣ́ры великолѣ́пїю

Exclamation: Singing the triumphal hymn, shouting, crying aloud, and saying:

Choir: Holy, Holy, Holy, Lord of Sabbaoth, heaven and earth are full of Thy glory. Hosanna in the highest. Blessed is He that cometh in the Name of the Lord. Hosanna in the highest.

And here the deacon, taking the holy star from the holy diskos, makes the sign of the Cross above it, and kissing it, lays it aside.

Then the deacon goes and stands on the right side, and having taken a fan in his right hand, fans gently, with all attentiveness and fear, over the Holy Gifts, lest flies or other such insects settle on them.

The priest prays silently:

With these blessed hosts, O Master, Lover of mankind, we sinners also cry aloud and say: Holy art Thou in truth, and Most holy, and there is no bound to the majesty of Thy holiness; and venerable art Thou

стⷮыни твоеѧ: и преподобенъ во всѣхъ
дѣлѣхъ твоихъ, ꙗкw правдою и сꙋдомъ
истиннымъ всѧ навелъ єси на ны: создавъ
бо человѣка, персть вземъ ѿ земли,
и ѻбразомъ твоимъ, бже, почетъ,
положилъ єси въ раи сладости, безсмертïе
жизни, и наслаждéнïе вѣчныхъ благъ въ
соблюдéнïе заповѣдей твоихъ ѡбѣщавъ
ємꙋ: но преслꙋшавша тебѐ истиннаго
бга, создавшаго єго, и прелестïю
ѕмïевою привлекшасѧ, оу҆мерцвлена же
своими прегрѣшéньми, изгналъ єси єго
праведнымъ твоимъ сꙋдомъ, бже, ѿ раѧ
въ мïръ сей, и ѿвратилъ єси въ землю ѿ
неѧже взѧтъ бысть, оу҆строѧѧ ємꙋ єже
ѿ пакибытïѧ спасéнïе, въ самѣмъ хрⷭ҇тѣ
твоемъ: не бо ѿвратилсѧ єси созданïѧ
твоегw въ конецъ, єже сотворилъ єси,
бл҃же, нижѐ забылъ єси дѣла рꙋкъ твоихъ,
но посѣтилъ єси многоѻбразнѣ, ради
милосéрдïѧ милости твоеѧ: пророки послалъ
єси, сотворилъ єси силы ст҃ыми твоими,

in all Thy works, for in righteousness and true
judgment hast Thou ordered all things for us;
for, having created man, taking him from the
dust of the earth, and having fashioned him
according to Thine image, O God, Thou didst
place him in a paradise of delight, promising
him life immortal, and delight in eternal bless-
ings in the keeping of Thy commandments;
but when he disobeyed Thee, the true God,
Who hadst created him, and was led astray
by the deception of the serpent, slain by his
own transgressions, Thou didst expel him, in
Thy righteous judgment, O God, from paradise into this world, and didst return him to
the earth whence he was taken, providing for
him salvation in Thy Christ Himself, through
regeneration; for not unto the end didst Thou
turn away from Thy creature whom Thou
hadst made, O Good One, neither didst Thou
forget the work of Thy hands, but didst visit
him in divers manners, for the sake of the
tender compassion of Thy mercy; Thou didst
send prophets, Thou didst perform mighty

въ ко́емждо ро́дѣ бл҃гоꙋго́ди́вшими тебѣ̀:
глаго́лалъ є҆сѝ на́мъ ѹ҆сты̀ ра̑бъ твои́хъ
проро́ковъ, предвозвѣща́ѧ на́мъ хотѧ́щее
бы́ти спасе́нїе: зако́нъ да́лъ є҆сѝ въ по́мощь:
а҆́гг҃лы поста́вилъ є҆сѝ храни́тели. є҆гда́ же
прїи́де и҆сполне́нїе време́нъ, гл҃а́лалъ є҆сѝ
на́мъ саме́мъ сн҃омъ твои́мъ, и҆́мже и҆
вѣ́ки сотвори́лъ є҆сѝ, и҆́же сы́й сїѧ́нїе
сла́вы твоеѧ̀ и҆ начерта́нїе ѵ҆поста́си твоеѧ̀,
носѧ́ же всѧ̑ глаго́ломъ си́лы своеѧ̀, не
хище́нїе непщева̀ є҆́же бы́ти ра́венъ тебѣ̀
бг҃ꙋ и҆ ѻ҆ц҃ꙋ̀: но бг҃ъ сы́й превѣ́чный, на
землѝ ꙗ҆ви́сѧ, и҆ человѣ́комъ спожи́ве: и҆
ѿ дв҃ы ст҃ы̑ѧ воплощь́сѧ, и҆стощѝ себѐ,
зра́къ раба̀ прїе́мь, соѻбра́зенъ бы́въ тѣ́лꙋ
смире́нїѧ на́шегѡ, да на́съ соѻбра́зны
сотвори́тъ ѻ҆́бразꙋ сла́вы своеѧ̀: поне́же
бо человѣ́комъ грѣ́хъ вни́де въ мі́ръ, и҆
грѣхо́мъ сме́рть, бл҃говолѝ є҆диноро́дный
тво́й сн҃ъ, сы́й въ нѣ́дрѣхъ тебѐ бг҃а и҆
ѻ҆ц҃а̀, бы́въ ѿ жены̀ ст҃ы̑ѧ бг҃оро́дицы, и҆
приснодв҃ы мр҃і́и, бы́въ подъ зако́номъ,

deeds by the saints, who in every generation were well-pleasing unto Thee; Thou didst speak to us by the mouths of Thy servants the prophets, foretelling to us the salvation to come; Thou didst give the Law as a help; Thou didst appoint angels. But when the fullness of the time was come, Thou didst speak to us by Thy Son Himself, by Whom also Thou didst create the ages, Who, being the Radiance of Thy glory, and the express image of Thy person, upholding all things by the word of His power, thought it not robbery to be equal with Thee, the God and Father; but being the pre-eternal God, yet He appeared on earth and dwelt among men; and was incarnate of a holy Virgin, didst empty Himself, taking on the form of a servant, being conformed to the body of our lowliness, that He might make us conformed to the image of His glory; for as by a man sin entered into the world, and death by sin, so Thine Only-begotten Son, Who is in the bosom of Thee, the God and Father, wast well-pleased to be born of a woman,

ѡсꙋди́ти грѣ́хъ во пло́ти свое́й, да во
ада́мѣ ѹмира́юще, ѡживотворѧ́тсѧ въ
само́мъ хр҃тѣ̀ твое́мъ: и̑ пожи́въ въ
мі́рѣ се́мъ, да́въ повелѣ́нїѧ спаси́тєльнаѧ,
ѿста́вивъ на́съ пре́лести і̑дѡльскі́ѧ, приведѐ
въ позна́нїе тебѐ и̑́стиннагѡ бг҃а и̑ ѻ̑ц҃а̀,
стѧжа́въ на́съ себѣ̀ лю́ди и̑збра́нны,
ца́рское сщ҃е́нїе, ꙗ̑зы́къ ст҃ъ: и̑ ѡчи́стивъ
водо́ю, и̑ ѡсти́въ дх҃омъ ст҃ымъ, дадѐ
себѐ и̑змѣ́нꙋ сме́рти, въ не́йже держи́ми
бѣ́хомъ, про́дани подъ грѣхо́мъ: и̑ соше́дъ
кр҃то́мъ во а̑́дъ, да и̑спо́лнитъ собо́ю всѧ̑,
разрѣши́ болѣ́зни сме́ртныѧ: и̑ воскр҃сѐ
въ тре́тїй де́нь, и̑ пꙋ́ть сотвори́въ всѧ́кой
пло́ти, къ воскр҃се́нїю є́же и̑зъ ме́ртвыхъ,
занѐ не бѧ́ше мо́щно держи́мꙋ бы́ти
тлѣ́нїемъ нача́льникꙋ жи́зни, бы́сть
нача́токъ ѹме́ршихъ, перворожде́нъ
и̑зъ ме́ртвыхъ, да бꙋ́детъ са́мъ всѧ̑,
во всѣ́хъ пе́рвенствꙋѧй: и̑ возше́дъ на
нб҃еса̀, сѣ́де ѡдеснꙋ́ю вели́чествїѧ твоегѡ̀
на высо́кихъ, и̑́же и̑ прїи́детъ возда́ти

the holy Theotokos and Ever-Virgin Mary; to be born under the law, to condemn sin in His flesh, that they who were dead in Adam mightest be made alive in Thy Christ Himself; and inhabiting this world, giving saving commandments, releasing us from the delusions of idols, He brought us unto knowledge of Thee, the true God and Father, acquiring us for Himself a chosen people, a royal priesthood, a holy nation; and purifying us with water, and sanctifying us by the Holy Spirit, He gave Himself a ransom to death, by which we were held, sold under sin; and descending through the Cross into hades, that He mightest fulfill all things in Himself, He loosed the pains of death; and He arose on the third day, and making a way for all flesh unto the resurrection from the dead, because it was not possible for the Author of Life to be held by corruption, He became the First-fruits of the dead, the First-born from the dead; that He might Himself be all, in all things preeminent;

комꙋ́ждо по дѣлѡ́мъ є҆гѡ̀. Ѡ҆ста́ви же
на́мъ воспоминáнïѧ спаси́тельнагѡ своегѡ̀
страда́нïѧ сïѧ̀, ꙗ҆́же предложи́хомъ по є҆гѡ̀
за́повѣдемъ: хотѧ̀ бо и҆зы́ти на во́льнꙋю
и҆ приснопа́мѧтнꙋю, и҆ животворѧ́щꙋю свою̀
смéрть, въ но́щь, въ ню́же предаѧ́ше себѐ
за живóтъ мíра, прïéмъ хлѣ́бъ на ст҃ы́ѧ
своѧ̀ и҆ пречⷭ҇тыѧ рꙋ́ки, показа́въ тебѣ̀
бг҃ꙋ и҆ ѻ҆ц҃ꙋ, благодари́въ, благослови́въ,
ѡ҆ст҃и́въ, преломи́въ,

Возглашéнïе: Дадѐ ст҃ы́мъ свои́мъ оу҆чн҃кѡ́мъ
и҆ а҆пⷭ҇лѡмъ, рéкъ: прïими́те, ꙗ҆ди́те, сïѐ
є҆́сть тѣ́ло моѐ, є҆́же за вы̀ ломи́мое во
ѡ҆ставлéнïе грѣхѡ́въ.

Ли́къ: А҆ми́нь.

Семꙋ́ же глаго́лемꙋ, показꙋ́етъ сщ҃éнникъ
дïа́конъ ст҃ы́й дíскосъ, держа̀ и҆ ѡ҆ра́рь тремѝ
пéрсты десни́цы. Подо́бнѣ, и҆ є҆гда̀ глаго́летъ

and ascending into heaven, He sat down at the right hand of Thy majesty on high, and shall come again to render unto every man according to his works. He hath left with us these memorials of His saving Passion, which we have offered according to His commandments; for when He was about to go forth to His voluntary and ever-memorable and life-creating death, in the night in which He gave Himself for the life of the world, taking bread in His holy and most pure hands, showing it to Thee, the God and Father, giving thanks, blessing it, sanctifying it, breaking it,

Exclamation: He gave it to His holy disciples and apostles, saying: Take, eat: this is My Body, which is broken for you for the remission of sins.

Choir: Amen.

When this is being said, the deacon points to the holy diskos, holding his orarion with three fingers of his right hand. Likewise,

сщ҃е́нникъ: Пі́йте ѿ неѧ̀ всѝ: споказꙋ́етъ и҆
са́мъ ст҃ы́й поти́ръ.

Сщ҃е́нникъ вта́й:

Подо́бнѣ и҆ ча́шꙋ ѿ плода̀ ло́знагѡ прїе́мь,
раствори́въ, благодари́въ, благослови́въ,
ѡ҆свѧти́въ:

Возглаше́нїе: Дадѐ ст҃ы́мъ свои́мъ ᲂу҆чн҃кѡ́мъ
и҆ а҆пⷭ҇лѡмъ, ре́къ: пі́йте ѿ неѧ̀ всѝ, сїѧ̀ є҆́сть
кро́вь моѧ̀ но́вагѡ завѣ́та, ꙗ҆́же за вы̀
и҆ за мнѡ́гїѧ и҆злива́емаѧ, во ѡ҆ставле́нїе
грѣхѡ́въ.

Ли́къ: А҆ми́нь.

Сщ҃е́нникъ приклони́въ главꙋ̀, мо́литсѧ вта́й:

Сїѐ твори́те въ моѐ воспомина́нїе:
Є҆ли́жды бо а҆́ще ꙗ҆́сте хлѣ́бъ се́й, и҆ ча́шꙋ
сїю̀ пїе́те, мою̀ сме́рть возвѣща́ете, моѐ
воскрⷭ҇нїе и҆сповѣ́даете. Помина́юще ᲂу҆́бѡ,
влⷣко, и҆ мы̀ спаси́тельнаѧ є҆гѡ̀ страда́нїѧ,
животворѧ́щїй крⷭ҇тъ, тридне́вное погребе́нїе,
є҆́же и҆зъ ме́ртвыхъ воскресе́нїе, є҆́же на нб҃са̀

when the priest says: **Drink of it, all of you,** he points to the holy chalice.

The priest prays secretly:

Likewise also taking the cup of the fruit of the vine, mingling it, giving thanks, blessing it, and sanctifying it:

Exclamation: He gave it to His holy disciples and apostles, saying: Drink of it, all of you: This is My Blood of the New Testament, which is shed for you and for many, for the remission of sins.

Choir: Amen.

The priest, bowing his head, prays secretly:

This do in remembrance of Me; for as often as ye eat this Bread and drink of this Cup, ye do proclaim My death, ye do confess My Resurrection. Therefore we also, Master, being mindful of His saving Passion, life-creating Cross, three-day burial, Resurrection from the dead, Ascension into the

возше́ствїе, є́же ѡдесну́ю тебѐ бг҃а и ѻ҆ц҃а̀
седѣ́нїе, и҆ сла́вное и҆ стра́шное є҆гѡ̀ второ́е
прише́ствїе.

Возглаше́нїе: Твоѧ̀ ѿ твои́хъ тебѣ̀
принося́ще, ѡ҆ всѣ́хъ и҆ за всѧ̀.

Сему̀ же глаго́лему, дїа́конъ ѿлага́етъ ри́пїду,
и҆ прело́жъ ру́цѣ крⷭ҇тоѻбра́знѣ, и҆ по́дємъ ст҃ы́й
дїскосъ, и҆ ст҃ы́й потирь, и҆
поклони́тсѧ оу҆миле́ннѣ.

Ли́къ: Тебѐ пое́мъ, тебѐ бл҃гословимъ, тебѣ̀
бл҃годаримъ гдⷭ҇и, и҆ мо́лимъ ти сѧ, бж҃е на́шъ.

Сщ҃е́нникъ приклони́въ главу̀, мо́литсѧ втай:
Сегѡ̀ ра́ди, влⷣко престы́й, и҆ мы̀
гре́шнїи, и҆ недосто́йнїи рабѝ твоѝ,
сподо́бльшїисѧ служи́ти ст҃о́му твоему̀
же́ртвенникꙋ, не ра́ди пра́вдъ на́шихъ, не бо̀
сотвори́хомъ что̀ бл҃го на землѝ, но ра́ди
ми́лости твоеѧ̀ и҆ щедро́тъ твои́хъ, ꙗ҆же
и҆злїѧ́лъ є҆сѝ бога́тнѡ на ны̀, дерза́юще
приближа́емсѧ ст҃о́му твоему̀ же́ртвенникꙋ

heavens, sitting at the right hand of Thee, the God and Father, and His glorious and fearsome Second Coming:

Exclamation: Thine Own of Thine Own, we offer unto Thee in behalf of all, and for all.

While this is being said, the deacon puts aside the fan, and having formed a cross with his arms, and having lifted the holy diskos and the holy chalice, he bows with compunction.

Choir: We praise Thee, we bless Thee, we give thanks unto Thee, O Lord, and we pray unto Thee, O our God.

The priest prays secretly:

Therefore, O Most-holy Master, having been vouchsafed to minister at Thy holy altar, not on account of our righteousness, for we have done nothing good on the earth, but because of Thy mercy and Thy compassions, which Thou hast poured out abundantly upon us, we sinners and Thine

и҆ предложше вмѣстоѻбразнаѧ ст҃а́гѡ тѣ́ла и҆ кро́ве хрⷭ҇та̀ твоегѡ̀, тебѣ̀ мо́лимсѧ, и҆ тебѐ призыва́емъ: сⷮе ст҃ы́хъ, бл҃говоле́нїемъ твое́ѧ бла́гости прїити дх҃ꙋ твоемꙋ̀ ст҃о́мꙋ на ны̀, и҆ на предлежа́щыѧ да́ры сїѧ̑, и҆ бл҃гослови́ти ѧ҆҆̀, ѡ҆ст҃и́ти, и҆ показа́ти

Дїа́конъ полага́етъ рїпі́дꙋ, ю҆же держа́ше, и҆лѝ покро́въ, и҆ прихо́дитъ бли́зъ сщ҃е́нника, и҆ покланѧ́ютсѧ ѻ҆́ба три́жды преⷣ ст҃о́ю трапе́зою, и҆ молѧ́щесѧ въ себѣ̀:

Бж҃е, ѡ҆чи́сти мѧ грѣ́шнаго, и҆ поми́лꙋй мѧ.

Сщ҃е́нникъ: Гдⷭ҇и, и҆́же прест҃а́гѡ твоегѡ̀ дх҃а въ тре́тїй ча́съ а҆пⷭ҇лѡмъ твои́мъ низпосла́вый, тогѡ̀, бл҃гі́й, не ѿимѝ ѿ на́съ: но ѡ҆бновѝ на́съ молѧ́щихъ ти сѧ.

Дїа́конъ стїⷯ: Се́рдце чи́сто сози́жди во мнѣ̀ бж҃е, и҆ дх҃ъ пра́въ ѡ҆бновѝ во оу҆тро́бѣ мое́й.

unworthy servants do also daringly draw nigh unto Thy holy altar; and having set forth the emblems of the holy Body and Blood of Thy Christ, we pray Thee, and we call upon Thee: O Holy of Holies, through the favor of Thy goodness send down Thy Holy Spirit upon us, and upon these gifts set forth, and bless them, sanctify, and show

The deacon lays aside the fan that he was holding, or the cover, and draws nigh to the priest, and both of them bow thrice before the Holy Table, praying within themselves:

O God, cleanse me a sinner, and have mercy on me.

Priest: O Lord, Who didst send down Thy Most-holy Spirit at the third hour upon Thine apostles: Take Him not from us, O Good One, but renew Him in us who pray unto Thee.

Deacon, the verse: Create in me a clean heart, O God, and renew a right spirit within me.

Па́ки сщⷢ҇е́нникъ: Гдⷭ҇и, и҆́же прест҃а́гѡ твоегѡ̀ дх҃а:

Дїа́конъ стї́хъ: Не ѿве́ржи менѐ ѿ лица̀ твоегѡ̀, и҆ дх҃а твоегѡ̀ ст҃а́гѡ не ѿимѝ ѿ менѐ.

И҆ па́ки сщⷢ҇е́нникъ: Гдⷭ҇и, и҆́же прест҃а́гѡ твоегѡ̀ дх҃а:

Та́же главꙋ̀ приклони́въ дїа́конъ, показꙋ́етъ ѡ҆раре́мъ ст҃ы́й хлѣ́бъ, и҆ глаго́летъ ти́химъ гла́сомъ:

Бл҃гословѝ влады́ко, ст҃ы́й хлѣ́бъ.

Сщⷢ҇е́нникъ же, зна́менꙋ́ѧ три́жды ст҃ы́ѧ да́ры, глаго́летъ та́йнѡ:

Хлѣ́бъ ѹ҆́бѡ се́й са́мое честно́е тѣ́ло гдⷭ҇а и҆ бг҃а и҆ спа́са на́шегѡ і҆и҃са хрⷭ҇та̀.

Дїа́конъ: А҆ми́нь.

И҆ па́ки дїа́конъ:

Бл҃гословѝ влады́ко, ст҃ꙋ́ю ча́шꙋ.

Again, the priest: O Lord, Who didst send down Thy Most-holy Spirit . . .

Deacon, the verse: Cast me not away from Thy presence, and take not Thy Holy Spirit from me.

And again, the priest: O Lord, Who didst send down Thy Most-holy Spirit . . .

Then bowing his head and pointing with his orarion to the Holy Bread, the deacon says quietly:

Bless, master, the Holy Bread.

And the priest makes the sign of the Cross over the Holy Bread three times, saying:

This Bread to be itself the precious Body of our Lord, and God, and Saviour, Jesus Christ.

Deacon: Amen.

And again, the deacon:

Bless, master, the Holy Cup.

Й сщⷬ҇енникъ блгословлѧ́ѧ глаго́летъ:

Ча́шꙋ же сїю̀, са́мꙋю чⷭ҇тнꙋю кро́вь гдⷭ҇а й бга̀ й спа́са на́шегѡ і҆нса хрⷭ҇та̀.

Дїа́конъ: А҆ми́нь.

Сщⷬ҇енникъ: И҆злїа́ннꙋю за живо́тъ мі́ра.

Дїа́конъ: А҆ми́нь.

Й па́ки дїа́конъ, показꙋ́ѧ й ѻ҆бою̀ стⷯ҇аѧ, глаго́летъ:

Блгословѝ влады́ко, ѻ҆бою̀.

Сщⷬ҇енникъ же, блгословлѧ́ѧ ѻ҆бою̀ стⷯ҇аѧ рꙋко́ю, глаго́летъ:

Преложи́въ дхⷯ҇омъ твои́мъ стⷯ҇ымъ.

Дїа́конъ: А҆ми́нь, а҆ми́нь, а҆ми́нь.

Й главꙋ̀ подклонⷤ҇ дїа́конъ ко сщⷬ҇енникꙋ, ре́къ:

Помѧни́ мѧ, стⷯ҇ый влады́ко, грѣ́шнаго.

Сщⷬ҇енникъ же глаго́летъ: Да помѧне́тъ тѧ̀ гдⷭ҇ь бгъ во црⷭ҇твїи свое́мъ, всегда̀, ны́нѣ й прⷭ҇нѡ, й во вѣ́ки вѣкѡ́въ.

And the priest, blessing, says:

And this cup to be itself the precious Blood of our Lord and God, and Saviour, Jesus Christ.

Deacon: Amen.

Priest: Which was shed for the life of the world.

Deacon: Amen.

And again the deacon, pointing to both the Holy Things, says:

Bless them both, master.

And the priest, blessing both the Holy Things, says:

Changing them by Thy Holy Spirit.

Deacon: Amen, amen, amen.

And the deacon, bowing his head to the priest, says:

Remember me, a sinner, holy master.

And the priest says: May the Lord God remember thee in His kingdom, always, now and ever, and unto the ages of ages.

Дїа́конъ же ре́къ: А҆ми́нь, преходи́тъ, на не́мже пе́рвѣе стоѧ́ше мѣ́стѣ, и҆ взе́мъ рі́підꙋ, ѡ҆ма́хиваетъ ст҃а́ꙗ́ ꙗ́кѡ и҆ пре́жде.

Сщ҃е́нникъ же мо́литсѧ:

На́съ же всѣ́хъ, ѿ є҆ди́нагѡ хлѣ́ба и҆ ча́ши причаща́ющихсѧ, соедини́ дрꙋ́гъ ко дрꙋ́гꙋ, во є҆ди́нагѡ дх҃а ст҃а́гѡ прича́стїе: и҆ ни є҆ди́наго на́съ въ сꙋ́дъ и҆ли во ѡ҆сꙋжде́нїе сотвори́ причасти́тисѧ ст҃а́гѡ тѣ́ла и҆ кро́ве хрⷭ҇та̀ твоегѡ̀: но да ѡ҆бра́щемъ ми́лость и҆ благода́ть со всѣ́ми ст҃ыми, ѿ вѣ́ка тебѣ̀ бл҃гоꙋгоди́вшими пра́ѻц҃ы, ѻ҆тц҃ы̀, патрїа́рхи, прⷪ҇ро́ки, а҆пⷭ҇лы, проповѣ́дники, бл҃говѣ́стники, мꙋ́ченики, и҆сповѣ́дники, оу҆чи́тельми, и҆ со всѧ́кимъ дх҃омъ пра́веднымъ, въ вѣ́рѣ сконча́вшимсѧ.

И҆ прїе́мъ кади́ло, сщ҃е́нникъ возглаша́етъ:

И҆зрѧ́днѡ ѡ҆ прест҃ѣ́й, пречⷭ҇тѣ́й, преблгⷭ҇ове́ннѣй, сла́внѣй влⷣчцѣ на́шей бцⷣѣ и҆ приснодв҃ѣ̀ мр҃і́н.

And the deacon says: **Amen**, and goes to the place where he first stood, and taking a fan, fans the Holy Things as before.

And the priest prays:

And all of us who partake of the one Bread and Cup, do Thou unite one to another, in one communion of the Holy Spirit; and cause not one of us to partake of the holy Body and Blood of Thy Christ unto judgment or condemnation; but may we find mercy and grace together with all the saints, who from the ages have been pleasing unto Thee, forefathers, fathers, patriarchs, prophets, apostles, preachers, evangelists, martyrs, confessors, teachers, and with every righteous soul made perfect in faith.

And taking the censer, the priest exclaims:

Especially for our most holy, most pure, most blessed, glorious Lady Theotokos and Ever-Virgin Mary.

И кади́тъ пред̾ ст҃ою трапе́зою
три́жды.

Ли́къ пое́тъ: Ѡ тебѣ̀ ра́дꙋетсѧ, бл҃года́тнаѧ,
всѧ́каѧ тва́рь, а́́гг҃льскїй собо́ръ, и человѣ́ческїй
ро́дъ, ѡсще́нный хра́ме, и раю̀ слове́сный,
дѣ́вственнаѧ похвало̀, и҆з̾ неѧ́же бг҃ъ
воплоти́сѧ, и мл҃нецъ бы́сть, пре́жде вѣ̑къ сы́й
бг҃ъ на́шъ: ложесна́ бо твоѧ̀ прⷭ҇то́лъ сотвори́,
и чре́во твоѐ простра́ннѣе небе́съ содѣ́ла: ѡ
тебѣ̀ ра́дꙋетсѧ бл҃года́тнаѧ, всѧ́каѧ тва́рь,
сла́ва тебѣ̀.

А҆́ще ли в̾ вели́кїй четверто́къ, и҆лѝ в̾
вели́кꙋю сꙋббѡ́тꙋ, тогда̀ пою́тъ і҆рмо́съ д҃-ѧ
пѣ́сни, днѐ тогѡ̀.

Сщ҃е́нникъ же мо́литсѧ: Ѡ ст҃ѣ́мъ і҆ѡа́ннѣ
прⷪ҇ро́цѣ, прⷣте́чи и крⷭ҇ти́тели, ѡ ст҃ы́хъ
сла́вныхъ и всехва́льныхъ а҆пⷭ҇лѣхъ, ѡ ст҃ѣ́мъ
и҆́мрекъ, є҆гѡ́же и па́мѧть соверша́емъ, и
ѡ всѣ́хъ ст҃ы́хъ твои́хъ: и҆́хже моли́твами
посѣти́ на́съ, бж҃е.

And he censes before the Holy Table
thrice.

The choir chants: In thee rejoiceth, O thou
who art full of grace, all creation, the angelic
assembly, and the race of man; O sanctified
temple and noetical paradise, praise of virgins,
of whom God was incarnate, and became a
child, He that was before the ages, even our
God; for, of thy body a throne He made, and
thy womb He made more spacious than the
heavens. In thee rejoiceth, O thou who art
full of grace, all creation: glory to thee.

But if it be Great Thursday, or Great
Saturday, then they chant the irmos
of the 9th ode of that day. The deacon
commemorates the names of the departed.

And the priest prays: For the holy Prophet,
Forerunner, and Baptist John, for the holy
and all-praised apostles; for Saint(s) N.,
whose memory we also celebrate, and for all
Thy saints: by their intercessions do Thou
visit us, O God.

Здѣ сщⷺнникъ помина́етъ, и҆́хже хо́щетъ живы́хъ и҆ ѹ҆ме́ршихъ, ѡ҆ живы́хъ ѹ҆́бѡ глаго́летъ:

Ѡ҆ спасе́нїи, посѣще́нїи, ѡ҆ставле́нїи грѣхѡ́въ, рабѡ́въ бж҃їихъ и҆́мрекъ.

Ѡ҆ ѹ҆ме́ршихъ же глаго́летъ:

Ѡ҆ поко́и, и҆ ѡ҆ставле́нїи грѣхѡ́въ дꙋшъ ра́бъ твои́хъ и҆́мрекъ: на мѣ́стѣ свѣ́тлѣ, ѿѻнꙋ́дꙋже ѿбѣ́же печа́ль и҆ воздыха́нїе, ѹ҆поко́й и҆́хъ, бж҃е на́шъ.

По си́хъ глаго́летъ:

Є҆щѐ мо́лимъ ти сѧ, помѧнѝ гдⷭ҇и, ст҃ꙋ́ю твою̀ собо́рнꙋю и҆ а҆пⷭ҇льскꙋ́ю цр҃ковь, ю҆́же ѿ конє́цъ да́же до конє́цъ вселе́нныѧ, и҆ ѹ҆мирѝ ю҆̀, ю҆́же назда́лъ є҆сѝ честно́ю кро́вїю хрⷭ҇та̀ твоегѡ̀, и҆ ст҃ый хра́мъ се́й ѹ҆твердѝ да́же до скончанїѧ вѣ́ка. Помѧнѝ гдⷭ҇и, и҆́же да́ры сїѧ̑ тебѣ̀ принє́сшихъ, и҆ ѡ҆ ни́хже, и҆ и҆́мже, и҆ за ни́хже сїѧ̑ принесо́ша.

And the priest commemorates by name whomever he wishes from among the living and the departed; for the living he says:

For the salvation, visitation, and remission of sins of the servants of God N.

And for the departed he says:

For the repose and remission of sins of the souls of Thy servants N. Grant them rest, O our God, in a place of light, whence sorrow and sighing have fled.

After this the priest says:

Again we pray Thee, remember, O Lord, Thy Holy Catholic and Apostolic Church, which is from one end of the world to the other end, and give peace unto her, whom Thou hast purchased with the precious Blood of Thy Christ, and establish this holy temple even unto the end of the age. Remember, O Lord, those who have offered these Gifts unto Thee, and those for whom, and through whom, and in behalf of whom they have offered them.

Помѧнѝ гдⷭ҇и, плодоносѧ́щихъ, ѝ добротворѧ́щихъ во ст҃ы́хъ твои́хъ цр҃квахъ ѝ помина́ющихъ ѹ҆бѡ́гїѧ: возда́ждь и҆мъ бога́тыми твои́ми ѝ небе́сными дарова́нїи, дарꙋ́й и҆мъ вмѣ́стѡ земны́хъ небе́снаѧ, вмѣ́стѡ вре́менныхъ вѣ́чнаѧ, вмѣ́стѡ тлѣ́нныхъ нетлѣ́ннаѧ.

Помѧнѝ гдⷭ҇и, и҆́же въ пꙋсты́нахъ ѝ гора́хъ, ѝ вертѣ́пахъ, ѝ про́пастѣхъ земны́хъ.

Помѧнѝ гдⷭ҇и, и҆́же въ дѣ́вствѣ ѝ бл҃гогове́нїи, ѝ по́стничествѣ, ѝ въ чи́стѣмъ жи́тельствѣ пребыва́ющихъ.

Помѧнѝ, гдⷭ҇и странꙋ̀ сїю̀ ѝ прави́телей є҆ѧ̀: дарꙋ́й и҆мъ глꙋбо́кїй ѝ неѿе́млемый мі́ръ: возглаго́ли въ сердца̀ и҆́хъ бл҃га́ѧ ѡ҆ цр҃кви твое́й ѝ всѣ́хъ лю́дехъ твои́хъ, да въ тишинѣ̀ и҆́хъ ти́хое ѝ безмо́лвное житїѐ поживе́мъ во всѧ́комъ бл҃гоче́стїи ѝ чистотѣ̀.

Помѧнѝ, гдⷭ҇и, всѧ́кое нача́ло ѝ вла́сть, ѝ и҆́же въ пала́тѣ бра́тїю на́шꙋ, ѝ всѐ

Remember, O Lord, those who bear fruit, and do good works in Thy holy churches, and those who are mindful of the poor; reward them with Thine abundant and heavenly gifts, grant them instead of earthly things, the heavenly; instead of temporal things, the eternal; instead of corruptible things, the incorruptible.

Remember, O Lord, those in deserts and mountains, and dens and caves of the earth.

Remember, O Lord, those who abide in virginity and piety, and in fasting, and in purity of life.

Remember, O Lord, this land and its authorities; grant them profound and inviolable peace; instill good in their hearts concerning Thy Church and all Thy people, that in their serenity we may lead a quiet and tranquil life in all piety and purity.

Remember, O Lord, every ruler and authority and our brethren who are in their council, and all the armed forces; do Thou

воинство: благ҃ѧ во блгости соблюдѝ,
лꙋка́выѧ благи сотворѝ бл҃гостїю твоею.

Помѧнѝ, гд҃и, предстоѧщыѧ лю́ди, и҆
ра́ди благослове́ныхъ вин́ъ ѡ҆ста́вльшихсѧ,
и҆ помилꙋй и҆хъ и҆ на́съ, по мно́жествꙋ
мл҃ости твоеѧ: сокрѡ́вища и҆хъ и҆спо́лни
всѧ́кагѡ бла́га: сꙋпрꙋ́жества и҆хъ въ ми́рѣ и҆
є҆диномы́слїи соблюдѝ: младе́нцы воспита́й,
ю́ность наста́ви, ста́рость поддержѝ,
малодꙋ́шныѧ ѹ҆тѣ́ши, расточе́нныѧ
соберѝ, прельще́нныѧ ѡ҆братѝ, и҆ совокꙋпѝ
ст҃ѣ́й твоей собо́рнѣй и҆ а҆пⷭ҇льстѣй цр҃кви,
стꙋжа́емыѧ ѿ дꙋхѡ́въ нечⷭ҇тыхъ свободѝ,
пла́вающымъ спла́вай, пꙋтеше́ствꙋющымъ
сше́ствꙋй, вдови́цамъ предста́ни, си́рыхъ
защитѝ, плѣне́ныѧ и҆зба́ви, недꙋ́гꙋющыѧ
и҆сцѣлѝ. На сꙋди́щи и҆ въ рꙋда́хъ, и҆ въ
заточе́нїихъ, и҆ въ го́рькихъ рабо́тахъ, и҆
всѧ́кой скорби, и҆ нꙋ́ждѣ, и҆ ѡ҆бстоѧ́нїи
сꙋ́щихъ помѧнѝ, бж҃е.

preserve the good, and do Thou make the evil good by Thy benevolence.

Remember, O Lord, the people here present, and those who are absent for reasonable cause, and have mercy on them and us, according to the multitude of Thy mercies; fill their treasuries with every good thing; preserve their marriages in peace and concord; rear the infants, teach the youth, support the aged, comfort the fainthearted, gather the scattered, turn back the ensnared from their wandering and unite them to Thy Holy Catholic and Apostolic Church, free those vexed by unclean spirits, sail with those who voyage, journey with those who travel; plead for the widows, defend the orphans, deliver the captives, heal the sick. Those under judgment and in the mines, and in prison, and in bitter labors, and in all affliction, necessity, and distress, do Thou remember, O God.

И҆ все́хъ тре́бꙋющихъ вели́кагѡ
твоегѡ̀ бл҃гоꙋтро́бїѧ, и҆ лю́бѧщихъ на́съ,
и҆ ненави́дѧщихъ и҆ запове́давшихъ на́мъ
недосто́йнымъ моли́тисѧ ѡ҆ ни́хъ, и҆ всѧ̀
лю́ди твоѧ̑ помѧнѝ, гд҃и бж҃е на́шъ, и҆ на
всѧ̑ и҆зле́й бога́тꙋю твою̀ ми́лость, все́мъ
пода́ѧ ꙗ҆́же ко спасе́нїю прошє́нїѧ. И҆ и҆́хже
мы̀ не помѧнꙋ́хомъ неве́дѣнїемъ, и҆лѝ
забве́нїемъ, и҆лѝ мно́жествомъ и҆ме́нъ, са́мъ
помѧнѝ, бж҃е, ве́дый коегѡ́ждо во́зрастъ и҆
и҆менова́нїе, ве́дый коегѡ́ждо ѿ ᲂу҆тро́бы
ма́тере є҆гѡ̀: ты̀ бо є҆сѝ гд҃ь, по́мощь
безпомо́щнымъ, наде́жда безнаде́жнымъ,
ѡ҆бꙋрева́ємымъ спаси́тель, пла́вающымъ
приста́нище, недꙋ́гꙋющымъ вра́чъ: са́мъ
все́мъ всѧ̑ бꙋ́ди, ве́дый, коегѡ́ждо, и҆
прошє́нїе є҆гѡ̀, до́мъ, и҆ потре́бꙋ є҆гѡ̀.
И҆зба́ви гд҃и, гра́дъ се́й, [и҆лѝ ве́сь сїю̀, и҆лѝ
ст҃ꙋю ѻ҆би́тель сїю̀] и҆ всѧ́кїй гра́дъ и҆ странꙋ̀
ѿ гла́да, гꙋби́тельства, трꙋ́са, пото́па,
ѻ҆гнѧ̀, меча̀, наше́ствїѧ и҆ноплеме́нныхъ,
и҆ междоꙋсо́бныѧ бра́ни.

And all in need of Thy great loving-kindness, those who love us, and those who hate us, and those who have charged us, the unworthy, to pray for them, and all Thy people, do Thou remember, O Lord our God, and do Thou pour out Thine abundant mercy upon all, granting unto each their petitions which are unto salvation. And those whom we have not remembered, through ignorance, or forgetfulness, or from the multitude of names, do Thou remember, O God, Who knowest the age and name of each, Who knowest each from his mother's womb; for Thou, O Lord, art the help of the helpless, the hope of the hopeless, the Saviour of the storm-tossed, the haven of the voyager, the physician of the ailing; be Thou all things to all men, Thou Who knowest every one, and his petition, his abode, and his need. Deliver, O Lord, this city (or this village, or this holy monastery) and ever city and country from famine, pestilence, earthquake, flood, fire, the sword, foreign invasion, and civil war.

Й возглашаетъ сщенникъ:

Въ пе́рвыхъ помѧни̑, гд҃и, вели́каго господи́на и̑ о̑тца̀ на́шего и҃мк, ст҃ѣ́йшаго патрїа́рха моско́вскаго и̑ всеѧ̀ рꙋ́си, и̑ господи́на на́шего, высокопресщен_ нѣ́йшаго и҃мк, митрополі́та восто́чно_ а̑мерика́нскаго и̑ нью_їо́ркскаго, первоіера́рха рꙋ́сскїѧ зарꙋбѣ́жныѧ цр҃кве, и̑ господи́на на́шего, высокопресщенѣ́йшаго и҃мк [и̑лѝ пресщенѣ́йшаго и҃мк], а̑рхїепі́скопа и̑лѝ є̑пі́скопа [є̑гѡ́же є̑сть о̑бласть] и̑хже дарꙋ́й ст҃ымъ твои̑мъ цр҃квамъ, въ ми́рѣ, цѣ́лыхъ, че́стныхъ, здра́выхъ, долгоде́нствꙋющихъ, пра́вѡ пра́вѧщихъ сло́во твоеѧ̀ и̑́стины.

Й пѣвцы̀ пою́тъ: И̑ всѣ́хъ, и̑ всѧ̑.

Сщенникъ же мо́литсѧ втай:

Помѧни̑, гд҃и, всѧ́кое є̑пі́скопство правосла́вныхъ, пра́вѡ пра́вѧщихъ сло́во твоеѧ̀ и̑́стины.

And the priest exclaims:

Among the first, remember, O Lord, our great lord and father N., the Most Holy Patriarch of Moscow and all Russia, and our lord, the Very Most Reverend N., Metropolitan of Eastern America and New York, First Hierarch of the Russian Church Abroad, and our lord, the Most [or Right] Reverend Archbishop [or Bishop] N. of [his see is commemorated here] whom do Thou grant unto Thy holy churches in peace, safety, honor, health and length of days, rightly dividing the word of Thy truth.

Choir: And each and every one.

The priest prays secretly:

Remember, O Lord, all the Orthodox episcopate that rightly divide the word of Thy truth.

Помѧни́ гдⷭ҇н, по мно́жествꙋ щедро́тъ
твои́хъ, и̇ моѐ недосто́инство, простѝ
ми́ всѧ́кое согрѣше́нїе, во́льное же и̇
нево́льное: и̇ да не мои́хъ ра́ди грѣхѡ́въ,
возбрани́ши бла҃года́ти ста҃гѡ твоегѡ̀ дх҃а
ѿ предлежа́щихъ дарѡ́въ.

Помѧни́ гдⷭ҇н, пресвꙋ́терство, є̑́же во
хрⷭ҇тѣ̀ дїа́конство, и̇ ве́сь сщ҃е́нническїй чи́нъ,
и̇ ни є̑ди́нагѡ же на́съ посрами́ши, ѻ̑́крестъ
стоѧ́щихъ ста҃гѡ твоегѡ̀ же́ртвенника.
Посѣти́ на́съ бла҃гостїю твое́ю, гдⷭ҇н, ꙗ̑ви́сѧ
на́мъ бога́тыми твои́ми щедро́тами,
благорастворе́ны и̇ поле́зны возаꙋ́хи
на́мъ дарꙋ́й: дожди́ ми́рны землѝ къ
плодоно́сїю дарꙋ́й: бла҃гословѝ вѣне́цъ лѣ́та
бла҃гости твоеѧ̀: оу̑толѝ раздо́ры цр҃кве́й,
оу̑гасѝ шата̑нїѧ ꙗ̑зы́ческаѧ, є̑рети́ческаѧ
возста̑нїѧ ско́рѡ разорѝ си́лою ста҃гѡ твоегѡ̀
дх҃а, всѣ́хъ на́съ прїимѝ въ цр҃тво твоѐ,
сы́ны свѣ́та и̇ сы́ны днѐ показа́вый, тво́й
ми́ръ и̇ твою̀ любо́вь дарꙋ́й на́мъ, гдⷭ҇н бж҃е
на́шъ, всѧ̑ бо возда́лъ є̑сѝ на́мъ.

Remember, O Lord, according to the multitude of Thy compassions, mine unworthiness, pardon me every transgression, voluntary and involuntary; and withhold not, on account of my sins, the grace of Thy Holy Spirit from the Gifts offered.

Remember, O Lord, the priesthood, the diaconate in Christ, and all the priestly rank, and put not to shame any of us who stand about Thy holy altar. Visit us with Thy goodness, O Lord, appear unto us through Thine abundant compassions, grant us seasonable and profitable weather; give gentle rain upon the earth unto fruitfulness; bless the crown of the year with Thy goodness; calm the dissensions of the churches, quench the raging of the nations, quickly destroy the risings of heresy by the power of Thy Holy Spirit, receive us all into Thy kingdom, showing us to be sons of light and sons of the day, grant us Thy peace and Thy love, O Lord our God, for all things hast Thou given unto us.

Возглаше́нїе: И да́ждь на́мъ є҆ди́нѣмъ
ѹ҆сты̀ и҆ є҆ди́нѣмъ се́рдцемъ сла́вити и҆
воспѣва́ти пречⷭ҇тно́е и҆ великолѣ́пое и҆́мѧ
твоѐ, Ѻ҆ц҃а̀, и҆ сн҃а, и҆ ст҃а́гѡ дх҃а, нн҃ѣ и҆
прⷭ҇нѡ, и҆ во вѣ́ки вѣкѡ́въ.

Ли́къ: А҆ми́нь.

Сщ҃е́нникъ, ѡ҆бра́щьсѧ ко две́ремъ и҆
бл҃гословлѧ́ѧ, глаго́летъ:

И҆ да бꙋ́детъ мⷧⷵти вели́кагѡ бг҃а и҆ сп҃са
на́шегѡ і҆и҃са хрⷭ҇та̀ со всѣ́ми ва́ми.

Ли́къ: И҆ со дх҃омъ твои́мъ.

Дїа́конъ, прїе́мъ бл҃гослове́нїе ѿ сщ҃е́нника
и҆ и҆зше́дъ, ста́въ на ѡ҆бы́чнѣмъ мѣ́стѣ,
глаго́летъ:

Всѧ̑ ст҃ы̑ѧ помѧнꙋ́вше, па́ки и҆ па́ки ми́ромъ
гдꙋ҃ помо́лимсѧ.

Ли́къ: Гдⷭ҇и поми́лꙋй.

Дїа́конъ: Ѡ принесе́нныхъ и҆ ѡ҆сщ҃е́нныхъ
честны́хъ дарѣ́хъ, гдꙋ҃ помо́лимсѧ.

Exclamation: And grant unto us that with one mouth and one heart we may glorify and hymn Thy most honorable and majestic name: of the Father, and of the Son, and of the Holy Spirit, now and ever, and unto the ages of ages.

Choir: Amen.

The priest turns toward the doors and blesses, saying:

And may the mercies of our great God and Saviour Jesus Christ be with you all.

Choir: And with thy spirit.

The deacon, having received a blessing from the priest, goes out and, standing in the usual place, says:

Having called to remembrance all the Saints, again and again, in peace let us pray to the Lord.

Choir: Lord, have mercy.

Deacon: For the precious Gifts set forth and sanctified, let us pray to the Lord.

Ли́къ: Гдⷭ҇и поми́лꙋй.

Дїа́конъ: Ꙗ҆́кѡ да чл҃вѣколю́бецъ бг҃ъ на́шъ, прїе́мъ ѧ҆̀ во ст҃ы́й и҆ пренбⷭ҇ный и҆ мы́сленный сво́й же́ртвенникъ, въ воню̀ бл҃гоꙋха́нїѧ дꙋхо́внагѡ, возниспо́слетъ на́мъ бж҃е́ственнꙋю бл҃года́ть и҆ да́ръ ст҃а́гѡ дх҃а, помо́лимсѧ.

Ли́къ: Гдⷭ҇и поми́лꙋй.

Дїа́конъ: Ѡ҆ и҆зба́витисѧ на́мъ ѿ всѧ́кїѧ ско́рби, гнѣ́ва и҆ нꙋ́жды, гдⷭ҇ꙋ помо́лимсѧ.

Ли́къ: Гдⷭ҇и поми́лꙋй.

Сщ҃е́нникъ мо́литсѧ вта́й:

Бж҃е на́шъ, бж҃е спаса́ти, ты̀ на́съ наꙋчи́ бл҃годари́ти тѧ̀ досто́йнѡ ѡ҆ благодѣ́нїихъ твои́хъ, и҆̀хже сотвори́лъ є҆сѝ, и҆ твори́ши съ на́ми. Ты̀, бж҃е на́шъ, прїе́мый да́ры сїѧ̑, ѡ҆чи́сти на́съ ѿ всѧ́кїѧ скве́рны пло́ти и҆ дꙋ́ха, и҆ наꙋчи́ соверша́ти ст҃ы́ню въ стра́сѣ твое́мъ, ꙗ҆́кѡ да чи́стымъ свидѣ́тельствомъ со́вѣсти

Choir: Lord, have mercy.

Deacon: That our God, the Lover of mankind, having accepted them upon His holy and noetic altar above the heavens as an odor of spiritual fragrance, will send down upon us divine grace and the gift of the Holy Spirit, let us pray.

Choir: Lord, have mercy.

Deacon: That we may be delivered from all tribulation, wrath, and necessity, let us pray to the Lord.

Choir: Lord, have mercy.

The priest prays secretly:

O our God, O God Who saveth, do Thou teach us to thank Thee worthily for Thy benefactions, which Thou hast bestowed and doth bestow upon us. Accepting these gifts, O our God, do Thou cleanse us of all defilement of flesh and spirit, and teach us to achieve holiness in Thy fear, that in the pure witness of our

на́шеѧ прїе́млюще ча́сть ст҃ы́нь твои́хъ,
соединни́мсѧ ст҃о́мꙋ тѣ́лꙋ и҆ кро́ви хрⷭ҇та̀
твоегѡ̀: и҆ прїе́мше и҆̀хъ досто́йнѣ, и҆́мамы
хрⷭ҇та̀ живꙋ́ща въ сердца́хъ на́шихъ, и҆ бꙋ́демъ
хра́мъ ст҃а́гѡ твоегѡ̀ дх҃а. Е҆́й, бж҃е на́шъ, и҆
да ни є҆ди́нагѡ же на́съ пови́нна сотвори́ши
стра́шнымъ твои́мъ си҆̀мъ и҆ нбⷭ҇нымъ
та́йнамъ, ниже́ не́мощна дꙋше́ю и҆ тѣ́ломъ,
ѿ є҆́же недосто́йнѣ си́хъ причаща́тисѧ: но
да́ждь на́мъ да́же до послѣ́днагѡ на́шегѡ
и҆здыха́нїѧ досто́йнѣ прїима́ти ча́сть
свѧты́нь твои́хъ, въ напꙋ́тїе жи́зни
вѣ́чныѧ, во ѿвѣ́тъ благопрїѧ́тенъ, и҆́же
на стра́шнѣмъ сꙋди́щи хрⷭ҇та̀ твоегѡ̀: ꙗ҆́кѡ
да и҆ мы̀ со всѣ́ми ст҃ы́ми, ѿ вѣ́ка тебѣ̀
бл҃гоꙋгоди́вшими, бꙋ́демъ прича́стницы
вѣ́чныхъ твои́хъ бла̑гъ, и҆̀хже оу҆готова́лъ
є҆сѝ лю́бѧщымъ тѧ̀ гдⷭ҇и.

Дїа́конъ: Застꙋпѝ, спасѝ, поми́лꙋй и҆ сохранѝ
на́съ бж҃е, твое́ю бл҃года́тїю.

Ли́къ: Гдⷭ҇и поми́лꙋй.

conscience, receiving a portion of Thy Holy Things, we may be united to the Holy Body and Blood of Thy Christ; and having received Them worthily, we may have Christ living in our hearts, and may become a temple of Thy Holy Spirit. Yea our God, and cause not any one of us to be condemned through these Thy fearsome and heavenly Mysteries, neither infirm in soul and body by partaking of them unworthily; but grant us even until our last breath to worthily receive a portion of Thy Holy Things, as a provision for life eternal, as an acceptable defense even at the dread judgment seat of Thy Christ; that we also together with all the saints who from the ages have been pleasing unto Thee, may be partakers of Thine eternal good things, which Thou hast prepared for them that love Thee, O Lord.

Deacon: Help us, save us, have mercy on us, and keep us, O God, by Thy grace.

Choir: Lord, have mercy.

Діа́конъ: Дне́ всегѡ̀ [а́ще літꙋргі́а соедина́етсѧ съ вече́рней, Ве́чера всегѡ̀] соверше́нна, ст҃а, ми́рна и безгрѣ́шна, ᲂу҆ гд҃а про́симъ.

Ли́къ: Пода́й гд҃и.

Діа́конъ: А҆́гг҃ла ми́рна, вѣ́рна наста́вника, храни́телѧ дꙋ́шъ и тѣле́съ на́шихъ, ᲂу҆ гд҃а про́симъ.

Ли́къ: Пода́й гд҃и.

Діа́конъ: Проще́нїѧ и ѡ҆ставле́нїѧ грѣхѡ́въ и прегрѣше́нїй на́шихъ, ᲂу҆ гд҃а про́симъ.

Ли́къ: Пода́й гд҃и.

Діа́конъ: До́брыхъ и поле́зныхъ дꙋша́мъ на́шымъ, и ми́ра мі́рови, ᲂу҆ гд҃а про́симъ.

Ли́къ: Пода́й гд҃и.

Діа́конъ: Про́чее вре́мѧ живота̀ на́шегѡ въ ми́рѣ и покаѧ́нїи сконча́ти, ᲂу҆ гд҃а про́симъ.

Ли́къ: Пода́й гд҃и.

Діа́конъ: Хрⷭтїа́нскїѧ кончи́ны живота̀ на́шегѡ, безболѣ́знены, непосты̂дны,

Deacon: That the whole day (but if it be a Vesperal Liturgy: whole evening) may be perfect, holy, peaceful, and sinless, let us ask of the Lord.

Choir: Grant this, O Lord.

Deacon: An angel of peace, a faithful guide, a guardian of our souls and bodies, let us ask of the Lord.

Choir: Grant this, O Lord.

Deacon: Pardon and remission of our sins and offenses, let us ask of the Lord.

Choir: Grant this, O Lord.

Deacon: Things good and profitable for our souls, and peace for the world, let us ask of the Lord.

Choir: Grant this, O Lord.

Deacon: That we may complete the remaining time of our life in peace and repentance, let us ask of the Lord.

Choir: Grant this, O Lord.

Deacon: A Christian ending to our life, painless, blameless, peaceful, and a good defense

мирны и добрагѡ ѿвѣ́та на стра́шнѣмъ сꙋди́щи хрⷭ҇то́вѣ про́симъ.

Ли́къ: Пода́й гдⷭ҇н.

Дїа́конъ: Соедине́нїе вѣ́ры, и причастїе стⷢ҇агѡ дх҃а испроси́вше, са́ми себѐ, и дрꙋ́гъ дрꙋ́га, и ве́сь живо́тъ на́шъ хрⷭ҇тꙋ̀ бг҃ꙋ предади́мъ.

Ли́къ: Тебѣ̀ гдⷭ҇н.

Сщ҃е́нникъ возглаше́нїе: И сподо́би на́съ, влⷣко, со дерзнове́нїемъ, неѡсꙋжде́ннѡ смѣ́ти призыва́ти тебѐ нбⷭ҇наго бг҃а ѻ҃ц҃а, и глаго́лати.

Лю́дїе: Ѻ́ч҃е на́шъ, и́же є҆сѝ на нб҃сѣ́хъ, да ст҃и́тсѧ и́мѧ твоѐ, да прїи́детъ ца́рствїе твоѐ: да бꙋ́детъ во́лѧ твоѧ̀, я҆́кѡ на нб҃сѝ, и на землѝ. Хлѣ́бъ на́шъ насꙋ́щный да́ждь на́мъ дне́сь, и ѡ҆ста́ви на́мъ до́лги на́ша, я҆́коже и мы̀ ѡ҆ставлѧ́емъ должнико́мъ на́шымъ: и не введѝ на́съ во и҆скꙋше́нїе, но и҆зба́ви на́съ ѿ лꙋка́вагѡ.

Сщ҃е́нникъ: Я҆́кѡ твоѐ є҆́сть црⷭ҇тво, и си́ла, и сла́ва, ѻ҃ц҃а, и сн҃а, и стⷢ҇агѡ дх҃а, нынѣ и при́снѡ, и во вѣ́ки вѣко́въ.

before the dread judgment seat of Christ, let us ask.

Choir: Grant this, O Lord.

Deacon: Having asked for the unity of the faith and the communion of the Holy Spirit, let us commit ourselves and one another and all our life unto Christ, our God.

Choir: To Thee, O Lord.

Exclamation: And vouchsafe us, O Master, that with boldness and without condemnation we may dare to call upon Thee, the heavenly God and Father, and to say:

People: Our Father, Who art in the heavens, hallowed be Thy Name. Thy Kingdom come, Thy will be done, on earth as it is in heaven. Give us this day our daily bread, and forgive us our debts, as we forgive our debtors; and lead us not into temptation, but deliver us from the evil one.

Priest: For Thine is the kingdom, and the power and the glory, of the Father, and of the Son, and of the Holy Spirit, now and ever, and unto the ages of ages.

Ли́къ: А҆ми́нь.

Сщⷷ́нникъ: Ми́ръ всѣ҃мъ.

Ли́къ: И҆ дꙋ́хови твоемꙋ̀.

Дїа́конъ: Главы̑ ва́шѧ гдⷭ҇ви приклони́те.

Ли́къ: Тебѣ̀, гдⷭ҇и.

Сщⷷ́нникъ же мо́литсѧ:

Вⷧⷣко гдⷭ҇и, О҆́че щедро́тъ и҆ бже҃ вса́кагѡ ᲂу҆тѣше́нїѧ, прикло́ньшыѧ тебѣ̀ своѧ̑ главы̑, благословѝ, ѡ҆свѧтѝ, соблюдѝ, ᲂу҆крѣпѝ, ᲂу҆твердѝ, ѿ вса́кагѡ дѣ́ла лꙋка́ва ѿста́ви, вса́комꙋ же дѣ́лꙋ благо́мꙋ сочета́й, и҆ сподо́би неѡсꙋжде́ннѡ причасти́тисѧ пречⷭ҇тыхъ си́хъ, и҆ животворѧ́щихъ твои́хъ та́инъ, во ѡ҆ставле́нїе грѣхѡ́въ, въ дх҃а ста҃гѡ прича́стїе.

Возглаше́нїе: Бл҃года́тїю, и҆ щедро́тами, и҆ чл҃вѣколю́бїемъ є҆диноро́днагѡ сн҃а твоегѡ̀, съ ни́мже бл҃гослове́нъ є҆сѝ, со престы́мъ и҆ бл҃ги́мъ и҆ животворѧ́щимъ твои́мъ дх҃омъ, ны́нѣ и҆ при́снѡ, и҆ во вѣ́ки вѣкѡ́въ.

Choir: Amen.

Priest: Peace be unto all.

Choir: And to thy spirit.

Deacon: Bow your heads unto the Lord.

Choir: To Thee, O Lord.

And the priest prays:

O Master and Lord, Father of bounties, and the God of every consolation, do Thou bless, sanctify, preserve, strengthen, and establish those who have bowed their heads unto Thee; remove them from every evil work, join them to every good work, and vouchsafe them to partake uncondemned of these, Thy most pure and life-creating Mysteries, unto the remission of sins, unto communion in the Holy Spirit.

Exclamation: Through the grace and compassions and love for mankind of Thine Only-begotten Son, with Whom Thou art blessed, together with Thine Most-holy and good and life-creating Spirit, now and ever, and unto the ages of ages.

Ли́къ: А҆ми́нь.

Сщⷻе́нникъ мо́литсѧ:

Вонмѝ, гдⷭ҇и і҆и҃се хрⷭ҇тѐ бж҃е на́шъ, ѿ ст҃а́гѡ жили́ща твоегѡ̀, и҆ ѿ прⷭ҇то́ла сла́вы црⷭ҇твїѧ твоегѡ̀, и҆ прїидѝ во є҆́же ѡ҆ст҃и́ти на́съ, и҆́же горѣ̀ со ѻ҆ц҃е́мъ сѣдѧ́й, и҆ здѣ̀ на́мъ неви́димѡ спребыва́ѧй: и҆ сподо́би держа́вною твое́ю рꙋко́ю препода́ти на́мъ пречⷭ҇тое тѣ́ло твоѐ и҆ чтⷭ҇нꙋ́ю кро́вь, и҆ на́ми всѣ́мъ лю́демъ.

Та́же покланѧ́етсѧ сщⷻе́нникъ, подо́бнѣ и҆ дїа́конъ, на не́мже стои́тъ мѣ́стѣ, глаго́люще та́йнѡ, три́жды: Бж҃е, ѡ҆чи́сти мѧ̀ грѣ́шнаго, и҆ поми́лꙋй мѧ̀.

Е҆гда́ же ви́дитъ дїа́конъ сщⷻе́нника простира́юща рꙋцѣ̀, и҆ прикаса́юща́сѧ ст҃о́мꙋ хлѣ́бꙋ, во є҆́же сотвори́ти ст҃о́е возноше́нїе, возглаша́етъ:

Во́нмемъ.

Choir: **Amen.**

The priest prays:

Attend, O Lord Jesus Christ our God, out of Thy holy dwelling-place, and from the glorious throne of Thy kingdom; and come and sanctify us, O Thou Who sittest with the Father on high, and invisibly abidest here with us; and vouchsafe by Thy strong right hand to impart unto us Thy most pure Body and precious Blood, and through us to all the people.

Then the priest bows, and likewise the deacon, at the place where he stands, while saying, thrice: **O God, cleanse me, a sinner, and have mercy on me.**

And when the deacon sees the priest stretch out his hands and touch the Holy Bread in order to make the holy elevation, he exclaims:

Let us attend.

Сщ҃енникъ же, вознося ст҃ый хлѣ́бъ,
возглаша́етъ:

Ст҃а҄я ст҃ы̑мъ.

Ли́къ: Є҆ди́нъ ст҃ъ, є҆ди́нъ гдⷭ҇ь, і҆и҃съ хрⷭ҇то́съ, во
сла́вꙋ бг҃а ѻ҆ц҃а̀. А҆ми́нь.

И҆ пою́тъ ли́цы кїнⷩ҇о́никъ днѐ,
и҆лѝ ст҃а́гѡ.

Дїа́конъ же входитъ во ст҃ый ѻ҆лта́рь, и҆
ста́въ ѡ҆десно́ю сщ҃енника, держа́щагѡ ст҃ый
хлѣ́бъ, глаго́летъ:

Раздробѝ, влады́ко, ст҃ый хлѣ́бъ.

Сщ҃енникъ же раздробля́я и҆ на четы́ре ча́сти
со внима́нїемъ и҆ бл҃гоговѣ́нїемъ, глаго́летъ:

Раздробля́ется и҆ раздѣля́ется а҆́гнецъ
бж҃їй, раздробля́емый и҆ неразⷣѣля́емый,
всегда̀ ꙗ҆до́мый и҆ никогда́же и҆жⷣива́емый,
но причаща́ющыяся ѡ҆сща́ꙗй.

And the priest, elevating the Holy Bread, exclaims:

Holy Things are for the holy.
Choir: One is holy, One is Lord, Jesus Christ, to the glory of God the Father. Amen.

And the choirs chant the communion verse of the day, or of the Saint.

And the deacon goes into the holy altar, and standing at the right hand of the priest, who holds the Holy Bread says:

Break the Holy Bread, master.

And the priest, breaking it into four parts with attentiveness and reverence, says:

Broken and distributed is the Lamb of God: broken, yet not divided; ever eaten, though never consumed, but sanctifying them that partake thereof.

Ѡ раздробле́нїи ст҃а́гѡ а́гнца.

Подоба́етъ тебѣ̀ вѣ́дати, ѽ і҆ере́е, ꙗ҆́кѡ, раздробла́ѧ ст҃ы́й а́гнецъ, полага́й ча́сти кр҃тнымъ зна́менїемъ до́лꙋ ко ст҃о́мꙋ ді́скосꙋ, закла́нїемъ же горѣ̀, ꙗ҆́коже пре́жде є҆гда̀ закала́шесѧ. І҆Н҃С, ᲂу҆́бѡ полага́й на вы́шнѣй странѣ̀ ст҃а́гѡ ді́скоса, ꙗ҆́же є҆́сть на восто́цѣ: ХС҃ же, ѽ до́лꙋ є҆́же є҆́сть на за́падѣ: а҆ є҆́же НІ, ѽ сѣ́верныѧ страны̀, КА҆ же, съ полꙋ́денныѧ страны̀, ꙗ҆́коже здѣ̀ и҆зѡбрази́сѧ.

On the Division of the Holy Lamb.

It is necessary for thee to know, O priest, that on breaking the Holy Lamb thou must place the part with the sign of the Cross downward on the holy diskos, the incised side upward, as before when it was cut. IC, therefore, is placed at the upper side of the holy diskos, which is toward the east. And XC, at the bottom, which is toward the west; and that which is NI, upon the north side; and KA, on the south side, as is depicted here:

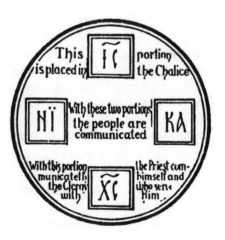

Іи҃съ ѹ҆́бѡ ча́сть взе́мъ, и҆сполнѧ́й ст҃ѹ́ю ча́шѹ. Хс҃ же, ча́сть, раздроблѧ́й сщ҃е́нникѡмъ и҆ дїа́конѡмъ. Ты́ѧ же двѣ̀ ча́сти ст҃ы̑ѧ, є҆́же НІ, и҆ є҆́же КА, причастникѡмъ да раздроблѧ́еши на ча́сти ма́лыѧ, є҆ли́кѡ бѹ́детъ дово́льно по разсмотре́нїю твоемѹ̀. А҆ ѿ ча́сти прест҃ы̑ѧ бц҃ы, и҆лѝ девѧти́хъ чинѡ́въ ст҃ы́хъ, и҆лѝ и҆́ныхъ є҆ли́кѡ во ст҃е́мъ дїскосѣ̀ сѹ́ть, никакоже кого̀ да причасти́ши: то́чїю ѿ двою̀ ча́стїю, ѡ҆ста́вшею ст҃а́гѡ а҆́гнца, да причаща́еши.

Къ томѹ́же тебѣ̀ вѣ́домо бѹ́детъ и҆ ѡ҆ се́мъ, ꙗ҆́кѡ є҆гда̀ растворѧ́еши ст҃ы́мъ ѹ҆кро́пцемъ бж҃е́ственнѹ́ю кро́вь влⷣчню, тогда̀ да вливаеши съ разсмотре́нїемъ, є҆ли́кѡ бы́ти дово́льно всѣ̑мъ хотѧ́щымъ причасти́тисѧ. Та́кожде и҆ ѿ вїна̀ и҆ воды̀, є҆гда̀ прободаеши ст҃ы́й а҆́гнецъ, тогда̀ да вливаеши толи́кѡ, є҆ли́кѡ бы́ти дово́льно всѣ̑мъ: послѣ́дй же никакоже что̀ да вливаеши, но то́чїю ѿ растворе́нїѧ є҆ди́ною,

Taking the portion IC, therefore, place it into the holy chalice. And divide the portion XC among the priests and deacons. Divide the other two portions, namely NI and KA, among the communicants in small particles, as many as may be sufficient according to thine own estimation.

But of the portion of the most-holy Theotokos, or of the nine orders of saints, or any others which are upon the holy diskos, thou shalt in no wise commune anyone; only of the two portions which remain of the Holy Lamb shalt thou give in Communion.

Furthermore, be it known unto thee also concerning this: that when thou dost dilute with the holy warm water the Divine Blood of the Master, then thou shalt pour with discretion so that there be enough for all that desire to partake. So also the wine and water, when thou dost pierce the Holy Lamb, then thou art to pour at that time an amount sufficient for all; after this, thou shalt pour no

е҆́же на Ст҃а́ѧ ст҃ы́мъ, и҆ та́кѡ причаща́й
всѣ́хъ ѿ си́хъ.

Дїа́конъ же, показꙋ́ѧ ѡ҆раре́мъ ст҃ы́й
поти́ръ, глаго́летъ:

И҆спо́лни влады́ко, ст҃ы́й поти́ръ.

Сщ҃е́нникъ же взе́мъ горѣ̀ лежа́щꙋю
ча́стицꙋ, ꙗ҆́же, І҆Н҃С, твори́тъ съ не́ю кр҃тъ
верхꙋ̀ ст҃а́гѡ поти́ра, глаго́лѧ:

И҆сполне́нїе дх҃а ст҃а́гѡ.
Дїа́конъ: А҆ми́нь.

И҆ та́кѡ влага́етъ во ст҃ы́й поти́ръ. И҆
прїе́млѧ теплотꙋ̀, глаго́летъ къ сщ҃е́нникꙋ:

Бл҃гословѝ влады́ко теплотꙋ̀.

Сщ҃е́нникъ же бл҃гословлѧ́етъ, глаго́лѧ:

Бл҃гослове́на теплота̀ ст҃ы́хъ твои́хъ,
всегда̀, ны́нѣ и҆ при́снѡ, и҆ во вѣ́ки вѣкѡ́въ.
А҆ми́нь.

more, but only that which is necessary for the dilution at: **Holy Things are for the holy,** and thus communicate all therefrom.

Then the deacon, pointing to the holy chalice with his orarion, says:

Fill the holy chalice, master.

The priest, taking the portion which lies at the top, that is, IC, makes a cross over the holy chalice therewith, saying:

The fullness of the Holy Spirit.
Deacon: **Amen.**

And thus places it in the holy chalice. And taking the warm water, he says to the priest:

Bless the warm water, master.

The priest blesses it, saying:

Blessed is the fervor of Thy saints, always, now and ever, and unto the ages of ages. Amen.

Ѝ дїаконъ вливаетъ, є҆ликш довольнѡ, кр҃тоѻбразнѡ внꙋтрь ст҃агш потира, глаголѧ:

Теплота̀ вѣ́ры, и҆сполнь дх҃а ст҃агш. А҆минь.

Ѝ ѿставивъ теплотꙋ́, стоитъ малш подалѣ̀. Сщ҃енникъ же глаголетъ:

Дїаконе, приступѝ.

Ѝ пришедъ дїаконъ творитъ поклонъ бл҃гоговѣ́йнѡ, просѧ̀ прощенїѧ.

Сщ҃енникъ же держа̀ ст҃ый хлѣ́бъ, даетъ дїаконꙋ: и҆ цѣловавъ дїаконъ подаю̀щꙋю є҆мꙋ̀ рꙋ́кꙋ, прїемлетъ ст҃ый хлѣ́бъ, глаголѧ:

Преподаждь мнѣ̀ влⷣко, чⷭтное и҆ ст҃ое тѣ́ло гдⷭа и҆ бг҃а и҆ сп҃са нашегш і҆и҃са хрⷭта̀.

Сщ҃енникъ же глаголетъ: А҆ми́къ, сщ҃еннодїаконꙋ преподаетсѧ чⷭтное и҆ ст҃ое и҆ пречⷭтое

And the deacon pours the water in the shape of a cross into the holy chalice, as much as is necessary, saying:

The fervor of faith, full of the Holy Spirit. Amen.

And having set aside the warm water, he stands a little aside. And the priest says:

Deacon, draw nigh.

And approaching, the deacon makes a bow, reverently, asking forgiveness.

The priest, holding the Holy Bread, gives it to the deacon; and the deacon having kissed the hand of him that gives, receives the Holy Bread, saying:

Impart unto me, master, the precious and holy Body of our Lord and God and Saviour Jesus Christ.

And the priest says: **To the Deacon N. is imparted the precious and holy and most**

тѣ́ло гд҃а и҆ бг҃а и҆ сп҃са на́шегѡ і҆и҃са хрⷭ҇та̀, во ѡ҆ставле́нїе грѣхѡ́въ є҆гѡ̀, и҆ въ жи́знь вѣ́чнꙋю.

И҆ ѿхо́дитъ дїа́конъ созадѝ ст҃ы́ѧ трапе́зы, приклони́въ главꙋ̀, и҆ мо́литсѧ ꙗ҆́кѡ и҆ сщ҃е́нникъ, глаго́лѧ: Вѣ́рꙋю, гд҃и, и҆ про́чаѧ.

Подо́бнѣ взе́мъ и҆ сщ҃е́нникъ є҆ди́нꙋ части́цꙋ ст҃а́гѡ хлѣ́ба, глаго́летъ:

Чⷭ҇тно́е и҆ прест҃о́е тѣ́ло гд҃а и҆ бг҃а и҆ сп҃са на́шегѡ і҆и҃са хрⷭ҇та̀ преподае́тсѧ мнѣ̀, и҆́мⷦ҇къ, сщ҃е́нникꙋ, во ѡ҆ставле́нїе грѣхѡ́въ мои́хъ, и҆ въ жи́знь вѣ́чнꙋю.

И҆ приклони́въ главꙋ̀ мо́литсѧ, глаго́лѧ:

Вѣ́рꙋю, гд҃и, и҆ и҆сповѣ́дꙋю, ꙗ҆́кѡ ты̀ є҆сѝ вои́стиннꙋ хрⷭ҇то́съ, сн҃ъ бг҃а жива́гѡ, прише́дый въ мі́ръ грѣ́шныѧ сп҃стѝ, ѿ ни́хже пе́рвый є҆́смь а҆́зъ. Є҆щѐ вѣ́рꙋю, ꙗ҆́кѡ сїѐ са́мое є҆́сть пречⷭ҇то́е тѣ́ло твоѐ, и҆ сїѧ̀ са́маѧ є҆́сть чⷭ҇тна́ѧ кро́вь твоѧ̀. Молю́сѧ

pure Body of our Lord and God and Saviour Jesus Christ, unto the remission of his sins, and life everlasting.

And bowing his head, the deacon goes behind the Holy Table and prays as does the priest, saying: I believe, O Lord..., and the rest.

Likewise the priest, taking one portion of the Holy Bread, says:

The precious and most holy Body of our Lord and God and Saviour Jesus Christ is imparted unto me, the Priest N., unto the remission of my sins, and life everlasting.

And bowing his head, he prays, saying:

I believe, O Lord, and I confess that Thou art truly the Christ, the Son of the living God, Who didst come into the world to save sinners of whom I am chief. Moreover, I believe that this is truly Thy most pure Body, and that this is truly Thine own precious

оу́бо тебѣ̀: помилꙋ́й мѧ̀, и҆ прости́ ми
прегрѣше́нїѧ моѧ̀ во́льнаѧ и҆ нево́льнаѧ,
ꙗ҆же сло́вомъ, ꙗ҆же дѣ́ломъ, ꙗ҆же вѣ́дѣнїемъ
и҆ невѣ́дѣнїемъ: и҆ сподо́би мѧ̀ неѡсꙋжде́ннѡ
причасти́тисѧ пречⷭ҇тыхъ твои́хъ та́инствъ,
во ѡ҆ставле́нїе грѣхѡ́въ и҆ въ жи́знь вѣ́чнꙋю.
А҆ми́нь.

Ве́чери твоеѧ̀ та́йныѧ дне́сь, сн҃е бж҃їй,
причастника мѧ̀ прїимѝ: не бо̀ врагѡ́мъ
твои́мъ та́йнꙋ повѣ́мъ, ни лобза́нїѧ
ти дамъ ꙗ҆́кѡ і҆ꙋ́да, но ꙗ҆́кѡ разбо́йникъ
и҆сповѣ́даю тѧ̀: помѧни́ мѧ, гдⷭ҇и, во цр҃тві́и
твое́мъ.

Да не въ сꙋ́дъ и҆лѝ во ѡ҆сꙋжде́нїе бꙋ́детъ
мнѣ̀ причаще́нїе ст҃ы́хъ твои́хъ та́инъ, гдⷭ҇и,
но во и҆сцѣле́нїе дꙋшѝ и҆ тѣ́ла.

И҆ та́кѡ причаща́ютсѧ въ рꙋка́хъ
держи́маго со стра́хомъ и҆ всѧ́цѣмъ
оу҆твержде́нїемъ.

Blood. Wherefore, I pray Thee: Have mercy on me and forgive me my transgressions, voluntary and involuntary, in word and deed, in knowledge and in ignorance. And vouchsafe me to partake without condemnation of Thy most pure Mysteries unto the remission of sins and life everlasting. Amen.

Of Thy Mystical Supper, O Son of God, receive me today as a communicant; for I will not speak of the Mystery to Thine enemies, nor will I give Thee a kiss as did Judas, but like the Thief do I confess Thee: Remember me, O Lord, in Thy kingdom.

Let not the communion of Thy holy Mysteries be unto me for judgment or condemnation, O Lord, but for healing of soul and body.

And thus they partake of that which they hold in their hands with fear and all heedfulness.

Та́же сщⷷнникъ воста́въ, прїе́млетъ ѻ҆бѣ́ма рꙋка́ма съ покро́вцемъ сты́й потѵ́рь, и҆ причаща́етсѧ три́жды и҆з̾ негѡ̀, глаго́лѧ:

Чⷭ҇тны́ѧ и҆ сты́ѧ кро́ве гдⷭ҇а бга и҆ спⷭ҇а на́шегѡ і҆и҃са хрⷭ҇та̀, причаща́юсѧ а҆́зъ ра́бъ бж҃їй, сщⷷнникъ и҆́мⷬ҇къ, во ѡ҆ставле́нїе грѣхѡ́въ мои́хъ и҆ въ жи́знь вѣ́чнꙋю. А҆ми́нь.

И҆ та́кѡ свои̑ ᲂу҆стнѣ̀, и҆ кра́й сщⷷннагѡ потѵ́ра въ рꙋкꙋ̀ держи́мымъ покро́вцемъ ѡ҆тё́ръ, и҆ глаго́летъ:

Сѐ прикоснꙋ́сѧ ᲂу҆стна́мъ мои̑мъ, и҆ ѿи́метъ беззакѡ́нїѧ моѧ̑, и҆ грѣхѝ моѧ̑ ѡ҆чи́ститъ.

Та́же призыва́етъ дїа́кона, глаго́лѧ:

Дїа́коне, пристꙋпѝ.

И҆ дїа́конъ прихо́дитъ и҆ покланѧ́етсѧ є҆ди́ною, глаго́лѧ:

Сѐ прихождꙋ̀ къ безсме́ртномꙋ цр҃ю̀ и҆ бг҃ꙋ на́шемꙋ.

Then rising, the priest takes the holy
chalice in both hands with the cloth, and
partakes thrice from it, saying:

Of the precious and holy Blood of our Lord
and God and Saviour Jesus Christ do I, the
servant of God, the Priest N., partake unto
the remission of my sins and life everlasting.

And thus, having wiped his lips and the
holy chalice with the cloth that he holds in
his hand, he says:

Behold, this hath touched my lips, and
taketh away mine iniquities, and purgeth
away my sins.

Then he calls the deacon, saying:

Deacon, draw nigh.

And the deacon approaches, and bows
down once, saying:

Behold, I approach unto the Immortal King
and our God.

Й: Преподаⷤждь мѝ, влады́ко, чⷵтнꙋ́ю и ст҃ꙋ́ю кро́вь гдⷵа и бг҃а и сп҃са на́шегѡ і҆и҃са хрⷵта̀.

И҆ глаго́летъ сщ҃е́нникъ:

Причаща́етсѧ ра́бъ бж҃їй, дїа́конъ и҆м҃к, чⷵтны́ѧ и҆ ст҃ы́ѧ кро́ве гдⷵа и҆ бг҃а и҆ сп҃са на́шегѡ і҆и҃са хрⷵта̀, во ѡ҆ставле́нїе грѣхѡ́въ свои́хъ и҆ въ жи́знь вѣ́чнꙋю.

Причасти́вшꙋсѧ же дїа́конꙋ, гл҃етъ сщ҃е́нникъ:

Сѐ прикоснꙋ́сѧ оу҆стна́мъ твои́мъ, и҆ ѿи́метъ беззакѡ́нїѧ твоѧ̀, и҆ грѣхѝ твоѧ̀ ѡ҆чи́ститъ.

Подоба́етъ вѣ́дати, ꙗ҆́кѡ а҆́ще сꙋ́ть хотѧ́щїи причаща́тисѧ ст҃ы́хъ та́инъ, раздробля́етъ сщ҃е́нникъ двѣ̀ ча́сти ст҃а́гѡ а҆́гнца ѡ҆ста́вшыѧ, є҆́же НІ, и҆ є҆́же КА, на ма́лыѧ ча́стицы, ꙗ҆́кѡ бы́ти всѣ̑мъ причаⷵтникѡмъ дово́льно: и҆ та́кѡ влага́етъ и҆̀хъ во ст҃ꙋ́ю ча́шꙋ.

And: Impart unto me, master, the precious and holy Blood of our Lord and God and Saviour Jesus Christ.

And the priest says:

The servant of God, the Deacon N., partaketh of the precious and holy Blood of our Lord and God and Saviour Jesus Christ unto the remission of his sins and life everlasting.

The deacon having partaken, the priest says:

Behold, this hath touched thy lips, and taketh away thine iniquities, and purgeth away thy sins.

It should be known, that if there be those that desire to partake of the Holy Mysteries, the priest breaks the two portions of the Holy Lamb that remain, that is, NI and KA, into small pieces, so that there be sufficient for all communicants, and then puts them into the holy chalice.

И҆ покрыва́етъ ст҃ый потѵ́рь покро́вцемъ, подо́бнѣ и҆ на ст҃ый ді́скосъ возлага́етъ ѕвѣздицꙋ̀ и҆ покро́вцы.

Та́же глаго́летъ мл҃твꙋ̀ бл҃года́рственнꙋю сщ҃е́нникъ:

Бл҃годари́мъ тѧ̀, гдⷭ҇и бж҃е на́шъ, ѡ҆ причаще́нїи ст҃ыхъ, пречⷭ҇тыхъ, безсме́ртныхъ, и҆ небе́сныхъ твои́хъ та́инъ, и҆̀хже да́лъ є҆сѝ на́мъ во благодѣѧ́нїе и҆ ѡ҆сщ҃е́нїе, и҆ и҆сцѣле́нїе дꙋ́шъ и҆ тѣле́съ на́шихъ. Са́мъ, влⷣко всѣ́хъ, да́ждь бы́ти на́мъ причⷭ҇тїю ст҃а́гѡ тѣ́ла и҆ кро́ве хрⷭ҇та̀ твоегѡ̀ въ вѣ́рꙋ непостыднꙋ̀, въ любо́вь нелицемѣ́рнꙋ, въ преꙋмноже́нїе премꙋ́дрости, во и҆сцѣле́нїе дꙋшѝ и҆ тѣ́ла, во ѿгна́нїе всѧ́кагѡ сопроти́внагѡ, въ снабдѣ́нїе за́повѣдей твои́хъ, во ѿвѣ́тъ благопрїѧ́тенъ, и҆̀же на стра́шнѣмъ сꙋди́щи хрⷭ҇та̀ твоегѡ̀.

And he covers the holy chalice with a veil, and also places the star and veils upon the holy diskos.

And the priest says this prayer of thanksgiving:

We give thanks unto Thee, O Lord our God, for the communion of Thy holy, most-pure, immortal, and heavenly Mysteries, which Thou gavest us unto well-being and sanctification, and healing of our souls and bodies. Do Thou Thyself, O Master of all, grant that the holy Body and Blood of Thy Christ may be unto us for faith unashamed, for love unfeigned, for the increase of wisdom, for healing of soul and body, for the driving away of every adversary, for the keeping of Thy commandments, for an acceptable defense, even at the dread judgment seat of Thy Christ.

И та́кѡ ѿверза́ютъ две́ри ст҃а́гѡ ѻлтара̀.
И дїа́конъ, поклони́всѧ є҆ди́ною, прїе́млетъ
потирь со блгогове́нїемъ, и҆ прихо́дитъ во
две́ри, и҆ возноса̀ ст҃ы́й потирь, показꙋетъ
и҆ лю́демъ, глаго́лѧ:

Со стра́хомъ бж҃їимъ и҆ ве́рою приступи́те.
Ли́къ: Блгослове́нъ грѧды́й во и҆мѧ гдⷭ҇не, бг҃ъ
гдⷭ҇ь, и҆ ꙗвисѧ на́мъ.

Та́же приступа́ютъ хотѧ́щїи причаща́тисѧ.
И҆ и҆дꙋ́тъ є҆ди́нъ по є҆ди́номꙋ, и҆
покланѧ́ютсѧ со всѧ́цемъ оу҆миле́нїемъ и҆
стра́хомъ, согбе́нне рꙋ́це къ пе́рсемъ и҆мꙋ́ще:
та́же прїе́млетъ ки́ждо бж҃е́ственныѧ
та́йны. Сщ҃е́нникъ же, причаща́ѧ є҆го̀,
глаго́летъ:

Причаща́етсѧ ра́бъ бж҃їй и҆мⷬ҇къ, чⷭ҇тна́гѡ и҆
ст҃а́гѡ те́ла и҆ кро́ве гдⷭ҇а и҆ бг҃а и҆ сп҃са
на́шегѡ і҆и҃са хрⷭ҇та̀, во ѡ҆ставле́нїе грехѡ́въ
и҆ въ жи́знь ве́чнꙋю.

And then they open the doors of the holy altar. And the deacon, bowing once, receives the holy chalice with reverence, and approaches the doors, and elevating the holy chalice, shows it to the people, saying:

With fear of God and with faith draw nigh. Choir: Blessed is He that cometh in the name of the Lord. God is the Lord, and hath appeared unto us.

Then those that desire to partake draw nigh. And they come one by one, and bow down with all compunction and fear, having their arms folded on their breast. Then each one receives the Divine Mysteries. The priest, as he communes every one, says:

The servant [or handmaiden] of God N., partaketh of the precious and holy Body and Blood of our Lord God and Saviour Jesus Christ, unto the remission of sins and life everlasting.

И дїа́конъ ѿира́етъ є҆мꙋ́ ᲂу҆стнѣ̀
пла́томъ, и҆ цѣлꙋ́етъ прича́стивыйсѧ
ст҃ꙋ́ю ча́шꙋ, и҆ поклони́всѧ
ѿхо́дитъ.

И҆ та́кѡ прича́щаютсѧ всѝ.

По прича́щенїи же, входитъ і҆ере́й во
ст҃ы́й ѻ҆лта́рь, и҆ поставлѧ́етъ ст҃а́ѧ на
ст҃ѣ́мъ пртⷭ҇о́лѣ.

Тогда̀ прїе́мъ дїа́конъ ст҃ы́й дїскосъ
верхꙋ̀ ст҃а́гѡ потира, и҆ глаго́лѧ воскрⷭ҇ныѧ
пѣ́сни сїѧ̑:

Воскрⷭ҇нїе хрⷭ҇то́во ви́дѣвше, поклони́мсѧ
ст҃о́мꙋ гдⷭ҇ꙋ і҆и҃ꙋ, є҆ди́номꙋ безгрѣ́шномꙋ.
крⷭ҇тꙋ̀ твоемꙋ̀ покланѧ́емсѧ хрⷭ҇тѐ, и҆ ст҃о́е
воскрⷭ҇нїе твоѐ пое́мъ и҆ сла́вимъ: ты́ бо є҆сѝ
бг҃ъ на́шъ, ра́звѣ тебѐ и҆но́гѡ не зна́емъ,
и҆́мѧ твоѐ и҆менꙋ́емъ. Прїиди́те всѝ вѣ́рнїи,
поклони́мсѧ ст҃о́мꙋ хрⷭ҇то́вꙋ воскрⷭ҇нїю: се́ бо
прїи́де крⷭ҇то́мъ ра́дость всемꙋ̀ мі́рꙋ. Всегда̀
бл҃гословѧ́ще гдⷭ҇а, пое́мъ воскрⷭ҇нїе є҆гѡ̀:

And the deacon wipes the communicant's lips with the cloth, and the communicant kisses the holy chalice, and bowing, withdraws.

And in this manner do all partake.

After communion, the priest enters the holy altar and places the Holy Things upon the Holy Table.

The deacon then holds the holy diskos over the holy chalice, and says these resurrectional hymns:

Having beheld the Resurrection of Christ, let us worship the holy Lord Jesus, the Only Sinless One. We worship Thy Cross, O Christ, and Thy holy Resurrection we hymn and glorify, for Thou art our God, and we know none other beside Thee; we call upon Thy name. O come, all ye faithful, let us worship Christ's holy Resurrection, for behold, through the Cross, joy hath come to all the world. Ever blessing the Lord, we hymn His

распѧ́тїе бо претерпѣ́въ, сме́ртїю сме́рть разрꙋши́.

Свѣти́сѧ, свѣти́сѧ, но́вый і҆ерⷭли́ме, сла́ва бо гдⷭнѧ на тебѣ̀ возсїѧ̀. Ликꙋ́й нынѣ̀, и҆ весели́сѧ сїѡ́не: ты́ же, чⷭтаѧ, красꙋ́йсѧ, бцⷣе, ѡ҆ воста́нїи ржⷭтва̀ твоегѡ̀.

Ѽ па́сха ве́лїѧ и҆ сщⷣе́ннѣйшаѧ, хрⷭтѐ! ѽ мꙋ́дросте, и҆ сло́ве бж҃їй, и҆ си́ло! подава́й на́мъ и҆стѣ́е тебѐ причаща́тисѧ, въ невече́рнѣмъ днѝ црⷭтвїѧ твоегѡ̀.

Ѿтира́етъ ст҃у́ю гꙋ́бою ѕѣлѡ̀ добрѣ̀, со внима́нїемъ и҆ блⷢгоговѣ́нїемъ, глаго́лѧ словеса̀ сїѧ̀:

Ѻ҆мы́й гдⷭи, грѣхѝ помина́вшихсѧ здѣ̀ кро́вїю твое́ю чⷭтно́ю, мл҃твами ст҃ы́хъ твои́хъ.

Сщⷣе́нникъ же блⷢгословлѧ́етъ лю́ди, возглаша́ѧ:

Resurrection, for having endured crucifixion, He hath destroyed death by death.

Shine, shine, O new Jerusalem, for the glory of the Lord has shone upon thee; dance now, and be glad, O Sion; and do thou exult, O pure Theotokos, in the arising of Him Whom thou didst bear.

O great and most sacred Pascha, O Christ! O Wisdom, and Word of God, and Power! Grant us more perfectly to partake of Thee, in the unwaning day of Thy kingdom.

The deacon wipes the holy diskos with the holy sponge exceedingly well, with attentiveness and reverence, saying these words:

Wash away by Thy precious Blood, O Lord, the sins of those here commemorated, through the prayers of Thy saints.

And the priest blesses the people, exclaiming:

Сп҃сѝ, бж҃е, лю́ди твоѧ̑, и҆ блгⷵловѝ доⷭ҇тоѧ́нїе твоѐ.

И҆ ѡ҆браща́етсѧ сщ҃е́нникъ ко ст҃е́й трапе́зѣ, и҆ кади́тъ сщ҃е́нникъ три́жды, глаго́лѧ въ себѣ̀:

Вознеси́сѧ на нб҃са̀ бж҃е, и҆ по все́й землѝ сла́ва твоѧ̑.

Ли́къ же пое́тъ: Ви́дѣхомъ свѣ́тъ и҆́стинный, прїѧ́хомъ дх҃а нбⷵнаго, ѡ҆брѣто́хомъ вѣ́рꙋ и҆́стиннꙋю, нераздѣ́льнѣй трⷪ҇цѣ покланѧ́емсѧ: та́ бо на́съ спасла̀ є҆́сть.

Та́же взе́мъ сщ҃е́нникъ ст҃ы́й ді́скосъ, возлага́етъ на главꙋ̀ дїа́кона, и҆ дїа́конъ прїе́мъ и҆̀ со блгоговѣ́нїемъ, зрѧ̀ внѣ̀ къ две́ремъ, ничто́же глаго́лѧ, ѿхо́дитъ въ предложе́нїе, и҆ поставлѧ́етъ и҆̀.

Сщ҃е́нникъ же поклони́всѧ, и҆ прїе́мъ ст҃ы́й поти́ръ, и҆ ѡ҆бра́щьсѧ къ две́ремъ, зрѧ̀ на лю́ди, глаго́летъ та́йнѡ:

Блгⷵве́нъ бг҃ъ на́шъ:

Save, O God, Thy people, and bless Thine inheritance.

And the priest turns back to the Holy Table, and censes it thrice, saying secretly:

Be Thou exalted above the heavens, O God, and Thy glory above all the earth.

Choir: We have seen the true Light, we have received the Heavenly Spirit, we have found the True Faith. We worship the indivisible Trinity, for He hath saved us.

Then the priest takes the holy diskos, places it on the deacon's head, and the deacon receives it with reverence; looking out through the doors, saying nothing, he goes to the table of oblation and places it thereon.

The priest bows, and takes the holy chalice, and turning to the doors, looking toward the people, he says secretly:

Blessed is our God:

И҆ возгла́снѡ: Всегда̀, ны́нѣ и҆ прⷭнѡ, и҆ во вѣ́ки вѣкѡ́въ.

И҆ ѿхо́дитъ ко ст҃о́мꙋ предложе́нїю и҆ поставлѧ́етъ та́мѡ ст҃а̑ѧ.

Ли́къ: А҆ми́нь. Да и҆спо́лнѧтсѧ ᲂу҆ста̀ на̑ша хвале́нїѧ твоегѡ̀ гдⷭи, ꙗ҆́кѡ да пое́мъ сла́вꙋ твою̀, ꙗ҆́кѡ сподо́билъ є҆сѝ на́съ причасти́тисѧ ст҃ы́мъ твои̑мъ, бж҃е́ственнымъ, безсме́ртнымъ и҆ животворѧ́щымъ та́йнамъ: соблюдѝ на́съ во твое́й ст҃ы́ни, ве́сь де́нь поꙋча́тисѧ пра́вдѣ твое́й. А҆ллилꙋ́їа, а҆ллилꙋ́їа, а҆ллилꙋ́їа.

И҆ и҆зше́дъ дїа́конъ сѣ́верною две́рїю, и҆ ста́въ на ѻ҆бы́чнѣмъ мѣ́стѣ, глаго́летъ:

Про́сти прїи́мше бж҃е́ственныхъ, ст҃ы́хъ, преч҇ты́хъ, безсме́ртныхъ, нбⷭныхъ и҆ животворѧ́щихъ, стра́шныхъ хрⷭто́выхъ та́йнъ, досто́йнѡ бл҃годари́мъ гдⷭа.

Ли́къ: Гдⷭи поми́лꙋй.

Дїа́конъ: Застꙋпѝ, спасѝ, поми́лꙋй и҆ сохранѝ на́съ, бж҃е, твое́ю бл҃года́тїю.

Ли́къ: Гдⷭи поми́лꙋй.

And aloud: Always, now and ever, and unto the ages of ages.

And he goes to the holy table of oblation and places the Holy Things on it.

Choir: Amen. Let our mouth be filled with Thy praise, O Lord, that we may hymn Thy glory, for Thou hast vouchsafed us to partake of Thy holy, divine, immortal and life-giving Mysteries. Keep us in Thy holiness, that we may meditate on Thy righteousness all the day long. Alleluia, alleluia, alleluia.

And the deacon comes out by the north door, and standing in the usual place, says:

Aright! Having partaken of the divine, holy, most pure, immortal, heavenly, and life-giving, fearful Mysteries of Christ, let us worthily give thanks unto the Lord.

Choir: Lord, have mercy.

Deacon: Help us, save us, have mercy on us, and keep us, O God, by Thy grace.

Choir: Lord, have mercy.

Дїа́конъ: **День** весь [а́ще лїтꙋргі́а соединѧ́етсѧ съ вече́рней, Ве́чера всегѡ̀] соверше́нъ, ст҃ъ, ми́ренъ и҆ безгрѣ́шенъ и҆спроси́вше, са́ми себѐ и҆ дрꙋ́гъ дрꙋ́га, и҆ ве́сь живо́тъ на́шъ хрⷭ҇тꙋ̀ бг҃ꙋ предади́мъ.

Ли́къ: Тебѣ̀ гдⷭ҇и.

І҆ере́й же, согнꙋ́въ а҆нтїми́нсъ и҆ прѧ́мѡ держа̀ є҆ѵⷢ҇лїе, твори́тъ над ни́мъ крⷭ҇тъ, и҆ возглаша́етъ:

Ꙗ҆́кѡ ты̀ є҆сѝ ѡ҆сщ҃е́нїе на́ше, и҆ тебѣ̀ сла́вꙋ возсыла́емъ, ѻ҆ц҃ꙋ, и҆ сн҃ꙋ, и҆ ст҃о́мꙋ дх҃ꙋ, ны́нѣ и҆ при́снѡ, и҆ во вѣ́ки вѣкѡ́въ.

Ли́къ: А҆ми́нь.

І҆ере́й: Съ ми́ромъ и҆зы́демъ.

Ли́къ: Ѡ҆ и҆́мени гдⷭ҇ни.

Дїа́конъ: Гдⷭ҇ꙋ помо́лимсѧ.

Ли́къ: Гдⷭ҇и поми́лꙋй.

Deacon: Having asked that the whole day (but if it be a Vesperal Liturgy: whole evening) may be perfect, holy, peaceful and sinless, let us commit ourselves and one another and all our life unto Christ, our God.

Choir: To Thee, O Lord.

The priest, having folded the antimension, and holding the Gospel upright, before laying it upon the antimension, makes the sign of the cross with it over the antimension and exclaims:

For Thou art our sanctification, and unto Thee do we send up glory, to the Father, and to the Son, and to the Holy Spirit, now and ever, and unto the ages of ages.

Choir: Amen.

Priest: Let us depart in peace.

Choir: In the name of the Lord.

Deacon: Let us pray to the Lord.

Choir: Lord, have mercy.

Мⷧтва заамвѡ́ннаѧ возгла́снѡ глаго́летсѧ
ѿ іере́а:

Б҃гословлѧ́ѧй благословѧ́щыѧ тѧ гдⷭи, и ѡсщ҃а́ѧй на тѧ оу҆пова́ющыѧ, спаси люди твоѧ̀, и҆ благослови̂ достоѧ́нїе твоѐ, и҆сполне́нїе цр҃кве твоеѧ̀ сохрани̂, ѡсти любѧ́щыѧ бл҃голѣ́пїе до́мꙋ твоегѡ̀: ты̀ тѣ́хъ воспросла́ви бж҃е́ственною твое́ю си́лою, и҆ не ѡста́ви на́съ оу҆пова́ющихъ на тѧ̀. Ми́ръ мíрови твоемꙋ̀ да́рꙋй, цр҃квамъ твои̂мъ, сщ҃е́нникѡмъ, и҆ всѣ́мъ лю́демъ твои̂мъ. Ꙗ҆́кѡ всѧ́кое даѧ́нїе бл҃го, и҆ всѧ́къ да́ръ соверше́нъ свы́ше е҆́сть, сходѧ́й ѿ тебѐ оц҃а̀ свѣ́тѡвъ: и҆ тебѣ̀ сла́вꙋ, и҆ бл҃годаре́нїе, и҆ поклоне́нїе возсыла́емъ, оц҃ꙋ̀, и҆ сн҃ꙋ, и҆ ст҃о́мꙋ дх҃ꙋ, ны́нѣ и҆ при́снѡ, и҆ во вѣ́ки вѣкѡ́въ.

Ли́къ: А҆ми́нь.

Та́же: Бꙋ́ди и҆́мѧ гдⷭне: три́жды и҆ ѱало́мъ а҃г, Благословлю̀ гдⷭа:

The priest says the Prayer behind the ambo aloud:

O Lord, Who dost bless them that bless Thee and sanctify them that put their trust in Thee: save Thy people and bless Thine inheritance. Preserve the fullness of Thy Church, sanctify them that love the beauty of Thy house. Do Thou glorify them by Thy divine power, and forsake us not that hope in Thee. Give peace to Thy world, to Thy churches, to the priests, and to all Thy people. For every good gift and every perfect gift is from above and cometh down from Thee, the Father of lights, and unto Thee do we send up glory and thanksgiving and worship: to the Father, and to the Son, and to the Holy Spirit, now and ever, and unto the ages of ages.

Choir: Amen.

Also the choir: Blessed be the Name of the Lord. (thrice), and Psalm 33: I will bless the Lord . . .

Моли́твѣ же глаго́лемѣй, дїа́конъ
стои́тъ на десн́ѣй стран́ѣ пред ѻ҆́бразомъ
влⷣки хрⷭ҇та̀, держа̀ и҆ ѡ҆ра́рь сво́й, главꙋ̀
приклон́ь, до соверше́нїѧ мл҃твы: се́й же
скончавшейсѧ, сщ҃е́нникъ ᲂу҆́бѡ входитъ
ст҃ы́ми две́рьми, и҆ ᲂу҆ше́дъ въ предложе́нїе,
глаго́летъ настоѧ́щꙋю мл҃твꙋ:

Мл҃тва, глаго́лемаѧ внегда̀ потреби́ти ст҃а̑ѧ:

И҆спо́лнисѧ и҆ соверши́сѧ є҆ли́кѡ по
на́шей си́лѣ, хрⷭ҇тѐ бж҃е на́шъ, твоегѡ̀
смотре́нїѧ та́инство: и҆мѣемъ бо сме́рти
твоеѧ̀ па́мѧть, ви́дѣхомъ воскресе́нїѧ
твоегѡ̀ ѻ҆́бразъ, напо́лнихомсѧ без-
коне́чныѧ твоеѧ̀ жи́зни, наслади́хомсѧ
неистоща́емыѧ твоеѧ̀ пи́щи, є҆́же и҆ въ
бꙋ́дꙋщемъ вѣ́цѣ, всѣ̑мъ на́мъ сподо́битисѧ
бл҃говолѝ, бл҃года́тїю безнача́льнагѡ тво-
егѡ̀ ѻ҆ц҃а̀ и҆ ст҃а́гѡ и҆ бл҃га́гѡ и҆ живот-
ворѧ́щагѡ твоегѡ̀ дх҃а, нн҃ѣ и҆ при́снѡ,
и҆ во вѣ́ки вѣкѡ́въ, а҆ми́нь.

While the Prayer behind the ambo is being said, the deacon stands on the right side before the icon of Christ the Master, holding his orarion, head bowed, until the completion of the Prayer. This being concluded, the priest then enters through the holy doors, and having gone to the table of oblation, he says the following prayer:

The Prayer said when the Holy Things are to be consumed:

The mystery of Thy dispensation, O Christ our God, hast been fulfilled and perfected as much as is in our power; for we have the memory of Thy death, we have seen the image of Thy Resurrection, we have been filled by Thy immortal life, we have delighted in Thy inexhaustible food, which do Thou deign to vouchsafe unto us all in the age to come, through the grace of Thine unoriginate Father and Thy holy and good and life-creating Spirit, now and ever, and unto the ages of ages, Amen.

Дїа́конъ же вше́дъ сѣ́верною страно́ю, потребла́етъ ст҃а҃ѧ со стра́хомъ, и҆ со вса́кимъ ᲂу҆твержде́нїемъ.

Сщ҃е́нникъ глаго́летъ:

Бл҃гослове́нїе гдⷭ҇не на ва́съ, того̀ бл҃года́тїю и҆ чл҃вѣколю́бїемъ, всегда̀, ны́нѣ и҆ при́снѡ, и҆ во вѣ́ки вѣкѡ́въ.

Ли́къ: А҆ми́нь.

Сщ҃е́нникъ: Сла́ва тебѣ̀, хрⷭ҇тѐ бж҃е, ᲂу҆пова́нїе на́ше, сла́ва тебѣ̀.

Ли́къ: Сла́ва, и҆ ны́нѣ: Гдⷭ҇и помилꙋ́й, три́жды. Бл҃гословѝ.

Сщ҃е́нникъ: Хрⷭ҇то́съ и҆́стинный бг҃ъ на́шъ, мл҃твами пречⷭ҇тыѧ своеѧ̀ мт҃ре [и҆ про́чаѧ], и҆́же во ст҃ы́хъ ѻ҆ц҃а̀ на́шегѡ васі́лїа вели́кагѡ, а҆рхїепⷭ҇кпа кесарі́и каппадокі́йскїѧ: и҆ ст҃а́гѡ и҆́мⷬ҇къ, [є҆гѡ́же є҆́сть хра́мъ и҆ є҆гѡ́же є҆́сть де́нь:], и҆ всѣ́хъ ст҃ы́хъ, помилꙋ́етъ и҆ спасе́тъ на́съ, ꙗ҆́кѡ бл҃гъ и҆ чл҃вѣколю́бецъ.

Ли́къ: А҆ми́нь.

The deacon, having entered by the north side, consumes the Holy Things with fear and with all heedfulness.

The priest says:

The blessing of the Lord be upon you, through His grace and love for mankind, always, now and ever, and unto the ages of ages.

Choir: Amen.

Priest: Glory to Thee, O Christ God, our hope, glory to Thee.

Choir: Glory, both now ... Lord, have mercy, (thrice). Father, bless.

Priest: May Christ our true God, through the intercessions of His most pure Mother; [and the rest]; of our father among the saints, Basil the Great, Archbishop of Caesarea in Cappadocia; of Saint(s) N.: [whose temple it is and whose day it is] and of all the Saints, have mercy on us and save us, for He is good and the Lover of mankind.

Choir: Amen.

Ликъ же многолѣтствꙋетъ.

И сщенникъ, вшедъ во стый олтарь, глаголетъ благодарныѧ молитвы.

Таже: Нынѣ ѿпꙋщаеши: Тристо́е. И по Оче нашъ:

Тропарь, гласъ а҃:

Во всю зе́млю изыде вѣщанїе твое́, ꙗкѡ прїемшꙋю слово твое́, имже бголѣпнѡ наꙋчилъ еси, естество сꙋщихъ оуѧснилъ еси: чл҃вѣческїѧ обычаи оукрасилъ еси. царское сщенїе, Оче преподобне, моли хрта, спастисѧ дꙋшамъ нашымъ.

Слава: Кондакъ, гласъ д҃.

Подобенъ: Явилсѧ еси:

Явилсѧ еси ѡснованїе непоколебимое цркве, подаѧ всѣмъ неꙋкрадомое гдство человѣкѡмъ, запечатлѣѧ твоими велѣньми, небоѧвленне васілїе преподобне.

And the choir sings the Polychronion.

And the priest, entering the holy altar,
  says the thanksgiving prayers.

Then, **Now lettest Thou...** The Trisagion.
  And after **Our Father...**

Troparion, 1st tone:

Thy fame hath gone forth into all the earth,
which hath receive thy word. Thereby thou
hast divinely taught the Faith; thou hast made
manifest the nature of created things; thou
hast made the moral life of men a royal priesthood. O Basil, our righteous father, intercede
with Christ God that our souls be saved.

Glory: Kontakion, 4th tone:

Prosomion: **Thou didst prove:**

Thou didst prove to be an unshakable foundation of the church, giving to all mortals
an inviolate lordship, and sealing it with
thy doctrines, O righteous Basil, revealer of
heavenly things.

И ны́нѣ, бг҃оро́диченъ: Предста́тельство хрⷭ҇тїа́нъ непосты́дное, хода́тайство ко творцꙋ̀ непрело́жное, не пре́зри грѣ́шныхъ моле́нїй гла́сы: но предвари́, ꙗ́кѡ бл҃га́, на по́мощь на́съ, вѣ́рнѡ зовꙋ́щихъ тѝ: оу҆скорѝ на мл҃твꙋ, и҆ потщи́сѧ на оу҆моле́нїе, предста́тельствꙋющи при́снѡ, бц҃е, чтꙋ́щихъ тѧ̀.

Гдⷭ҇и поми́лꙋй, в҃і. Честнѣ́йшꙋю: Сла́ва, и҆ ны́нѣ:

и҆ твори́тъ ѿпꙋ́стъ.

Потреби́вшꙋ же дїа́конꙋ ст҃а̑ѧ со всѧ́кимъ ѡ҆пасе́нїемъ, ꙗ́кѡ ничемꙋ̀ ѿ ѕѣлѡ̀ дробнѣ́йшихъ па́сти крꙋ́пицъ, и҆лѝ ѡ҆ста́тисѧ, налїа́въ во ст҃ꙋ́ю ча́шꙋ ѿ вїна̀ и҆ воды̀, и҆ потреби́въ, и҆ сопра́тавъ гꙋ́бою всю̀ мокротꙋ̀.

Та́же слага́етъ ст҃ы̑ѧ сосꙋ́ды вкꙋ́пѣ, и҆ ѡ҆бвѧза́въ и҆̀хъ, полага́етъ на ѻ҆бы́чнемъ

Both now, The Theotokion: O protection of Christians that cannot be put to shame, O mediation unto the Creator unfailing: disdain not the supplicant voices of sinners; but be thou quick, O good one, to help us who in faith cry unto thee; hasten to intercession and speed thou to make supplication, thou who dost ever protect, O Theotokos, them that honor thee.

Lord, have mercy (twelve times).   More honorable: . . . Glory, Both now . . .

And he gives the dismissal.

The deacon, having consumed the Holy Things with all diligence, so that no smallest particle fall or remain, pours into the holy chalice some wine and water, and consumes it, and wipes away all moisture with the sponge.

Then he puts the holy vessels together, and wrapping them, sets them in their usual

мѣстѣ, глаголѧ: Ны́нѣ ѿпꙋща́еши: и
про́чаѧ, ꙗ́коже и сщ҃е́нникъ. И ѡмыва́етъ
рꙋ́ки на ѻбы́чнемъ мѣстѣ, и поклони́всѧ
вкꙋ́пѣ со сщ҃е́нникомъ, творѧ́тъ ѿпꙋ́стъ, и
бл҃годарѧ́ще бг҃а ѡ всѣ́хъ, исхо́дѧтъ.

Коне́цъ бжⷭ҇твенныѧ лїтꙋргíи
вели́кагѡ васíлïа.

place, saying: **Now lettest Thou**, and the rest, as did the priest, and washes his hands in the usual place, and bowing together with the priest, they make the dismissal, and giving thanks unto God for all things, they depart.

The End of the Divine Liturgy
of St. Basil the Great

Мл҃твы бл҃года́рственныѧ по ст҃ѣ́мъ причаще́нїи

Е҆гда́ же полꙋчи́ши до́браго причаще́нїѧ животворѧ́щихъ та́инственныхъ дарова́нїй, воспо́й а҆́бїе, бл҃года́ри вельмѝ, и҆ сїѧ̑ те́плѣ ѿ дꙋшѝ бг҃ꙋ глаго́ли:

Сла́ва тебѣ̀, бж҃е. Сла́ва тебѣ̀, бж҃е. Сла́ва тебѣ̀, бж҃е.

Та́же бл҃года́рственнꙋю сїю̀ мл҃твꙋ:

Бл҃годарю́ тѧ, гдⷭ҇и бж҃е мо́й, ꙗ҆́кѡ не ѿри́нꙋлъ мѧ̀ є҆сѝ грѣ́шнаго, но ѻ҆́бщника мѧ̀ бы́ти ст҃ы́нь твои́хъ сподо́билъ є҆сѝ. Бл҃годарю́ тѧ, ꙗ҆́кѡ менѐ недосто́йнаго причасти́тисѧ пречⷭ҇ты́хъ твои́хъ и҆ нбⷭ҇ныхъ дарѡ́въ

Prayers of Thanksgiving
After Communion

When you will have received the good
Communion of the life-giving Mystical
Gifts, give praise at once, give thanks
greatly, and from the soul say fervently
unto God these things:

Glory to Thee, O God. Glory to Thee, O
God. Glory to Thee, O God.

Then this Prayer of Thanksgiving:

I thank Thee, O Lord my God, that Thou
hast not rejected me, a sinner, but hast
vouchsafed me to be a communicant of Thy
Holy Things. I thank Thee that Thou hast
vouchsafed me, the unworthy, to partake

сподобилъ є҆сѝ. Но, влⷣко чл҃вѣколю́бче, на́съ
ра́ди ѹ҆ме́рый же и҆ воскр҃сый, и҆ дарова́вый
на́мъ стра́шнаѧ сїѧ̑ и҆ животворѧ̑щаѧ
та̑инства во бл҃годѣѧ́нїе и҆ ѡ҆сщ҃е́нїе дꙋ́шъ
и҆ тѣле́съ на́шихъ, да́ждь бы́ти си̑мъ и҆ мнѣ̀
во и҆сцѣле́нїе дꙋшѝ же и҆ тѣ́ла, во ѿгна́нїе
всѧ́кагѡ сопроти́внагѡ, въ просвѣще́нїе
ѻ҆́чїю се́рдца моегѡ̀, въ ми́ръ дꙋше́вныхъ
мои́хъ си́лъ, въ вѣ́рꙋ непосты́днꙋ, въ любо́вь
нелицемѣ́рнꙋ, во и҆сполне́нїе премꙋ́дрости,
въ соблюде́нїе за́повѣдей твои́хъ, въ
приложе́нїе бж҃е́ственныѧ твоеѧ̀ бл҃года́ти,
и҆ твоегѡ̀ цр҃твїѧ присвое́нїе: да во ст҃ы́ни
твое́й тѣ́ми сохранѧ́емь, твою̀ бл҃года́ть
помина́ю всегда̀, и҆ не ктомꙋ̀ себѣ̀ живꙋ̀, но
тебѣ̀ на́шемꙋ влⷣцѣ и҆ бл҃годѣ́телю, и҆ та́кѡ
сегѡ̀ житїѧ̀ и҆зше́дъ ѡ҆ наде́жди живота̀
вѣ́чнагѡ, въ присносꙋ́щный дости́гнꙋ поко́й,
и҆дѣ́же пра́зднꙋющихъ гла́съ непреста́нный,
и҆ безконе́чнаѧ сла́дость, зрѧ́щихъ твоегѡ̀
лица̀ добро́тꙋ неизрече́ннꙋю: ты́ бо є҆сѝ
и҆́стинное жела́нїе и҆ неизрече́нное весе́лїе

of Thy most pure and heavenly Gifts. But, O Master, Lover of mankind, Who for our sake didst die and didst rise again, and didst bestow upon us these dread and life-giving Mysteries for the well-being and sanctification of our souls and bodies, grant that these may be even unto me for the healing of both soul and body, for the averting of everything hostile, for the enlightenment of the eyes of my heart, for the peace of the powers of my soul, for faith unashamed for love unfeigned, for the fullness of wisdom, for the keeping of Thy commandments, for an increase of Thy divine grace, and for the attainment of Thy Kingdom; that being preserved by Them in Thy holiness, I may always remember Thy grace, and no longer live for myself, but for Thee, our Master and Benefactor; and thus when I shall have departed this life in hope of life eternal, I may attain unto everlasting rest, where the sound of them that keep festival is unceasing and the delight is endless of

любѧщихъ тѧ, хрⷭ҇тѐ бж҃е нашъ, и҆ тѧ
пое́тъ всѧ̀ тва́рь во вѣ́ки. А҆ми́нь.

Вели́кагw Васі́лїа, втора́ѧ:

Влⷣко хрⷭ҇тѐ бж҃е, цр҃ю̀ вѣкẃвъ и҆ содѣ́телю
всѣ́хъ, бл҃годарю̀ тѧ ѡ҆ всѣ́хъ, я҆́же мѝ є҆сѝ
по́далъ, бл҃ги́хъ, и҆ ѡ҆ причаще́нїи пречⷭ҇тыхъ и҆
животворѧ́щихъ твои́хъ та́инствъ. Молю̀
ᲂу҆́бw тѧ̀, бл҃же и҆ чл҃вѣколю́бче: сохранѝ
мѧ подъ кро́вомъ твои́мъ и҆ въ сѣ́ни
крилᲂу҆ твоє́ю, и҆ да́рᲂу҆й мѝ чи́стою со́вѣстїю,
да́же до послѣ́днѧгw моегẁ и҆здыха́нїѧ,
досто́йнw причаща́тисѧ ст҃ы́нь твои́хъ во
ѡ҆ставле́нїе грѣхẃвъ и҆ въ жи́знь вѣ́чнᲂу҆ю.
Ты̀ бо є҆сѝ хлѣ́бъ живо́тный, и҆сто́чникъ
ст҃ы́ни, пода́тель бл҃ги́хъ: и҆ тебѣ̀ сла́вᲂу҆
возсыла́емъ, со Ѻ҆ц҃е́мъ, и҆ ст҃ы́мъ дх҃омъ,
ны́нѣ и҆ при́снw и҆ во вѣ́ки вѣкẃвъ. А҆ми́нь.

them that behold the ineffable beauty of Thy countenance. For Thou art the true desire and the unutterable gladness of them that love Thee, O Christ our God, and all creation doth hymn Thee unto the ages. Amen.

Of St. Basil the Great, 2:

O Master Christ our God, King of the ages and Creator of all things, I thank Thee for all the good things which Thou hast bestowed upon me and for the communion of Thy most pure and life-giving Mysteries. I pray Thee, therefore, O Good One and Lover of mankind: Keep me under Thy protection and in the shadow of Thy wings and grant me, even unto my last breath, to partake worthily, with a pure conscience, of Thy holy Things unto the remission of sins and life eternal. For Thou art the Bread of Life, the Source of Holiness, the Giver of good things, and unto Thee do we send up glory, together with the Father and the Holy Spirit, now and ever, and to the ages of ages. Amen.

Метафра́ста по стїхѡ́мъ, тре́тїа.

Да́вый пищꙋ мнѣ̀ пло́ть твою̀ во́лею,
ѻ҆́гнь сый, и҆ ѡ҆паля́й недосто́йныѧ, да
не ѡ҆пали́ши менѐ, содѣ́телю мо́й. Па́че
же пройдѝ во ᲂу҆́ды моѧ̑, во всѧ̑ соста́вы,
во ᲂу҆тро́бꙋ, въ се́рдце. Попалѝ те́рнїе
всѣ́хъ мои́хъ прегрѣше́нїй. Дꙋ́шꙋ ѡ҆чи́сти,
ѡ҆стѝ помышле́нїѧ. Соста́вы ᲂу҆твердѝ
съ костьмѝ вкꙋ́пѣ. Чꙋ́вствъ просвѣтѝ
просты̀ю пѧтери́цꙋ. Всего́ мѧ спригвоздѝ
стра́хꙋ твое́мъ. При́снѡ покры́й, соблюдѝ
же и҆ сохранѝ мѧ ѿ вся́кагѡ дѣ́ла и҆
сло́ва дꙋшетлѣ́ннагѡ. Ѡ҆чи́сти, и҆ ѡ҆мы́й,
и҆ ᲂу҆краси́ мѧ: ᲂу҆добрѝ, вразꙋмѝ, и҆ просвѣтѝ
мѧ. Покажи́ мѧ твоѐ селе́нїе є҆ди́нагѡ
дх҃а, и҆ не ктомꙋ̀ селе́нїе грѣха̀. Да ꙗ҆́кѡ
твоегѡ̀ до́мꙋ вхо́домъ прича́щенїа, ꙗ҆́кѡ
ѻ҆гнѧ̀ менѐ бѣ́житъ всѧ́къ злодѣ́й, всѧ́ка
стра́сть. Моли́твенники тебѣ̀ приношꙋ̀
всѧ̑ ст҃ы̑ѧ, чинонача́лїѧ же безпло́тныхъ,
предте́чꙋ твоего̀, мꙋ́дрыѧ а҆пⷭлы, къ си̑мъ

Verses of Metaphrastes, 3:

O Thou Who givest me willingly Thy Flesh as food, Thou Who art fire that doth consume the unworthy, burn me not, O my Creator. But rather, enter Thou into my members, into all my joints, my reigns, my heart. Burn up the thorns of all my sins. Purify my soul, sanctify my thoughts. Strengthen my substance together with my bones. Enlighten my simple five senses. Nail down the whole of me with Thy fear. Ever protect, preserve, and keep me from every soul-corrupting deed and word. Purify, cleanse and adorn me; make me comely, give me understanding and enlighten me. Show me to be the dwelling-place of Thy Spirit alone, and no longer a habitation of sin, that from me as Thine abode through the entry of Communion, every evildoer, every passion may flee as from fire. As intercessors I offer unto Thee all the saints, the commanders of the bodiless hosts, Thy Forerunner,

же твою нескверную чт҃ую мт҃рь, йхже
мольбы, бл҃гоутробне, прїимй, хрⷭ҇те мой, й
сы́номъ свѣта содѣлай твоегѡ̀ служи́теля.
Ты бо є҆ди́нъ є҆сѝ и ѡ҆сщ҃е́нїе на́шихъ, бл҃же,
дꙋшъ и свѣ́тлость, и тебѣ̀ лѣпоподо́бнѡ,
ꙗ҆́кѡ бг҃у и влⷣцѣ, сла́вꙋ всѝ возсыла́емъ
на всꙗ́къ де́нь.

Мл҃тва ина́а:

Тѣ́ло твоѐ ст҃о́е, гдⷭ҇н і҆и҃се хрⷭ҇тѐ бж҃е на́шъ,
да бꙋ́детъ мѝ въ живо́тъ вѣ́чный, и кро́вь
твоꙗ̀ чⷭ҇тна́а во ѡ҆ставле́нїе грѣхѡ́въ: бꙋ́ди
же мѝ бл҃годаре́нїе сїѐ въ ра́дость, здра́вїе и
весе́лїе, въ стра́шное же и второ́е прише́ствїе
твоѐ сподо́би мꙗ̀ грѣ́шнаго ста́ти ѡ҆десну́ю
сла́вы твоеꙗ̀, мл҃твами пречⷭ҇тыꙗ твоеꙗ̀
мт҃ре и всѣ́хъ ст҃ы́хъ.

Мл҃тва ина́а, ко престѣ́й бц҃ѣ:

Престⷶ́а влⷣчце бц҃е, свѣ́те помраче́нныꙗ
моеꙗ̀ дꙋшѝ, наде́жде, покро́ве, прибѣ́жище,

the wise apostles, and Thine undefiled pure Mother, whose entreaties do Thou accept, O my compassionate Christ, and make Thy servant a child of light. For Thou alone art the sanctification and radiance of our souls, O Good One, and unto Thee as God and Master, we all send up glory as is meet, every day.

Another Prayer:

O Lord Jesus Christ our God, may Thy Holy Body be unto me for life eternal, and Thy Precious Blood for the remission of sins; and may this Eucharist be unto me for joy, health, and gladness. And at Thy dread Second Coming, vouchsafe me, a sinner, to stand at the right hand of Thy glory, through the intercessions of Thy most pure Mother and of all the saints.

Another Prayer, to the Most Holy Theotokos:

O most-holy Lady, Theotokos, light of my darkened soul, my hope, protection, refuge,

оутѣшéнïе, рáдованïе моѐ: бл҃годарю̀ тѧ, ꙗ҆́кѡ сподóбила мѧ̀ є҆сѝ недостóйнаго, причáстника бы́ти пречⷭ҇таго тѣ́ла, и҆ чⷭ҇ты́ныѧ крóве сн҃а твоегѡ̀. Но рóждшаѧ и҆́стинный свѣ́тъ, просвѣтѝ моѧ̀ оу҆́мныѧ ó҆чи сéрдца: ꙗ҆́же и҆стóчникъ безсмéртïѧ рóждшаѧ, ѡ҆животворѝ мѧ оу҆мерцвлéннаго грѣхóмъ: ꙗ҆́же милостивагѡ бг҃а любоблгⷪутрóбнаѧ мт҃и, помилꙋ́й мѧ̀, и҆ дáждь мѝ оу҆миléнïе, и҆ сокрꙋшéнïе въ сéрдцѣ моéмъ, и҆ смирéнïе въ мы́слехъ моѝхъ, и҆ воззвáнïе въ плѣнéнïихъ помышлéнïй моѝхъ: и҆ сподóби мѧ̀ до послѣ́днагѡ и҆здыхáнïѧ, неѡсꙋждéннѡ прïимáти пречⷭ҇ты́хъ тáйнъ ѡ҆сщ҃éнïе, во и҆сцѣлéнïе дꙋшѝ же и҆ тѣ́ла: и҆ подáждь мѝ слéзы покаѧ́нïѧ и҆ и҆сповѣ́данïѧ, во є҆́же пѣ́ти и҆ слáвити тѧ̀ во всѧ̑ дни́ животá моегѡ̀, ꙗ҆́кѡ бл҃гословéнна и҆ препрослáвленна є҆сѝ во вѣ́ки. А҆ми́нь.

Конéцъ бл҃годáрственныхъ мл҃твъ по ст҃ѣмъ причащéнïи.

consolation, my joy; I thank thee that thou hast vouchsafed me, who am unworthy, to be a partaker of the most pure Body and precious Blood of thy Son. O thou who gavest birth to the True Light, do thou enlighten the spiritual eyes of my heart; thou who gavest birth to the Source of Immortality, revive me who am dead in sin; thou who art the lovingly-compassionate Mother of the merciful God, have mercy on me and grant me compunction and contrition in my heart, and humility in my thoughts, and the recall of my thoughts from captivity. And vouchsafe me until my last breath to receive without condemnation the sanctification of the most pure Mysteries for the healing of both soul and body; and grant me tears of repentance and confession, with which to hymn and glorify thee all the days of my life, for blessed and most glorified art thou unto the ages. Amen.

The end of the thanksgiving prayers
after Holy Communion.

Ѿпꙋ́сты влады́чнихъ
пра́здникѡвъ, глаго́лемїи є҆гда̀
быва́етъ бж҃е́ственнаѧ лїтꙋ́ргїа
ст҃и́телѧ васі́лїа вели́кагѡ.

На ржⷭ҇тво̀ хрⷭ҇то́во:

И҆́же въ верте́пѣ роди́выйсѧ, и҆ въ ꙗ҆́слѣхъ
возлеги́й, на́шегѡ ра́ди спⷭ҇е́нїѧ, хрⷭ҇то́съ
и҆́стинный бг҃ъ на́шъ: и҆ про́чее до конца̀.

На ѡ҆брѣ́занїе:

И҆́же во ѻ҆́смый де́нь пло́тїю ѡ҆брѣ́затисѧ
и҆зво́ливый, на́шегѡ ра́ди спⷭ҇е́нїѧ, хрⷭ҇то́съ
и҆́стинный бг҃ъ на́шъ:

Dismissals for Feasts of the Lord, which are said when the Divine Liturgy of Saint Basil the Great is served.

On the Nativity of Christ:

May Christ our true God, Who was born in a cave, and lay in a manger for our salvation … and the rest unto the end.

On the Circumcision:

May Christ our true God, Who on the eighth day deigned to be circumcised for our salvation…

На бгоꙗвле́нїе:

И҆́же во і҆ѻрда́нѣ крⷭ҇ти́тисѧ и҆зво́ливый ѿ і҆ѡа́нна, на́шегѡ ра́ди спⷭ҇е́нїѧ, хрⷭ҇то́съ и҆́стинный бг҃ъ на́шъ:

Въ вели́кїй четверто́къ:

И҆́же за превосходѧ́щꙋю бл҃гость пꙋ́ть добрѣ́йшїй смире́нїѧ показа́вый, внегда̀ оу҆мы́ти но́ги оу҆ченикѡ́въ, да́же и҆ до крⷭ҇та̀ и҆ погребе́нїѧ снизше́дый на́мъ, хрⷭ҇то́съ и҆́стинный бг҃ъ на́шъ:

On Theophany:

May Christ our true God, Who for our salvation deigned to be baptized by John in the Jordan...

On Great Thursday:

May Christ our true God, Who by His surpassing goodness did show the most excellent way of humility when He washed the feet of His disciples, and did condescend even unto the Cross and burial for us...

Прошє́нїѧ на ра́зныѧ потрє́бы

Є҆щѐ мо́лимсѧ тебѣ̀, гд҃у бг҃у на́шему, є҆́же оу҆слы́шатисѧ гла́су моле́нїѧ на́шегѡ, и҆ мл҃твѣ, и҆ поми́ловати рабѡ́въ твои́хъ и҆́мⷬ҇къ: бл҃года́тїю и҆ щедро́тами твои́ми, и҆ и҆спо́лнити всѧ̑ проше́нїѧ и҆́хъ, и҆ прости́ти и҆̀мъ всѧ̑ согрѣше́нїѧ во́льнаѧ и҆ нево́льнаѧ: бл҃гопрїѧ́тнымъ же бы́ти мольба́мъ и҆ ми́лостынамъ и҆́хъ предъ престо́ломъ влⷣчествїѧ твоегѡ̀, и҆ покры́ти и҆̀хъ ѿ вра̑гъ ви́димыхъ и҆ неви́димыхъ, ѿ всѧ́кїѧ напа́сти, бѣды̀ и҆ ско́рби, и҆ недꙋ́гѡвъ и҆зба́вити, и҆ пода́ти здра́вїе съ долгоде́нствїемъ: рце́мъ всѝ, гд҃и, оу҆слы́ши и҆ поми́луй.

Ли́къ: Гд҃и, поми́луй, г҃-жды.

Petitions for Various Needs

Again we pray Thee, O Lord our God, that Thou wouldst hearken unto the voice of our supplication and prayer, and have mercy on Thy servants N. through Thy grace and compassions, and fulfill all their petitions, and pardon them all transgressions voluntary and involuntary, let their prayers and alms be acceptable before the throne of Thy dominion, and protect them from enemies visible and invisible, from every temptation, harm, and sorrow, and deliver them from diseases, and grant them health and length of days: let us all say, O Lord, hearken and have mercy.

Choir: Lord, have mercy (thrice).

Призри, влко чл҃вѣколюбче, милостивнымъ
ти ѻкомъ на рабѡвъ твоихъ и҃мк: и
оу́слыши моле́нїѧ на́ша съ вѣ́рою
приносима̑ѧ, ꙗ́кѡ са́мъ ре́клъ є́си: всѧ̑
є҆лика молѧ́щесѧ проси́те, вѣ́руйте, ꙗ́кѡ
прїи́мете, и бу́детъ ва́мъ, и па́ки: проси́те
и да́стсѧ ва́мъ: сегѡ̀ ра́ди и мы̀, а́ще и
недосто́йнїи, оу҆пова́юще на ми́лость твою̀,
про́симъ: пода́ждь бл҃гость твою̀ рабѡ́мъ
твои́мъ и҃мк: и исполни бл҃га̑ѧ желанїѧ
и́хъ, ми́рнѡ же и ти́хѡ въ здра́вїи, и
долгоде́нствїи всѧ̑ дни̑ и́хъ соблюдѝ: рце́мъ
всѝ, скорѡ оу҆слы́ши и ми́лостивнѡ помилу́й.

Ли́къ: Г҃ди, поми́лу́й, г҃-жды.

Є҆щѐ мо́лимсѧ ѡ҆ предстоѧ́щихъ лю́дехъ,
ѡ҆жида́ющихъ ѿ тебѐ вели́кїѧ и бога́тыѧ
ми́лости, за всю̀ бра́тїю, и за всѧ̑ хр҇тїа́ны.

Ли́къ: Г҃ди, поми́лу́й, г҃-жды.

Look down, O Master, Lover of mankind, with Thy merciful eye, upon Thy servants N. and hearken unto our supplication which is offered with faith, for Thou Thyself hast said: "All things whatsoever ye shall ask in prayer, believe that ye shall receive, and it will be done unto you," and again: "Ask, and it shall be given to you." Therefore we, though we be unworthy, yet hoping in thy mercy, ask: bestow Thy kindness upon Thy servants N. and fulfill their good desires, preserve them all their days peacefully and calmly in health and length of days: let us all say, quickly hearken and graciously have mercy.

Choir: Lord, have mercy (thrice).

Again we pray for the people here present that await of Thee great and abundant mercy, for all the brethren, and for all Christians.

Choir: Lord, have mercy (thrice).

Е́ктенїа̀ ѡ̀ болѧ́щихъ:

Врачꙋ̀ дꙋ́шъ и̑ тѣле́съ, со оу̑миле́нїемъ въ се́рдцѣ сокрꙋше́нномъ къ тебѣ̀ припа́даемъ, и̑ стена́ще вопїе́мъ тѝ: и̑сцѣлѝ болѣ́зни, оу̑врачꙋ́й стра́сти дꙋ́шъ и̑ тѣле́съ рабѡ́въ твои́хъ и̑м҃къ: и̑ простѝ и̑мъ , ꙗ̑кѡ бл҃госе́рдъ, всѧ̑ прегрѣше́нїѧ, во́льнаѧ и̑ нево́льнаѧ, и̑ ско́рѡ воздви́гни ѿ о̑дра̀ болѣ́зни, мо́лимъ ти сѧ, оу̑слы́ши и̑ поми́лꙋй.

Ли́къ: Гд҃и, поми́лꙋй, г҃-жды.

Не хотѧ́й сме́рти грѣ́шныхъ, но є̑́же ѡ̑брати́тисѧ и̑ живы̑мъ и̑мъ бы́ти, пощадѝ и̑ поми́лꙋй рабѡ́въ твои́хъ и̑м҃къ: ми́лостиве, запретѝ болѣ́зни, ѿ ста́ви всю̀ стра́сть, и̑ ве́сь недꙋ́гъ, оу̑толѝ зи́мꙋ и̑ о̑́гнь, и̑ прострѝ крѣ́пкꙋю твою̀ рꙋ́кꙋ, и̑ ꙗ̑коже і̑аі́ровꙋ дще́рь ѿ о̑дра̀ болѣ́зни воздви́гни, и̑ здра́выхъ предста́ви, мо́лимъ ти сѧ, оу̑слы́ши и̑ поми́лꙋй.

Litany for the Sick:

O Physician of souls and bodies, with compunction and broken hearts we fall down before Thee, and groaning we cry unto Thee: heal the sicknesses, heal the passions of the soul and body of Thy servants N., and pardon them, for Thou art kindhearted, all transgressions, voluntary and involuntary, and quickly raise them up from the bed of sickness, we pray thee, hearken and have mercy.

Choir: Lord, have mercy (thrice).

O Thou Who desirest not the death of sinners, but rather that they should return to Thee, and live: Spare and have mercy on Thy servants N., O Merciful One, banish sickness, drive away all passion, and all ailments, assuage chill and fever, and stretch forth Thy mighty arm and, as Thou didst raise up Jairus' daughter from the bed of sickness, restore them to health, we pray Thee, hearken and have mercy.

Ли́къ: Гд҃и, поми́луй, г҃-жды.

Ѻ҆гненнꙋю бол́езнь петро́вой те́щи прикоснове́нїемъ твои́мъ и҆сц́ели́вый, и҆ ны́н́е лю́т́е стра́ждꙋщихъ рабѡ́въ твои́хъ и҆́мⷬ҇къ: бол́езнь благосе́рдїемъ твои́мъ и҆сц́ели́, здра́вїе и҆́мъ ско́рѡ подава́ѧ, прил́ежнѡ мо́лимъ ти сѧ, и҆сто́чниче ц́ельба́мъ, оу҆слы́ши и҆ поми́лꙋй.

Ли́къ: Гд҃и, поми́лꙋй, г҃-жды.

Є҆щѐ мо́лимсѧ гдꙋ҃ бг҃ꙋ на́шемꙋ, ѡ е́же оу҆слы́шати гла́съ моле́нїѧ на́съ гр́ешныхъ, и҆ поми́ловати рабѡ́въ свои́хъ, и҆́мⷬ҇къ и҆ покры́ти и҆́хъ ѿ всѧ́кїѧ ско́рби, б́еды̀, гн́ева и҆ нꙋ́жды, и҆ ѿ всѧ́кїѧ бол́езни дꙋше́вныѧ и҆ т́еле́сныѧ, дарова́ти же и҆́мъ здра́вїе съ долгоде́нствїемъ, рце́мъ всѝ: ско́рѡ оу҆слы́ши и҆ ми́лтивнѡ поми́лꙋй.

Ли́къ: Гд҃и, поми́лꙋй, г҃-жды.

Choir: Lord, have mercy (thrice).

O Thou Who by thy touch didst heal Peter's mother-in-law who was sick with fever: do Thou now, in Thy loving-kindness, heal Thy terribly-suffering servants of their malady, quickly granting them health, we diligently pray Thee, O Fount of healing, hearken and have mercy.

Choir: Lord, have mercy (thrice).

Again we pray to the Lord our God, that He may hearken unto the voice of the supplications of us sinners, and have mercy on His servants N., and protect them from all tribulation, harm, wrath, and necessity, and from every sickness of soul and body, granting them health with length of days, let us all say, quickly hearken and graciously have mercy.

Choir: Lord, have mercy (thrice).

Ѽ пꙋтешє́ствꙋющихъ:

Стѡпы̀ человѣ́ческїѧ исправлѧ́ѧй, гдⷭ҇и, при́зри ми́лостивнѡ на рабы̀ твоѧ̀ и҆́мⷬ҇къ, и прости́въ и҆̀мъ всѧ́кое прегрѣше́нїе, во́льное же и невольное, блгⷭ҇овѝ бл҃го́е намѣ́ренїе совѣ́та и҆́хъ, и и҆схо́ды и входы со пꙋтьшє́ствїемъ испра́ви, прилѣ́жнѡ мо́лимъ ти сѧ, оу҆слы́ши и помилꙋ́й.

Ли́къ: Гдⷭ҇и, поми́лꙋй, г҃-жды.

Ї҆ѡси́фа ѿ ѡ҆ѕлобле́нїѧ бра́тїй є҆гѡ̀ пресла́внѡ свободи́вый гдⷭ҇и, и во є҆гѵ́петъ тогѡ̀ наста́вивый, и блгⷭ҇ове́нїемъ твоеѧ̀ бл҃гости во все́мъ блгополꙋ́чна сотвори́вый: и си́хъ рабѡ́въ твои́хъ пꙋтьшє́ствовати хотѧ́щихъ блгⷭ҇овѝ, и ше́ствїе и҆́хъ безмате́жно и блгополꙋ́чно сотворѝ, мо́лимъ ти сѧ, оу҆слы́ши и помилꙋ́й.

Ли́къ: Гдⷭ҇и, поми́лꙋй, г҃-жды.

For Those Who Journey:

O Lord, Who dost guide the footsteps of mankind, graciously look upon Thy servants N., and pardoning them every transgression, both voluntary and involuntary, bless the good intention of their counsel, and guide their goings out and comings in on the journey, we earnestly pray Thee, hearken and have mercy.

Choir: Lord, have mercy (thrice).

O Lord, Who didst most gloriously deliver Joseph from the animosity of his brethren, and didst lead him to Egypt, and through the blessing of Thy goodness didst make him to prosper in all things: Bless also these Thy servants who desire to travel, and cause their journey to be safe and tranquil, we pray Thee, hearken and have mercy.

Choir: Lord, have mercy (thrice).

Блгодарє́нїе ѡ полꙋчє́нїи прошє́нїѧ:

Блгодара́ще со стра́хомъ и трепе́томъ ꙗ́кѡ
раби̂ непотрє́бнїи, твоемꙋ̀ блгоꙋтро́бїю, спсе
и влⷣко на́шъ гдⷭ҇и, ѡ твои́хъ блгодѣѧ́нїихъ,
ꙗ́же изліа́лъ є҆сѝ и҆зоби́льнѡ на рабѣ́хъ
твои́хъ, и припа́даемъ и славосло́вїе тебѣ̀
ꙗ́кѡ бгꙋ прино́симъ, и ꙋ҆милє́ннѡ вопїє́мъ:
и҆зба́ви ѿ всѣ́хъ бѣ́дъ рабы̀ твоѧ̂, и всегда̀,
ꙗ́кѡ млⷭ҇тивъ, и҆спо́лни во блги́хъ жела́нїе
всѣ́хъ на́съ, прилѣ́жнѡ мо́лимъ ти сѧ,
ꙋ҆слы́ши и поми́лꙋй.

Ли́къ: Гдⷭ҇и, поми́лꙋй, г҃-жды.

Ꙗ́коже нынѣ̀ млⷭ҇тивнѡ ꙋ҆слы́шалъ є҆сѝ
мл҃твы рабѡ́въ твои́хъ гдⷭ҇и, и ꙗ҆ви́лъ є҆сѝ
на ни́хъ блгоꙋтро́бїе члвѣколю́бїѧ твоегѡ̀,
си́це и въ прє́дняѧ не презира́й, и҆спо́лни во
сла́вꙋ твою̀ всѧ̂ блга̂ѧ хотѣ́нїѧ вѣ́рныхъ
твои́хъ, и ꙗ҆вѝ всѣ́мъ на́мъ бога́тꙋю млⷭ҇ть

Thanksgiving for Petitions Granted:

Giving thanks with fear and trembling, as unprofitable servants, unto Thy loving-kindness, O Lord our Saviour and Master, for Thy benefits which Thou hast poured out abundantly on Thy servants, we fall down in worship and offer a doxology unto Thee as God, and fervently cry aloud to Thee: deliver Thou Thy servants from all misfortune, and, as Thou art merciful, always fulfill the desires of us all unto good, we diligently pray Thee, hearken and have mercy.

Choir: Lord, have mercy (thrice).

In that Thou now hast mercifully hearkened unto the prayers of Thy servants, O Lord, and hast manifested upon us the tender compassion of Thy love for mankind, so also, in time to come, disdaining us not, do Thou fulfill, unto Thy glory, all good desires of Thy faithful, and show unto all of us Thine

твою̀, всѧ̑ на́мъ согрѣше́нїѧ презира́ѧ: мо́лимъ ти сѧ, ᲂу҆слы́ши и҆ поми́луй.

Ли́къ: Гдⷭ҇и, поми́луй, г҃-жды.

abundant mercy, disregarding all our iniquities, we pray Thee, hearken and have mercy.

Choir: Lord, have mercy (thrice).

Чи́нъ бж҃е́ственныѧ літꙋргі́и, когда̀ соедина́етсѧ съ вече́рней

Слꙋчи́вшейсѧ въ вели́кїй четверто́къ, вели́кꙋю сꙋббѡ́тꙋ, и̑ про́чихъ дне́й въ годꙋ̀.

Проскомі́дїа соверша́етсѧ по ѻ̑бы́чаю. А҆ще цр҃кїе часы̀ не пою́тсѧ, часы̀ г҃ій, и̑ ѕ҃ый, и̑ ѳ҃ый чте́мъ вкꙋ́пѣ съ и̑зѡбрази́тельными. По ѿпꙋ́стѣ и̑зѡбрази́тельныхъ, вре́мени же наста́вшꙋ, сщ҃е́нникъ со дїа́кономъ, ста́вше вкꙋ́пѣ пред̾ ст҃о́ю трапе́зою, покланѧ́ютсѧ три́жды, въ себѣ̀ молѧ́щесѧ, и̑ глаго́люще:

Сщ҃е́нникъ: Цр҃ю̀ небе́сный: и̑ про́чее какъ ѻ̑бы́чно.

The Order of the Vesperal Liturgy

As appointed on Holy Thursday, Holy Saturday, and certain other days of the year

The priest performs the proskomedia as directed in the Service Book, and we serve the 3rd, 6th, and 9th hours together with the Typica. After the dismissal of the Typica, at the appointed time, the priest and deacon gather before the Holy Table and bow down thrice, while praying secretly, saying:

Priest: **O Heavenly King….** and the rest as usual.

дїа́конъ и҆схо́днтъ пре́дъ ст҃ы́мн две́рьмн, и҆
глаго́летъ: Бл҃гословн̀, влады́ко.

І҆ере́й: Бл҃гослове́но цр҃тво:

    Ли́къ: А҆ми́нь.

И҆ чте́цъ: Сла́ва тебѣ̀, бж҃е на́шъ, сла́ва
тебѣ́. Цр҃ю̀ небе́сный: Трист҃о́е: Прест҃а́ѧ тр҃це:
О́ч҃е на́шъ:

Сщ҃е́нннкъ: Га́кѡ твоѐ є́сть цр҃тво:

    І҆ере́й же поклони́вса ст҃ѣ́й трапе́зѣ
и҆схо́днтъ сѣ́верною две́рью. Сва̃ще́нннкъ и҆
дїа́конъ стоѧ́тъ на а҆мвѡ́нѣ и҆ кла́нѧютса
тр́нжды пре́дъ ст҃ы́мъ а҆лтаре́мъ, н дрꙋ́гъ
дрꙋ́гꙋ. Посе́мъ дїа́конъ вхо́днтъ въ а҆лта́рь и҆
чте́цъ глаго́летъ ѱало́мъ р҃г:

И҆ ѱало́мъ р҃г: Благословѝ, дꙋ́шѐ моѧ̀, гд҃а, гд҃н
бж҃е мо́й:

    І҆ере́й же пре́дъ ст҃ы́мн две́рьмн ста́въ
ꙋ҆крове́нною главо́ю, глаго́летъ моли́твы
свѣти́льннчныѧ.

And the deacon goes out before the holy doors, and says: **Bless Master.**

And the priest: **Blessed is the Kingdom . . .**
  Choir: **Amen.**
And the reader: **Glory to Thee, Our God, Glory to Thee. O Heavenly King . . .** Trisagion to **Our Father...**

Priest: **For Thine is the Kingdom....**

And the priest venerates the Holy Table and exits the altar through the north deacon's door. The priest and deacon stand on the ambon and make three bows toward the altar, and one to each other. Then the deacon enters the altar and the reader chants Psalm 103:

Bless the Lord, O my soul. O Lord my God ...

And the priest, having stood bareheaded before the holy doors, saith the Lamp-lighting Prayers.

Моли́тва а҃.

Г҃ди ще́дрый и ми́лостивый, долготерпѣ_ли́ве и многоми́лостиве, внꙋши́ моли́твꙋ на́шꙋ и вонми́ гла́сꙋ моле́нїѧ на́шегѡ, сотвори́ съ на́ми зна́менїе во бла́го: наста́ви на́съ на пꙋ́ть тво́й, є҆́же ходи́ти во и҆́стинѣ твое́й, возвесели́ сердца̀ на́ша, во є҆́же боѧ́тисѧ и҆́мене твоегѡ̀ ст҃а́гѡ: занѐ ве́лїй є҆си́ ты̀ и творѧ́й чꙋдеса̀, ты̀ є҆си́ бг҃ъ є҆ди́нъ, и҆ нѣ́сть подо́бенъ тебѣ̀ въ бозѣ́хъ, гд҃и: си́ленъ въ ми́лости и҆ бла́гъ въ крѣ́пости, во є҆́же помога́ти, и҆ ѹ҆тѣша́ти, и҆ спаса́ти всѧ̑ ѹ҆пова́ющыѧ во и҆́мѧ ст҃о́е твоѐ.

Ꙗ҆́кѡ подоба́етъ тебѣ̀ всѧ́каѧ сла́ва, че́сть и҆ поклоне́нїе, ѻ҆ц҃ꙋ̀ и҆ сн҃ꙋ и҆ ст҃о́мꙋ дх҃ꙋ, ны́нѣ и҆ при́снѡ и҆ во вѣ́ки вѣкѡ́въ, а҆ми́нь.

Моли́тва в҃.

Г҃ди, да не ꙗ҆́ростїю твое́ю ѡ҆бличи́ши на́съ, нижѐ гнѣ́вомъ твои́мъ нака́жеши на́съ,

First Prayer

O Lord, compassionate and merciful, long-suffering and plenteous in mercy, give ear unto our prayer and attend to the voice of our supplication; work in us a sign unto good; guide us in Thy way, that we may walk in Thy truth; gladden our heart that we may fear Thy holy name; for Thou art great and workest wonders, Thou alone art God, and there is none like unto Thee among the gods, O Lord: strong in mercy and good in might, to help and comfort, and to save all that hope in Thy holy name.

For unto Thee is due all glory, honor, and worship: to the Father, and to the Son, and to the Holy Spirit now and ever, and unto the ages of ages. Amen.

Second Prayer

O Lord, rebuke us not in Thine anger, nor chasten us in Thy wrath, but deal

но сотвори съ нами по милости твоей, врачꙋ
й исцѣлителю дꙋшъ нашихъ: настави насъ
ко пристанищꙋ хотѣнїѧ твоегѡ: просвѣти
ѻчи сердецъ нашихъ въ познанїе твоеѧ
истины: и дарꙋй намъ прочее настоѧщагѡ
дне мирное и безгрѣшное, и все времѧ
живота нашегѡ, молитвами стыѧ бцы
и всѣхъ стыхъ.

Ꙗкѡ твоѧ держава, и твое єсть
царство, и сила, и слава, ѻца и сна и
стагѡ дха, нынѣ и приснѡ и во вѣки
вѣкѡвъ, Аминь.

Молитва г҃.

Гди, бже нашъ, помѧни насъ грѣшныхъ
и непотребныхъ рабъ твоихъ, внегда
призывати намъ стое покланѧемое имѧ
твое, и не посрами насъ ѿ чаѧнїѧ милости
твоеѧ: но дарꙋй намъ, всѧ ꙗже ко спасенїю
прошенїѧ, и сподоби насъ любити, и

with us according to Thy mercy, O Physician and Healer of our souls. Guide us to the haven of Thy will; enlighten the eyes of our hearts to the knowledge of Thy truth; and grant unto us that the remainder of the present day and the whole time of our life may be peaceful and sinless, through the intercessions of the holy Theotokos and of all the saints.

For Thine is the dominion, and Thine is the kingdom, and the power, and the glory, of the Father, and of the Son, and of the Holy Spirit, now and ever, and unto the ages Of ages. Amen.

Third Prayer

O Lord our God, remember us, Thy sinful and unprofitable servants, when we call upon Thy holy, venerable name, and turn us not away in shame from the expectation of Thy mercy; but grant us, O Lord, all our requests which are unto salvation, and

боѧ́тисѧ тебѐ ѿ всегѡ̀ се́рдца на́шегѡ, и̂
твори́ти во все́хъ во́лю твою̀.

Ꙗ҆́кѡ бла́гъ и̂ человѣ́колю́бецъ бг҃ъ є҆сѝ,
и̂ тебѣ̀ сла́вꙋ возсыла́емъ, ѻ҆ц҃ꙋ̀ и̂ сн҃ꙋ и̂
ст҃о́мꙋ дх҃ꙋ, ны́нѣ и̂ при́снѡ и̂ во вѣ́ки
вѣкѡ́въ, а҆ми́нь.

Моли́тва д҃.

Н е́молчными пѣ́сньми и̂ непреста́нными
славословле́ньми ѿ ст҃ы́хъ си́лъ вос-
пѣва́емый, и̂спо́лни оу҆ста̀ на́ша хвале́нїѧ
твоегѡ̀, є҆́же пода́ти вели́чествїе и̂́мени
твоемꙋ̀ ст҃о́мꙋ: и̂ да́ждь на́мъ оу҆ча́стїе
и̂ наслѣ́дїе со всѣ́ми боѧ́щимисѧ тебѐ
и҆́стиною и̂ храня́щими за́повѣди твоѧ̀,
моли́твами ст҃ы́ѧ бц҃ы и̂ всѣ́хъ ст҃ы́хъ
твои́хъ.

Ꙗ҆́кѡ подоба́етъ тебѣ̀ всѧ́каѧ сла́ва,
че́сть и̂ поклоне́нїе, ѻ҆ц҃ꙋ̀ и̂ сн҃ꙋ и̂ ст҃о́мꙋ
дх҃ꙋ, ны́нѣ и̂ при́снѡ и̂ во вѣ́ки вѣкѡ́въ,
а҆ми́нь.

vouchsafe us to love and fear Thee with our whole heart, and to do Thy will in all things.

For a good God art Thou, and the Lover of mankind, and unto Thee do we send up glory: to the Father, and to the Son, and to the Holy Spirit, now and ever, and unto the ages of ages. Amen

Fourth Prayer

O Thou Who art praised in song with perpetual hymns and unceasing doxologies of the holy hosts, fill our mouth with Thy praise, that we may magnify Thy holy name. And grant unto us a portion and an inheritance with all that truly fear Thee and keep Thy commandments, through the intercessions of the holy Theotokos and all Thy saints.

For unto Thee is due all glory, honor, and worship, to the Father, and to the Son, and to the Holy Spirit, now and ever, and unto the ages of ages. Amen.

Моли́тва є҃.

Гдⷭ҇и, гдⷭ҇и, пречⷭ҇тою твое́ю дла́нїю содержа́й всѧ́ческаѧ, долготерпѧ́й на всѣ́хъ на́съ и҆ ка́ѧйсѧ ѡ҆ ѕло́бахъ на́шихъ, помѧни̑ ще́дрѡты твоѧ̑ и҆ ми́лость твою̀, посѣти́ ны твое́ю бла́гостїю, и҆ да́ждь на́мъ и҆збѣжа́ти и҆ про́чее настоѧ́щагѡ днѐ, твое́ю благода́тїю, ѿ разли́чныхъ ко́зней лꙋка́вагѡ, и҆ ненавѣ́тнꙋ жи́знь на́шꙋ соблюди̑ благода́тїю всест҃а́гѡ твоегѡ̀ дх҃а.

Мⷭ҇тїю и҆ человѣколю́бїемъ є҆диноро́днагѡ твоегѡ̀ сн҃а, съ ни́мже благослове́нъ є҆сѝ, со всест҃ы́мъ и҆ благи́мъ и҆ животворѧ́щимъ твои́мъ дх҃омъ, ны́нѣ и҆ прⷭ҇нѡ и҆ во вѣ́ки вѣкѡ́въ. А҆ми́нь.

Моли́тва ѕ҃.

Бж҃е вели́кїй и҆ ди́вный, неиспⷭ҇вѣди́мою бла́гостїю и҆ бога́тымъ про́мысломъ ѹ҆правлѧ́ѧй всѧ́ческаѧ: и҆ мїрска́ѧ на́мъ

Fifth Prayer

O Lord, O Lord, Who holdest all things in the most pure hollow of Thy hand, Who art long-suffering toward us all and repentest Thee at our wickedness, remember Thy compassions and Thy mercy. Visit us with Thy goodness, and grant unto us during the remainder of the present day, by Thy grace, to flee the various snares of the evil one, and keep our life unassailed through the grace of Thine all-holy Spirit.

Through the mercy and love for mankind of Thine Only-begotten Son, with Whom Thou art blessed, together with Thine all-holy and good and life-creating Spirit, now and ever, and unto the ages of ages. Amen.

Sixth Prayer

O God, great and wondrous, Who with unsearchable goodness and abundant providence orderest all things, and grantest unto us earthly good things; Who hast

блага̑ѧ дарова́вый, и̑ спорꙋ́чивый на́мъ
ѡ̑бѣща́нное ца́рство, ѡ̑бѣща́нными бл҃ги́ми
пꙋтесотвори́вый на́мъ и̑ днѐ преше́дшꙋю
ча́сть ѿ всѧ́кагѡ ꙋ̑клони́тисѧ ѕла̀: да́рꙋй
на́мъ и̑ про́чее непоро́чнѡ соверши́ти предъ
ст҃о́ю сла́вою твое́ю, пѣ́ти тѧ̀ є̑ди́наго
блага́гѡ и̑ человѣколюби́вагѡ бг҃а на́шегѡ.

Ꙗ̑́кѡ ты̀ є̑сѝ бг҃ъ на́шъ, и̑ тебѣ̀ сла́вꙋ
возсыла́емъ, ѻ̑ц҃ꙋ и̑ сн҃ꙋ и̑ ст҃о́мꙋ дх҃ꙋ, ны́нѣ
и̑ при́снѡ и̑ во вѣ́ки вѣкѡ́въ. А̑ми́нь.

Моли́тва з҃.

Б҃же вели́кїй и̑ вы́шнїй, є̑ди́нъ и̑мѣ́ѧй
безсме́ртїе, во свѣ́тѣ живы́й непри
стꙋ́пнѣмъ, всю̀ тва́рь премꙋ́дростїю
созда́вый, раздѣли́вый междꙋ̀ свѣ́томъ
и̑ междꙋ̀ тмо́ю, и̑ со́лнце положи́вый во
ѻ̑́бласть но́щи, сподо́бивый на́съ грѣ́шныхъ
и̑ въ настоѧ́щїй ча́съ предвари́ти лицѐ твоѐ

given us a pledge of the promised kingdom through the good things already bestowed upon us; and hast made us to shun all evil during that part of the day which is past: grant us also to fulfill the remainder of this day blamelessly before Thy holy glory and to hymn Thee, our God, the only good and the Lover of mankind.

For Thou art our God, and unto Thee do we send up glory: to the Father, and to the Son, and to the Holy Spirit, now and ever, and unto the ages of ages. Amen

Seventh Prayer

O great and most high God, Who alone hast immortality, and dwellest in light unapproachable; Who hast fashioned all creation in wisdom; Who hast divided the light from the darkness, and hast set the sun for dominion over the day, the moon and stars for dominion over the night, Who hast vouchsafed unto us sinners at this

исповѣданіемъ и вечéрнее тебѣ славослóвїе
принести: самъ, человѣколю́бче, испрáви
молитвꙋ нáшꙋ ꙗ́кѡ кадило предъ тобóю
и прїими ю̀ въ воню̀ благоꙋхáнїа: подáждь
же нáмъ настоѧ́щїй вéчеръ и приходѧ́щꙋю
нóщь мирнꙋ: ѡблецы́ ны во ѻрꙋжїе свѣ́та:
избáви ны ѿ стрáха нощнáгѡ и всѧ́кїѧ вéщи
во тмѣ̀ преходѧ́щїѧ: и дáждь сóнъ, єгóже
во оу̑покоéнїе нéмощи нáшей даровáлъ є̑сѝ,
всѧ́кагѡ мечтáнїѧ дїáвола ѿчꙋждéнный.
Є́й, влⷣко, благи́хъ подáтелю, да и на лóжахъ
нáшихъ оу̑милѧ́ющеся, помнáемъ въ нощѝ
и́мѧ твоѐ, и поꙋчéнїемъ твои́хъ зáповѣдей
просвѣщáеми, въ рáдости дꙋшéвнѣй востá-
немъ ко славослóвїю твоеѧ̀ блáгости,
молéнїѧ и молитвы твоемꙋ̀ благоꙋтрóбїю
принося́ще ѡ свои́хъ согрѣшéнїихъ и всѣ́хъ
людéй твои́хъ, ꙗ́же, молитвами стⷯы́ѧ
бцⷣы, ми́лостїю посѣтѝ.

present hour to come before Thy presence with thanksgiving and to offer unto Thee our evening doxology: do Thou Thyself, O Lover of mankind, direct our prayer as incense before Thee and accept it as a sweet-smelling savor; grant unto us that the present evening and the coming night be peaceful. Clothe us with the armor of light. Deliver us from the terror by night and from every-thing that walketh in darkness. And grant that the sleep which Thou hast given for the repose of our infirmity may be free from all fantasies of the devil. Yea, O Master, Giver of good things, may we, being moved to compunction upon our beds, remember Thy name in the night, and, enlightened by meditation on Thy commandments, arise in joyfulness of soul to the glorification of Thy goodness, offering prayers and suppli-cations to Thy lovingkindness for our own sins and for those of all Thy people, whom do Thou visit in mercy, through the interces-sions of the holy Theotokos.

Ꙗ́кѡ бла́гъ и҆ человѣколю́бецъ бг҃ъ є҆сѝ, и҆ тебѣ̀ сла́вꙋ возсыла́емъ, ѻ҆ц҃ꙋ и҆ сн҃ꙋ и҆ ст҃о́мꙋ дх҃ꙋ, ны́нѣ и҆ при́снѡ и҆ во вѣ́ки вѣкѡ́въ, а҆ми́нь.

И҆спо́лншꙋсѧ же предначина́тельномꙋ ѱалмꙋ̀, дїа́конъ, и҆зше́дъ сѣ́верною страно́ю, твори́тъ вкꙋ́пѣ со сщ҃éнникомъ къ восто́кꙋ пред ст҃ы́ми две́рьми поклонéнїѧ трѝ, и҆ посе́мъ дрꙋ́гъ ко дрꙋ́гꙋ покло́нъ є҆ди́нъ. сщ҃éнникъ вхо́дитъ въ а҆лта́рь, и҆ дїа́конъ, ста́въ на ѻ҆бы́чномъ мѣ́стѣ, глаго́летъ є҆ктенїю̀ сїю̀:

Ми́ромъ гд҃ꙋ помо́лимсѧ.

Ли́къ: Гд҃и, поми́лꙋй.

Ѡ҆ свы́шнѣмъ ми́рѣ, и҆ спасéнїи дꙋ́шъ на́шихъ, гд҃ꙋ помо́лимсѧ.

Ли́къ: Гд҃и, поми́лꙋй.

Ѡ҆ ми́рѣ всегѡ̀ мі́ра, благостоѧ́нїи ст҃ы́хъ бж҃їихъ церквéй, и҆ соединéнїи всѣ́хъ, гд҃ꙋ помо́лимсѧ.

For a good God art Thou, and the Lover of mankind, and unto Thee do we send up glory: to the Father, and to the Son, and to the Holy Spirit, now and ever, and unto the ages of ages. Amen.

When the Introductory Psalm is finished, the deacon having come out by the northern door, together with the priest makes three bows toward the altar, and one to each other, and the priest enters the holy altar. The deacon stands before the Royal Doors and intones the Great Litany:

In peace let us pray to the Lord.

Choir: Lord, have mercy.

For the peace from above, and the salvation of our souls, let us pray to the Lord.

Choir: Lord, have mercy.

For the peace of the whole world, the good estate of the holy churches of God, and the union of all, let us pray to the Lord.

Ли́къ: Гдⷭ҇и, поми́лꙋй.

Ѡ҆ ст҃ѣ́мъ хрⷶ́мѣ сéмъ, и҆ съ вѣ́рою, бл҃го_
говѣ́нїемъ и҆ стрⷶ́хомъ бж҃їимъ входѧ́щихъ
въ ѻ҆́нь, гдⷭ҇ꙋ помо́лимсѧ.

Ли́къ: Гдⷭ҇и, поми́лꙋй.

Ѡ҆ вели́комъ господи́нѣ и҆ ѻ҆тцѣ̀ нáшемъ
ст҃ѣ́йшемъ патрїáрсѣ и҆м҃къ, и҆ ѡ҆ господи́нѣ
нáшемъ высокопреѡсщ҃éннѣ́йшемъ митро_
поли́тѣ и҆м҃къ, первоїерáрсѣ рꙋ́сскїѧ зарꙋбѣ́жныѧ
цр҃кве, и҆ ѡ҆ господи́нѣ нáшемъ высокопреѡс_
сщ҃éннѣ́йшемъ а҆рхїепі́скопѣ [и҆лѝ
преѡсщ҃éннѣ́йшемъ є҆пі́скопѣ] и҆м҃къ [є҆гѡ́же
є҆́сть ѻ҆́бласть], честнѣ́мъ пресвꙋ́терствѣ,
во хрⷭ҇тѣ̀ дїáконствѣ, ѡ҆ всéмъ при́чтѣ и҆
лю́дехъ, гдⷭ҇ꙋ помо́лимсѧ.

Ли́къ: Гдⷭ҇и, поми́лꙋй.

Ѡ҆ странѣ̀ сéй, властéхъ и҆ во́инствѣ є҆ѧ̀,
гдⷭ҇ꙋ помо́лимсѧ.

Ли́къ: Гдⷭ҇и, поми́лꙋй.

Ѡ҆ бг҃охрани́мѣй странѣ̀ рѡссі́йстѣй и҆ ѡ҆
правослáвныхъ лю́дехъ є҆ѧ̀ во ѻ҆тéчествїи

Choir: Lord, have mercy.

For this holy temple, and for them that with faith, reverence, and the fear of God enter herein, let us pray to the Lord.

Choir: Lord, have mercy.

For our great lord and father, the Most Holy Patriarch N.; for our lord, the Very Most Reverend Metropolitan N., First Hierarch of the Russian Church Abroad; for our lord, the Most Reverend Archbishop [or Bishop] N. (whose diocese this is); for the honorable priesthood, the diaconate in Christ, for all the clergy and people, let us pray to the Lord.

Choir: Lord, have mercy.

For this land, its authorities, and armed forces, and for all who with faith and piety dwell therein, let us pray to the Lord.

Choir: Lord, have mercy.

For the God-preserved Russian land and its Orthodox people both in the homeland and

й разсѣ́ѧнїи су́щихъ, и ѡ спасе́нїи и҆̀хъ, гд҃у
помо́лимсѧ.

Ли́къ: Гд҃и, поми́лу́й.

Ѡ є҆́же и҆зба́вити лю́ди своѧ̀ ѿ вра̑гъ
ви́димыхъ и҆ неви́димыхъ, въ на́съ же
оу҆тверди́ти є҆диномы́слїе, братолю́бїе и҆
благоче́стїе, гд҃у помо́лимсѧ.

Ли́къ: Гд҃и, поми́лу́й.

Ѡ гра́дѣ се́мъ [и҆лѝ ѡ ве́си се́й, и҆лѝ ѡ ст҃ѣ́й
о҆би́тели се́й], всѧ́комъ гра́дѣ, странѣ̀ и҆
вѣ́рою живу́щихъ въ ни́хъ, гд҃у помо́лимсѧ.

Ли́къ: Гд҃и, поми́лу́й.

Ѡ благорастворе́нїи возду́ховъ, ѡ и҆зоби́лїи
плодѡ́въ земны́хъ и҆ време́нѣхъ ми́рныхъ,
гд҃у помо́лимсѧ.

Ли́къ: Гд҃и, поми́лу́й.

Ѡ пла́вающихъ, путеше́ствующихъ,
недугу́ющихъ, стра́ждущихъ, плѣне́нныхъ
и҆ ѡ спасе́нїи и҆̀хъ, гд҃у помо́лимсѧ.

Ли́къ: Гд҃и, поми́лу́й.

in the diaspora, and for their salvation, let us pray to the Lord.

Choir: Lord, have mercy.

That He may deliver His people from enemies visible and invisible, and confirm in us oneness of mind, brotherly love, and piety, let us pray to the Lord.

Choir: Lord, have mercy.

For this city, (or village, or holy monastery), for every city and country, and the faithful that dwell therein, let us pray to the Lord.

Choir: Lord, have mercy.

For seasonable weather, abundance of the fruits of the earth, and peaceful times, let us pray to the Lord.

Choir: Lord, have mercy.

For travelers by sea, land, and air; for the sick, the suffering, the captives, and for their salvation, let us pray to the Lord.

Choir: Lord, have mercy.

Ѽ избавитисѧ нáмъ ѿ всѧкїѧ скóрби, гнѣва и нꙋжды, гдꙋ помóлимсѧ.

Лнкъ: Гдн, помилꙋй.

Застꙋпѝ, спасѝ, помилꙋй и сохранѝ нáсъ, бже, твоéю благодáтїю.

Лнкъ: Гдн, помилꙋй.

Престꙋю, пречнстꙋю, преблагословéннꙋю, слáвнꙋю влчцꙋ нáшꙋ бцꙋ и приснодвꙋ мрїю, со всѣми стыми помѧнꙋвше, сáми себѐ и дрꙋгъ дрꙋга, и вéсь живóтъ нáшъ хртꙋ бгꙋ предадимъ.

Лнкъ: Тебѣ, гдн.

Возглашéнїе: Ꙗкѡ подобáетъ тебѣ всѧкаѧ слáва, чéсть и поклонéнїе, ѻцꙋ и снꙋ и стомꙋ дхꙋ, нынѣ и приснѡ и во вѣки вѣкѡвъ. Аминь.

Лнкъ: Аминь.

И дїакóнъ, вшéдъ же во святый ѻлтáрь, прїéмлетъ кадильницꙋ, и прїéмъ благословéнїе, кадитъ хрáмъ вéсь. Лнкъ же поéтъ гдн воззвáхъ на глáсъ стїхиръ, и

That we may be delivered from all tribulation, wrath, and necessity, let us pray to the Lord.

Choir: Lord, have mercy.

Help us, save us, have mercy on us, and keep us, O God, by Thy grace.

Choir: Lord, have mercy.

Calling to remembrance our most holy, most pure, most blessed, glorious Lady Theotokos and Ever-Virgin Mary with all the saints, let us commit ourselves and one another and all our life unto Christ our God.

Choir: To Thee, O Lord.

Exclamation: For unto Thee is due all glory, honor and worship, to the Father, and to the Son, and to the Holy Spirit, now and ever, and unto the ages of ages.

Choir: Amen.

And the deacon, entering the holy altar, takes the censer and, receiving a blessing, begins to cense the temple. The choir sings "Lord, I have cried" and the lamp-lighting

при́чїѧ ѱалмы̀. Та́же стїхи́ры.
Сла́ва, и҆ ны́нѣ:

И҆ сщ҃е́нникъ со дїа́кономъ творѧ́тъ вхо́дъ
со є҆ѵⷢлїемъ.

Моли́тва вхо́да:

Ве́черъ, и҆ за́ꙋтра, и҆ по́лꙋдне, хва́лимъ,
пое́мъ, благослови́мъ, благодари́мъ
и҆ мо́лимсѧ тебѣ̀, влⷣко всѣ́хъ: и҆спра́ви
моли́твꙋ на́шꙋ, ꙗ҆́кѡ кади́ло пре́дъ тобо́ю,
и҆ не ꙋ҆клонѝ серде́цъ на́шихъ во словеса̀, и҆лѝ
въ помышлє́нїѧ лꙋка́вствїѧ: но и҆зба́ви
на́съ ѿ всѣ́хъ ловѧ́щихъ дꙋ́шы на́шѧ,
ꙗ҆́кѡ къ тебѣ̀, гдⷭ҇и, гдⷭ҇и, о҆́чи на́ши, и҆ на
тѧ̀ ꙋ҆пова́хомъ, да не посрами́ши на́съ,
бж҃е на́шъ. Ꙗ҆́кѡ подоба́етъ тебѣ̀ всѧ́каѧ
сла́ва, че́сть и҆ поклоне́нїе, о҆ц҃ꙋ̀, и҆ сн҃ꙋ, и҆
стⷨ҇омꙋ дх҃ꙋ, ны́нѣ и҆ при́снѡ, и҆ во вѣ́ки
вѣкѡ́въ, а҆ми́нь.

Та́же бл҃гословлѧ́етъ вхо́дъ.

И҆ возглаша́етъ дїа́конъ:

Премꙋ́дрость, про́сти.

psalms, together with the appointed stichera. Then: **Glory. . . both now. . .**

And the priest and deacon make an entrance with the Holy Gospel.

The Prayer of the Entrance:

Evening, morning, and noonday we praise Thee, we bless Thee, we give thanks unto Thee, and we pray Thee O Master of all: Direct our prayer as incense before Thee, and incline not our hearts unto words or thoughts of evil, but deliver us from all that hunt after our souls; for unto Thee, Lord, O Lord, do we lift up our eyes, and in Thee have we hoped, let us not be put to shame, O our God. For unto Thee is due all glory, honor, and worship: to the Father, and to the Son, and to the Holy Spirit, now and ever, and unto the ages of ages. Amen.

Then he blesseth the entrance.

And the deacon exclaimeth:

Wisdom! Aright!

Ли́къ же: Свѣ́те ти́хїй ст҃ы́а сла́вы, безсме́ртнагѡ, ѻ҆ц҃а̀ небе́снагѡ, ст҃а́гѡ бл҃же́ннагѡ, і҆и҃се хрⷭ҇тѐ: прише́дше на за́падъ со́лнца, ви́дѣвше свѣ́тъ вече́рнїй пое́мъ ѻ҆ц҃а̀, сн҃а и҆ ст҃а́гѡ дх҃а, бг҃а. Досто́инъ є҆сѝ во всѧ̑ времена̀ пѣ́тъ бы́ти гла́сы преподо́бными, сн҃е бж҃їй, живо́тъ даѧ́й: тѣ́мже мі́ръ тѧ̀ сла́витъ.

По вхо́дѣ же дїа́конъ: Во́нмемъ.
Сщ҃е́нникъ: Ми́ръ всѣ́мъ.
Дїа́конъ: Премꙋ́дрость.

И҆ глаго́летсѧ прокі́менъ днѐ и҆лѝ и҆з трїѡ́ди по́стной и҆лѝ вели́кїй прокі́менъ пра́здника, по чи́нꙋ.

Въ сꙋббѡ́тꙋ ве́чера, гла́съ ѕ҃:
Гдⷭ҇ь воцари́сѧ, въ лѣ́потꙋ ѡ҆блече́сѧ.
Сті́хъ: Ѡ҆блече́сѧ гдⷭ҇ь въ си́лꙋ и҆ препоѧ́сасѧ.
Сті́хъ: И҆́бо оу҆твердѝ вселе́ннꙋю, ꙗ҆́же не подви́жетсѧ.

Choir: O gentle Light of the holy glory of the immortal, heavenly, holy, blessed Father, O Jesus Christ: having come to the setting of the sun, having beheld the evening light, we praise the Father, the Son, and the Holy Spirit: God. Meet it is for Thee at all times to be hymned with reverent voices, O Son of God, Giver of life. Wherefore, the world doth glorify Thee.

After the entrance, Deacon: Let us attend.
Priest: Peace be unto all.
Deacon: Wisdom!

And the prokeimenon of the day is said, or of the Triodion, or the Great Prokeimenon of the feast, as appointed.

On Saturday evening, Sixth Tone:
The Lord is King, He is clothed with majesty.
Verse: The Lord is clothed in strength, and hath girt Himself.
Verse: For He hath made the whole world so sure, that it shall not be moved.

Сті́хъ: До́мꙋ твоемꙋ̀ подоба́етъ ст҃ы́нѧ, гд҃и, въ долготꙋ̀ дні́й.

Й па́ки: Гд҃ь воцари́сѧ:

Ли́къ: Въ лѣ́потꙋ ѡблече́сѧ.

Въ недѣ́лю ве́чера, гла́съ и҃:

Сѐ ны́нѣ благослови́те гд҃а, всѝ рабѝ гд҃ни.

Сті́хъ: Стоѧ́щїи во хра́мѣ гд҃ни, во дво́рѣхъ до́мꙋ бг҃а на́шегѡ.

Въ понедѣ́льникъ ве́чера, гла́съ д҃:

Гд҃ь оу҆слы́шитъ мѧ̀, внегда̀ воззва́ти мѝ къ немꙋ̀.

Сті́хъ: Внегда̀ призва́ти мѝ, оу҆слы́ша мѧ̀ бг҃ъ пра́вды моеѧ̀.

Въ вто́рникъ ве́чера, гла́съ а҃:

Ми́лость твоѧ̀, гд҃и, поженетъ мѧ̀ всѧ̑ дни̑ живота̀ моегѡ̀.

Сті́хъ: Гд҃ь пасетъ мѧ̀, и҆ ничто́же мѧ̀ лиши́тъ: на мѣ́стѣ ѕла́чнѣ, та́мѡ всели́ мѧ.

Verse: Holiness becometh Thine house, O Lord, unto length of days.

And again. . . The Lord is King . . .

Choir: He is clothed with majesty.

On Sunday evening, Eighth Tone:

Behold now, bless ye the Lord, all ye servants of the Lord.

Verse: Ye that stand in the house of the Lord, in the courts of the house of our God.

On Monday evening, Fourth Tone:

The Lord will hearken unto me when I cry unto Him.

Verse: When I called, the God of my righteousness hearkened unto me.

On Tuesday evening, First Tone:

Thy mercy, O Lord, shall pursue me all the days of my life.

Verse: The Lord is my shepherd, and I shall not want; He maketh me to lie down in a place of green pasture.

Въ сре́дꙋ ве́чера, гла́съ г҃:

Бж҃е, во и҆́мѧ твоѐ спаси́ мѧ, и҆ въ си́лѣ твое́й сꙋди́ ми.

Сті́хъ: Бж҃е, ᲂу҆слы́ши моли́твꙋ мою̀, внꙋши́ глаго́лы ᲂу҆́стъ мои́хъ.

Въ четверто́къ ве́чера, гла́съ г҃:

По́мощь моѧ̀ ѿ гд҃а, сотво́ршагѡ не́бо и҆ зе́млю.

Сті́хъ: Возведо́хъ о҆́чи моѝ въ го́ры, ѿню́дꙋже прїи́детъ по́мощь моѧ̀.

Въ пѧто́къ ве́чера, гла́съ з҃:

Бж҃е, застꙋ́пникъ мо́й е҆сѝ ты̀, и҆ ми́лость твоѧ̀ предвари́тъ мѧ̀.

Сті́хъ: И҆зми́ мѧ ѿ вра̑гъ мои́хъ, бж҃е, и҆ ѿ востаю́щихъ на мѧ̀ и҆збáви мѧ̀.

Ѡ҆браща́ьсѧ же свѧще́нникъ къ за́падꙋ согбе́нѣ и҆мѣ́ай рꙋ́цѣ, стои́тъ ѡ҆жида́ай и҆сполне́нїѧ проки́мна, та́же покланѧ́етсѧ и҆ ѿхо́дитъ на мѣ́сто своѐ.

On Wednesday evening, Fifth Tone:
O God, in Thy name save me, and in Thy strength do Thou judge me.
Verse: O God, hearken unto my prayer, give ear unto the words of my mouth.

On Thursday evening, Sixth Tone:
My help cometh from the Lord, Who hath made heaven and the earth.
Verse: I have lifted up mine eyes to the mountains, from whence cometh my help.

On Friday evening, Seventh Tone:
O God, my helper art Thou, and Thy mercy shall go before me.
Verse: Rescue me from mine enemies, O God, and from them that rise up against me redeem me.

And the priest, facing westward, having his hands folded, standeth awaiting the completion of the prokeimenon, then maketh a reverence and goeth back to his place.

И чте́цъ чте́нїя пра́здника, и́ли трїѡ́ди, по чи́нꙋ и́хъ.

То́кмѡ же во ст҃ꙋ́ю и вели́кꙋю сꙋббѡ́тꙋ, проки́менъ не глаго́летсѧ, а̀ по Свѣ́те тꙗхꙗ́й дїа́конъ глаго́летъ а́бїе: Премꙋ́дрость. И чтенїѧ.

Конча́ющꙋсѧ чте́нїю, і҆ере́й же глаго́летъ та́йнѡ моли́твꙋ сїю́:

Мл҃тва трист҃а́гѡ пѣ́нїѧ:

Б҃же ст҃ы́й, и́же во ст҃ы́хъ почива́ѧй, трист҃ы́мъ гла́сомъ ѿ серафі́мѡвъ воспѣва́емый и ѿ херꙋві́мѡвъ славосло́вимый, и ѿ всѧ́кїѧ нбⷭ҇ныѧ си́лы покланѧ́емый, и́же ѿ небытїѧ̀ во є́же бы́ти приведы́й всѧ́чесꙙкаѧ, созда́вый человѣ́ка по ѡ́бразꙋ твоемꙋ́ и по подо́бїю, и всѧ́кимъ твои́мъ дарова́нїемъ оу҆краси́вый, даѧ́й просѧ́щемꙋ премꙋ́дрость и ра́зꙋмъ, и не презира́ѧй согрѣ́ша́ющагѡ, но полага́ѧй на спⷭ҇е́нїе

And the reader intones the appointed
readings from the Old Testament.

Only on Holy Saturday a prokeimenon is
not said, but immediately after **O Gentle
Light**... the deacon proclaims "**Wisdom**"
and the Old Testament readings begin.

And nearing the end of the appointed
readings, the priest says this prayer
secretly:

The Prayer of the Trisagion Hymn:

O Holy God, Who restest in the saints,
Who art praised with the thrice-holy
hymn by the Seraphim, and art glorified by
the Cherubim, and art worshipped by all the
heavenly hosts, Who from non-existence
hast brought all things into being, Who
hast created man according to Thine image
and likeness, and hast adorned him with
Thine every gift; Who givest wisdom and
understanding to him that asketh, and Who

покланїе, сподобивый насъ, смиренныхъ
и недостойныхъ рабъ твоихъ, и въ часъ
сей стати предъ славою стагѡ твоегѡ
жертвенника, и должное тебѣ поклоненїе
и славословїе приносити: самъ, влко, приими
и ѿ оустъ насъ грѣшныхъ тристую пѣснь,
и посѣти ны блгостїю твоею, прости
намъ всякое согрѣшенїе вольное же и
невольное, ѡсти наша дꙋшы и тѣлеса,
и даждь намъ въ преподобїи служити
тебѣ вся дни живота нашегѡ, млтвами
стыя бцы, и всѣхъ стыхъ, ѿ вѣка тебѣ
блгоꙋгодившихъ.

И по єже исполнитися чтенїемъ, дїаконъ
же ставъ предъ стыми дверми глаголетъ
дїаконства сїя:

Паки и паки миромъ гдꙋ помолимся.
Ликъ: Гдн, помилꙋй.

disdainest not him that sinneth, but hast appointed repentance unto salvation; Who hast vouchsafed us, Thy lowly and unworthy servants, to stand even in this hour before the glory of Thy holy altar, and to offer the worship and glory due unto Thee: Do Thou Thyself, O Master, accept even from the lips of us sinners the thrice-holy hymn, and visit us in Thy goodness. Pardon us every sin, voluntary and involuntary; sanctify our souls and bodies, and grant us to serve Thee in holiness all the days of our life, through the intercessions of the holy Theotokos, and of all the saints, who from ages past have been pleasing unto Thee.

And when the readings have ended, the deacon stands before the Royal Doors and intones these petitions:

Again and again, in peace let us pray to the Lord.

Choir: Lord, have mercy.

Застꙋпѝ, спасѝ, поми́лꙋй и сохранѝ на́съ, Бж҃е, твое́ю благода́тїю.

Ли́къ: Гд҃и, поми́лꙋй.

Прест҃ꙋю, пречи́стꙋю, преблагослове́ннꙋю, сла́внꙋю влⷣчцꙋ на́шꙋ бц҃ꙋ и приснодв҃ꙋ мр҃і́ю, со всѣ́ми ст҃ы́ми помянꙋ́вше, са́ми себѐ и дрꙋ́гъ дрꙋ́га, и ве́сь живо́тъ на́шъ хрⷭ҇тꙋ́ бг҃ꙋ предади́мъ.

Ли́къ: Тебѣ̀, гд҃и.

Їере́й глаго́летъ:

Ꙗ҆́кѡ ст҃ъ є҆сѝ бж҃е на́шъ, и тебѣ̀ сла́вꙋ возсыла́емъ, ѻ҆ц҃ꙋ, и сн҃ꙋ, и ст҃о́мꙋ дх҃ꙋ, нынѣ̀ и при́снѡ.

И дїа́конъ показꙋ́я ѡ҆ра́ремъ, пе́рвѣе ѹ҆́бѡ ко і҆кѡ́нѣ хрⷭ҇то́вѣ глаго́летъ:

Гд҃и, спс҃ѝ бл҃гочести́выѧ, и҆ ѹ҆слы́ши ны̀.

Help us, save us, have mercy on us, and keep us, O God, by Thy grace.

Choir: Lord, have mercy.

Calling to remembrance our most holy, most pure, most blessed, glorious Lady Theotokos and Ever-Virgin Mary with all the saints, let us commit ourselves and one another and all our life unto Christ our God.

Choir: To Thee, O Lord.

And the priest, the exclamation:

For holy art Thou, our God, and unto Thee do we send up glory, to the Father, and to the Son, and to the Holy Spirit, now and ever, and unto the ages of ages.

And standing on the ambo and pointing with his orarion, first to the icon of Christ, the deacon says:

O Lord, save the pious, and hearken unto us.

Та́же наво́дитъ, глаго́ля ко внѣ̀
стоѧ́щымъ велегла́снѡ:

И҆ во вѣ́ки вѣкѡ́въ.

Ли́къ: А҆ми́нь

и҆ Трист҃о́е (и҆ли̑ Е҆ли́цы во хрⷭ҇та̀ крⷭ҇ти́стесѧ,
во хрⷭ҇та̀ ѡ҆блеко́стесѧ): а҆ллилꙋ́їа. И҆
бж҃е́ственнаѧ лїтꙋргі́а слѣ́дꙋетъ по ѡ҆бы́чаю.
Страни́ца р҃.

Then he points to all the people, saying in a
loud voice:

And unto the ages of ages.
Choir: **Amen**

and the Trisagion, or "As Many As Have
Been Baptized into Christ." And the
Divine Liturgy proceeds from here as
usual. See page 101.

HOLY TRINITY
PUBLICATIONS
JORDANVILLE, NEW YORK

All-Night Vigil
Clergy Service Book
Slavonic-English Parallel

ISBN: 9780884654636

The Divine Liturgy of Our
Father Among the Saints
John Chrysostom:
Slavonic-English Parallel

ISBN: 9780884653523

The Divine Liturgies
of The Holy Apostle James,
Brother of the Lord
Slavonic-English Parallel

ISBN: 9780884654308